Copyright © 2000 Aerospace Publishing Ltd

Produced by Aerospace Publishing Ltd and published
jointly in the UK in 2000 with Airlife Publishing Ltd.
Second impression 2001

British Library Cataloguing-in-Publication Data
A catalogue record for this book is available from the
British Library

ISBN 1 84037 064 5

Compiled and designed by:
Robert Hewson

Printed in Hong Kong

Airlife Publishing Ltd
101 Longden Road
Shrewsbury SY3 9EB
England
E-mail: airlife@airlifebooks.com
Website: www.airlifebooks.com

THE VITAL GUIDE TO

COMMERCIAL AIRCRAFT AND AIRLINERS

SECOND EDITION
FULLY REVISED, EXPANDED AND UPDATED

EDITOR: ROBERT HEWSON

The ATR story began in October 1981 when Aeritalia (now Alenia) of Italy and Aerospatiale of France, set out to develop a new family of turboprop regional airliners. The **ATR 42** designation was derived from Avion de Transport Régional (the new company name) and the intended number of seats (42). The first of two **ATR 42-200** prototypes flew on 16 August 1984, and type certification was received on 24 September 1985, in both France and Italy.

The ATR 42 features a high-set wing, mounted above the fuselage so that the carry-through structure does not reduce cabin height. The tailplane is mounted near the top of the swept-back fin, while the undercarriage is housed in sponsons on the fuselage side. The flight deck is configured for two-crew operations, with a Honeywell EVZ-820 EFIS cockpit now as standard. Between 42 and 50 passengers can be carried.

France's Air Littoral received the fourth production aircraft, dubbed **ATR 42-300** for customers, and put the ATR 42 into service on 9 December 1985. The basic -300 version was powered by PW120 turboprops driving four-blade Hamilton Standard 14SF propellers. It was joined, in 1987, by the **ATR 42-320**, with more powerful PW121 engines for improved 'hot-and-high' performance. Both versions were phased out of production in 1996.

Olympic Aviation is an affiliate of the Greek national carrier Olympic Airways, for which it provides regional services. Its fleet includes four ATR 42-320s.

The ATR 42-500 is the current production model. It uses PW127E turboprops, each driving six-blade Ratier-Figeac/Hamilton Standard 568F propellers.

On 12 July 1995, the **ATR 42-400** made its first flight, powered by PW121A engines fitted with six-blade props. This model entered service with CSA in March 1996, but it proved only to be an interim development. From 1995 onwards, the baseline production model became the **ATR 42-500**, which flew on 1 June 1995. Powered by more powerful PW127 engines, the ATR 42-500 (service designation **ATR 42-512**) has a reinforced wing and strengthened landing gear allowing higher operating speeds and weights. First deliveries were made to Italy's Air Dolomiti in October 1995 and Continental Express, in the USA, in May 1996

Other variants include; **ATR 42 Cargo**, with reconfigurable cabin and cargo door; **ATR 42F**, military freighter with air-opening side door; **ATR 42L**, lateral cargo door freighter; **ATR 42 Calibration**, for navigational aid testing; **ATR 42MP**, maritime patrol aircraft in service with Italian customs service; and **SAR 42** proposed surveillance/rescue version.

In 1995 ATR joined with the regional aircraft arms of British Aerospace to undertake joint marketing and the development of future designs. This partnership, the AI(R) Group, dissolved in early 1998 after disagreement on a future strategy for regional jets (see ATR 72). By September 1999 ATR 42 orders stood at 356, with 344 delivered.

SPECIFICATION:
ATR 42-500
Powerplant: two 2,160-hp (1610-kW) Pratt & Whitney Canada PW127E turboprops
Accommodation: two (flight deck), maximum of 50 passengers, standard layout for 48
Dimensions: span 80 ft 7½ in (24.57 m); height 24 ft 10½ in (7.58 m); length 74 ft 4½ in (22.67 m)
Weights: operating empty 24,802 lb (11250 kg); maximum take-off 41,005 lb (18600 kg)
Performance: cruising speed 304 kt (563 km/h, 350 mph); service ceiling 18,000 ft (5485 m); maximum range with reserves 1,000 nm (1852 km, 1,151 miles)

ATR 72

Noting customer demand for a larger aircraft, ATR launched the **ATR 72-200** in 1985. The '72-seat' airliner made its first flight on 27 October 1988. Three prototypes were built, all of which were flying by April 1989. Structurally, the ATR 72 is similar to the ATR 42, but its fuselage is extended by 4.5 m (14 ft 7 in). The resultant larger aircraft, also with a reinforced wing, offered more engine power, more fuel and more range. Powered by Pratt & Whitney Canada PW124B turboprops, the cabin can accommodate 64-74 passengers. For the first time in an ATR design, the ATR 72 introduced composite materials in its wing and skin construction.

Kar-Air of Finland, took delivery of the first ATR 72-200 (known as the **ATR 72-202** in service) on 27 October 1989. The next variant to appear was the **ATR 72-210** (or **ATR 72-212**), with PW127 engines for improved 'hot-and-high' performance. The first ATR 72-210 flew on 10 July 1992. This version could carry up to 19 additional passengers, compared to the ATR 72-200, in critical WAT (Weight And Temperature) limited conditions. The ATR 72-210 was certified in December 1992 by both French and US authorities, and deliveries commenced in December 1992, to American Airlines' American Eagle regional partner airlines.

A further improved version of the the -210, the **ATR 72-210A** (or **ATR 72-212A**) followed in 1996, when the first aircraft flew on 24 July. This variant is powered by uprated PW127F turboprops with six-blade all-composite propellers. The type was

Britain's Gill Airways operates a mix of ATR 42s and ATR 72s from its base at Newcastle. It took delivery of the first of its four ATR 72-202s in 1995.

certified in France on 14 January 1997 and the first delivery was made to American Eagle (Simmons Airlines) on 31 July 1997. The ATR 72-210A has now been redesignated the **ATR 72-500**, to highlight its commonality (in powerplant, systems, spares and maintenance) with the ATR 42-500. The two aircraft also share a common pilot and crew type-rating. The ATR 72-500 has adopted a carbon fibre composite rudder for further weight savings.

In 1992 ATR announced the ATR72-derived **ATR 52C** military freighter with rear ramp, but none have yet been built. An **ATR 72 Cargo** version is now available with a 2.95-m (116-in) wide side cargo door. The proposed 'next-generation' **ATR 82** (an Allison AE2100-powered 80/86-seater), once hoped to fly in 1996, has now been cancelled. Future ATR designs will instead focus on regional jets – the 60- to 100-seat **AIRJET** family – perhaps with another partner. Leasing of second-hand ATRs to new customers is handled by ATR Asset Management, established in July 1998, which has a portfolio of 100 aircraft. By September 1999 ATR 72 orders stood at 249, with 226 delivered.

ATR 72-201s serve on Finnair's regional and domestic routes. The world's highest-timed ATR 72 is a Finnair aircraft with 20,000 hours and 31,000 take-offs.

SPECIFICATION:
ATR 72-500
Powerplant: two 2,160-shp (1610-kW) Pratt & Whitney Canada PW127E turboprops
Accommodation: two (flight deck), maximum of 74 passengers, standard layout for 68
Dimensions: span 88 ft 9 in (27.05 m); height 25 ft 1¼ in (7.65 m); length 89 ft 1¼ in (27.17 m)
Weights: operating empty 27,558 lb (12500 kg); maximum take-off 47,400 lb (21500 kg)
Performance: maximum cruising speed at 15,000 ft (4575 m) 284 kt (526 km/h, 327 mph); maximum operating altitude 25,000 ft (7620 m); maximum range with reserves and 66 passengers 1,200 nm (2222 km, 1,381 miles)

Airbus A300 and A300ST

U nveiled in the mid-1960s, the **A300**, (and with it Airbus Industries) grew from an informal requirement expressed by several European carriers for a new wide-bodied airliner. The aircraft that became the A300 had its roots in the Anglo-French **HBN100**, a design proposed by Hawker Siddeley, Breguet and Nord. Sud-Aviation and a conglomeration of German manufacturers joined the project, and by 1967 the planned design was renamed A300.

In 1968 the A300 was fixed as a 252-seat, 275,500-lb (124966-kg) design renamed the **A300B**. In 1969 France and Germany announced they would proceed with this aircraft, in the face of British apathy towards the project, but British Aerospace (then BAC) did later become an important manufacturing partner in Airbus Industrie, which was founded in December 1970. Currently, work is divided between Aérospatiale (37.9 per cent), Daimler Benz Aerospace (37.9 per cent), BAe (20 per cent) and CASA (4.2 per cent), with other contributions made by Fokker.

The first A300 to fly, an **A330B1**, took to the air on 28 October 1972. Air France took delivery of two, but the dominant early production version was the slightly stretched **A300B2**. A longer-range version, the **A300B4**, followed in 1974 along with the **A300C4** convertible passenger/freight version.

There is no mistaking the impressive size and shape of the A300-600ST Super Transporter, more commonly known as the 'Beluga'.

Iran Air has operated a small fleet of early-model A300B2s since 1980. In 1994 it added two more modern A300-605Rs.

The current production version is the **A300-600** (initially named the **Advanced A300B2/B4**) and the extended-range **A300-600R**, which features a fin fuel tank and a computerised fuel trimming system. The A300-600 offers a fully 'glass' EFIS cockpit for two-crew operations, increased use of composite materials and much improved aerodynamics. Spurred by interest from Federal Express (which placed a major order for 36), Airbus developed the **A300-600F** freighter. The first of these was delivered to FedEx on 27 April 1994. Though A300 production had slowed to a trickle in recent years – on a strict 'build-to-order' basis – a major order for up to 60 A300-600Fs from UPS, confirmed in September 1998, ensures a production future for the type.

An Aerospatiale/DASA partnership company, SATIC (special aircraft transport international) was established to build the **A300-600ST** (Super Transporter) '**Beluga**' to replace the Aerospacelines Super Guppies used to transport Airbus parts to Toulouse and Hamburg for final assembly. The first 'Beluga', the widest civil jet ever at 24 ft 2 in (7.4 m) across, flew in September 1994 and the fourth aircraft was delivered in July 1998. A fifth aircraft has now been ordered for delivery in 2000.

By September 1999, Airbus A300 firm orders stood at 520 aircraft with 485 delivered.

SPECIFICATION: Airbus A300-600R
Powerplant: two 61,500-lb (273.6-kN) General Electric CF6-80C2A5 or 58,000-lb (258-kN) Pratt & Whitney PW4158 turbofans
Accommodation: two (flight deck), maximum of 375 passengers, typical layout for 266
Dimensions: span 147 ft 1 in (4.84 m); height 54 ft 3 in (16.53 m); length 177 ft 5 in (54.08 m)
Weights: (with CF6-80C2A5s) operating, empty 200,700 lb (91040 kg); maximum take-off 378,535 lb (171700 kg)
Performance: max cruising speed at 30,000 ft (9150 m) Mach 0.82 (897 km/h, 557 mph); max operating altitude 40,000 ft (12200 m); max range with reserves 4,718 miles (7593 km)

Airbus A310

Customer experience with the A300 highlighted the need for a smaller, short-range Airbus, initially proposed as the **A300B10**. Interest was expressed by Swissair, Lufthansa and Eastern Airlines, and the design that emerged was launched in 1978 as the **A310**. The main cabin is 11 frames shorter than the A300, while retaining the same cross-section, and features a new advanced technology wing, modified undercarriage, and increased use of composites. A two-crew EFIS cockpit was standard and engine choices included General Electric CF6, Pratt & Whitney JT9D and Rolls-Royce RB.211 turbofans. In the event, no orders were received for the Rolls-Royce-powered version.

The first A310 flew on 3 April 1982. Airbus had intended to offer two versions, the 2,300-mile (3704-km) range **A310-100** and the **A310-200**, which could cover an additional 1,150 miles (1852 km) with 210 passengers. Swissair placed the first orders, for 10 series -200 aircraft with 10 options, and all subsequent orders were for A310-200s. No A310-100s were ever built. The last A310-200 was delivered to Cyprus Airways on 28 February 1989.

In 1982 Airbus announced a third version, the **A310-300**, aimed at even longer routes than the previous models. The programme was announced during the handover of Swissair's first A310, and that same airline again became the launch customer. Outwardly, the A310-300 is almost identical to previous versions, although it does carry small, but distinctive winglets (which were subsequently

The distinctive cedar tree emblem of Lebanon marks the A310s of Middle East Airlines, which operates a mix of A310-200s and A310-300s.

introduced on some late production A310-200s also). Power is provided by either General Electric CF6 or Pratt & Whitney PW4000-series engines. Internally, the aircraft is fitted with a fin fuel tank. Optional tanks can be carried in the hold.

Airbus developed a cargo-convertible version, the **A310-200C**, but only one example was sold, to Dutch airline Martinair. DASA Airbus is converting 30 A310-200s, for FedEx, to **A310-200F** freighter configuration with a large side-cargo door. The first was delivered on 18 July 1994. In June 1999 Airbus formally announced a partnership with Raytheon to develop a military **Multi-Role Tanker Transport** (**MRTT**) version of the A310 with a side-cargo door and wing-mounted refuelling pods. Raytheon and Elta used the A310 airframe as the platform for an AEW&C aircraft offered to Australia and Turkey. A stretched A310 may also serve as the basis for a new regional airliner, the **Airbus P305** (a follow-on to the cancelled **AE31X** for China). An outline design for this project is now on offer by Airbus Asia.

By September 1999, 261 A310s of all versions had been ordered, with 255 delivered.

TAP Air Portugal is an important Airbus customer with a fleet ranging in size from the A319 to the A340. It became an A310 operator in 1988.

SPECIFICATION: Airbus A310-300
Powerplant: two 59,000-lb (262.4-kN) General Electric CF6-80C2A8 or 56,000-lb (249.1-kN) Pratt & Whitney PW4156A turbofans
Accommodation: two (flight deck), maximum of 280 passengers, standard layout 210-250
Dimensions: span 144 ft (43.89 m); height 51 ft 10 in (15.80 m); length 153 ft 1 in (46.66 m)
Weights: (with CF6-80C2A8 engines) operating, empty 179,920 lb (81610 kg); maximum take-off 330,675 lb (150000 kg)
Performance: cruising speed at 31,000 ft+ (9150 m+) Mach 0.80; max operating altitude 40,000 ft (1220 m); max range, at max weight with PW4156A engines 5,984 miles (9630 km)

Airbus A319

As with the A320 and A321 before it, the **A319** can trace its design heritage back to the SA (single aisle) concepts of the early 1980s, in particular the 130/140-seat **SA1**. By 1990 Airbus was ready to launch a shortened A320, dubbed the A319 or **A320 M-7** (minus seven seat rows). BAe agreed to drop a development of its 146 regional airliner (the 146 NRA) and to proceed with the A319, however Aerospatiale and DASA were less enthusiastic as the new Airbus would compete with their proposed 'Regioliner' family. In 1992 the Airbus project was further delayed when DASA took over Fokker and inherited the Fokker 100 programme.

A dispute over the final production location of the A319 (finally allocated to Hamburg along with the A321, while the A320 remained at Toulouse) further delayed the launch of the aircraft. Airbus began marketing the A319 in May 1992, as the third member of the A320 family. It was not until 10 June 1993 that the A319 was formally launched, with just six orders and two options from ILFC.

Using similar systems, avionics and structure to the A320, the 120/130-seat A319 offers the same engine choices as the A321, but is optimised for 124-seat 2,000-nm (3695-km, 2,296-mile) routes. The A319 is 12 ft 3 in (3.73 m) shorter than the A320, though the wingspan of both is the same.

Swissair was Airbus's launch customer for the A319 and has a fleet of nine A319-112s. It was also the first airline to operate the A319, A320 and A321 together.

Air Canada took delivery of the last of its substantial fleet of 35 A319-114s in April 1998. The airline is now the world's largest A319 operator, by far.

The A319 first flew on 25 August 1995, the day after its official roll-out. A total of 650 hours of flight tests with CFM56-5B engines led to type certification on 10 April 1996, followed by the V2524-A5 certification on 18 December. The first delivery was made to Swissair (via ILFC) on 30 April 1996 and the A319 entered service on 8 May. Other 1996 deliveries were made to Air Inter (21 June), Lufthansa (19 July) and Air Canada (12 December) – which had placed a significant (initial) order for 25 aircraft as DC-9 replacements. Another important North American order came from United Airlines which has signed for 48 A319s since 1996. In August 1998 British Airways placed orders and options for up to 188 A319/A320/A321 aircraft, including firm orders for 39 A319s, for delivery from September 1999.

At the 1997 Paris air show Airbus launched its **Corporate Jetliner**, based on the A319. This aircraft can carry 10 passengers over a maximum distance of 7,208 miles (11600 km) with the addition of extra fuel tankage. The first **A319CJ** was delivered to a Kuwaiti customer in 1999 and 10 are currently on order. In September 1998, Airbus announced a 100-seat A319 'shrink, the **A318** which will enter service in 2002. It will be powered by Pratt & Whitney's new PW6000 turbofan. By July 1999 A319 orders stood at 603 with 155 delivered.

SPECIFICATION: Airbus A319
Powerplant: two 22,000-lb (97.9-kN) IAE V2522-A5 or CFM International CFM56-5A4 turbofans. Higher powered options available
Accommodation: two (flight deck), maximum of 148 passengers, standard layout for 124
Dimensions: span 111 ft 3 in (33.91 m); height 38 ft 9½ in (11.80 m); length 110 ft 10¾ in (33.80 m)
Weights: operating, empty 88,537 lb (40160 kg); maximum take-off 166,450 lb (7550 kg)
Performance: cruising speed 824 km/h (512 mph); max cruising altitude 39,000 ft (11887 m); max range, at special maximum take-off weight (above) with reserves and standard load 4,085 miles (6574 km)

Airbus A320

Seeing that American dominance of the airliner market had clearly been shaken by the A300/A310 family, Airbus launched a rival for the Boeing 737 and McDonnell Douglas MD-80 families in the form of the **A320**. Airbus made a firm decision to use as much new technology as possible to dramatically reduce operating costs, and it worked hard to persuade the world airline market to accept something new. The design had its roots in a myriad of European small airliner studies dating back to the early 1970s, but when Airbus launched the definitive A320 in 1981 it was built around a then-unique fly-by-wire (FBW) control system and a choice of two new turbofan engines. Three fuselage lengths were initially proposed, but the team at Toulouse settled on just two for production aircraft: the 130/140-seat **A320-100** and the 150-160 seat **A320-200**.

Air France announced a letter of intent for both versions at the Paris air show of 1981, where Boeing was also exhibiting the new 737-300. In the face of strong airline interest, Airbus decided to concentrate on a single fuselage length, seating approximately 150, while offering two versions still dubbed A320-100 and -200. The difference now was in payload/range, as the 'new' A320-100 had wing fuel tanks only, as opposed to the higher MTOW A320-200 with its additional fuselage centrebody fuel tanks. The A320 was finally launched in 1984, with an order from British Caledonian Airways. Orders continued to grow until the A320 first flew on 22 February 1984. The first

Condor is the charter subsidiary of Lufthansa. Its Schoenefeld-based offshoot, Condor Berlin, operates a fleet of eight A320-212s with four more on order.

deliveries were made to Air France in March 1988, these being of the lightweight A320-100 version (only 21 of which were built). The first A320-200 was delivered to Ansett Airways in June 1988.

Airbus offers several versions of the CFM International CFM56-5A engine for the A320, along with the newly developed International Aero Engines (IAE) V2500-A1, which claims a much improved fuel burn. A more radical innovation is the five-computer, quadruplex Thomson-CSF/Sfena digital FBW control system that provides the pilot with a side-stick controller instead of a more normal control column. The cockpit features colour, multi-function displays, a unique Electronic Centralised Aircraft Monitor system and only 13 main panel instruments.

Perhaps the ultimate compliment came in May 1994 when Boeing tried to acquire a (second-hand) A320 for display in Seattle, to 'motivate its employees'. Airbus now offers its customers tremendous flexibility within its A319/320/321 range, allowing orders and options to be swapped from larger to smaller aircraft (and *vice versa*), as required. By September 1999 A320 orders totalled 1,220 with 752 delivered.

Syrianair's re-equipment with modern airliners, to replace its elderly Soviet-era aircraft, began in 1998 with the delivery of the first of six A320-232s.

SPECIFICATION: Airbus A320-200
Powerplant: two 25,000-lb (111.2-kN) IAE V2525-A5 or 26,500-lb (117.9-kN) CFM International CFM56-5B4 turbofans
Accommodation: two (flight deck), maximum of 180 passengers, standard layout for 150
Dimensions: span 111 ft 3 in (33.91 m); length 123 ft 3 in (37.57 m)
Weights: (with CFM56 engines) operating, empty 91,675 lb (41583 kg); maximum take-off 169,765 lb (77000 kg)
Performance: cruising speed at 31,000 ft (9150 m) Mach 0.80; max operating altitude 40,000 ft (1220 m); max range, with reserves and standard load 3,222 miles (5190 km)

Airbus A321

In the early years of the A320 several developed models were proposed. A higher-capacity design initially referred to as the '**Stretched A320**' or '**A320 Stretch**', was the first to emerge. In November 1989 this new aircraft was officially launched as the **A321**, a minimum-change version of the A320, with a revised wing, higher operating weights and more powerful engines. The aircraft is 6.93 m (273 in) longer than its antecedent, with a reinforced centre fuselage and landing gear, and redesigned trailing-edge flaps. The fuselage stretch, accommodating a normal load of 176/185 passengers, comprises two plugs forward and aft of the wing. This has led to the repositioning of the four emergency exits to either side of the wing leading- and trailing-edges.

Airbus initially offered one version, the **A321-100**, with a choice of CFM56-5B or IAE V2530-A5 turbofans. The A321 become the first Airbus to be assembled in Germany, at DASA's Otto Lilienthal facility, Hamburg – where it has since been joined by the A319. The first A321 was rolled out on 3 March 1993 and its maiden flight (with V2530 engines) took place on 11 March 1993. Four aircraft underwent an 850-hour flight test programme that led to the type's European JAA certification in December 1993, with CFM56 approval following on 15 February 1994.

Air Macau operates a mix of A320s and A321s. The airline was established in 1994, in the Portuguese colony which is now due for return to China.

All Nippon Airways, like most Japanese carriers, has been an enthusiastic supporter of special schemes for its aircraft, like this A321-211.

Launch customers were Lufthansa, which chose the higher-powered V2530 for its aircraft (20), and Alitalia (40). Lufthansa took delivery of the first production A321 on 27 January 1994 (which entered service in March), followed by deliveries to Alitalia (with CFM56-5B engines) on 22 March.

A second version of the A321, the **A321-200**, was launched in April 1995, when Hapag Lloyd placed an order for up to 10 aircraft, via leasing company ILFC. The A321-200 is an increased MTOW version which takes advantage of structural reinforcements to boost maximum take-off weight by 13,200 lb (5987 kg), to 196,200 lb (88996 kg). An additional centre tank (ACT) can be fitted in the rear cargo hold to increase fuel capacity by 766 US gal (2900 litres), to 7,026 US gal (26596 litres). This extends the range of the A321-200 to approximately 2,750 nm (5080 miles, 3,157 miles) – only slightly less than the smaller, lighter A320. The A321-200 is offered with two engine choices, the 31,100-lb (138-kN) CFM International CFM56-5B2 and the 33,300-lb (148-kN) IAE V2533-A5.

The first A321-200, powered by V2533-A5 engines flew on 12 December 1996. The type entered service with Germany's Hapag Lloyd in March 1997. By September 1999 total A321 orders stood at 264, with 139 delivered.

SPECIFICATION: Airbus A321-100
Powerplant: two 30,000-lb (133.4-kN) CFM International CFM56-5B or 31,000 (137.9-kN) IAE V2530-A5 turbofans
Accommodation: two (flight deck), maximum of 220 passengers
Dimensions: span 111 ft 10 in (34.09 m); height 38 ft 9 in (11.81 m); length 146 ft (44.51 m)
Weights: operating, empty 104,746 lb (47512 kg); maximum take-off 182,984 lb (83000 kg)
Performance: cruising speed at 31,000 ft (9150 m) Mach 0.80; maximum operating altitude 40,000 ft (12200 m); maximum range, with reserves and standard load 2,648 miles (4260 km)

Airbus A330

Needing to build up a family of long-range airliners, Airbus took a design study from the early 1970s (the **A300B9**) and brought it back to the drawing board in the early 1980s. The new aircraft emerged as the **TA9** (TA=twin aisle) and shared its design roots with the A340. In 1986 the TA9 became the A330 and received its official launch in 1987. The initial production version was named the **A330-300**.

Market forces were behind Airbus' decision to launch the A340 several years ahead of the A330. The A330 and A340 are a common design. Both use a wing swept to 30° with distinctive 9-ft (2.74-m) winglets. The A330 wing needs only small structural changes to carry the A340's extra engines. The A330 was the first Airbus design to be offered with powerplants from all three major manufacturers. Current options include the General Electric 67,500-lb (300-kN) thrust CF6-80A1; Pratt & Whitney's 64,000-lb (284.8-kN) PW4-6164, with the 68,000-lb (302.6-kN) PW4168 also available; and the 67,500-lb (300-kN) Rolls-Royce Trent 768, which has been developed into the 71,100-lb (316.4-kN) Trent 772-60, for Cathay Pacific's A330-300s.

The A330-300 prototype made its maiden flight on 2 November 1987. The CF6-powered A330 was certified by the FAA and JAA on 2 June 1994, and entered revenue service with Air Inter on 17 January 1994. The PW4168-powered version was certified on June 2 1994. The first PW4168-powered aircraft entered service with Thai International on 19 December 1994. The Trent-powered A330 was

Hong Kong's Cathay Pacific Airways has a fleet of 12 A330-342s and was the launch customer for the Trent 700-powered version of the A33-300.

certified on 22 December 1994 and deliveries began to Cathay Pacific on 27 February 1995.

In 1995 Airbus announced a major development of the basic A330, the shorter-fuselage, increased range **A330-200**. Its overall length has been reduced to 59 m (193 ft 6¾ in), but its wing remains unchanged. The A330-200 is a 256-seat aircraft with a 6,400-nm (11824-km, 7,347-mile) range. It is fitted with an additional centre wing fuel tank, a revised tail fin and has a maximum take-off weight of 507,055-lb (230000 kg).

The A330-200 made its first flight on 13 August 1997, received simultaneous US FAA, European JAA and Transport Canada certification on 31 March 1998. The first customer aircraft was handed over to Canada 3000 (via ILFC) on 30 April 1998. All initial production A330s is powered by CF6-80E1A4 turbofans, which together with the PW4168 were the first engines to be certified on the type. On 24 June 1998 the first Rolls-Royce Trent-powered A330-200 made its maiden flight. By September 1999 Airbus had 260 orders for all versions of the A330, with 112 delivered.

Garuda Indonesia operates a fleet of Trent 768-powered A330-341s. Deliveries began in December 1996 and six are in service with three more on order.

SPECIFICATION: Airbus A330-300
Powerplant: two 67,5000-lb (300-kN) class General Electric CF6, Pratt & Whitney PW4000, or Rolls- Royce Trent 700 turbofans
Accommodation: two (flight deck), maximum of 440 passengers (standard layout for 335)
Dimensions: span 197 ft 10 in (60.3 m); height 54 ft 11 in (16.74 m); length 209 ft 11½ in (63.69 m)
Weights: (with CF6-80E1A2 engines) operating, empty 268,675 lb (121870 kg); maximum take-off 467,375 lb (212000 kg)
Performance: max operating speed Mach 0.86; max operating altitude 40,000 ft (1220 m); max range, with reserves 6,329 miles (10186 km)

Airbus A340

Airbus used the A300 as the basis for the **A340** design – but it changed beyond all recognition. The A340 started as the **A300B11**, becoming the **TA11** in 1980. By 1982 the TA11 had become a four-engined airliner with a design range of 6,830 nm (12650 km; 7,860 miles). In 1986, the TA11 was renamed as the A340.

Airbus had hoped to power the A340 with a 'SuperFan' – an ultra-high bypass development of the CFM56 or V2500. This was unsuccessful and Airbus had to rely on improved versions of existing engines to achieve its promised range. Interest had been received on the understanding that such new engines, or at least an aircraft with their performance, would be available. To solve its problems, Airbus increased the A340's wingspan and added winglets, while CFM International announced an uprated version of its CFM56, the CFM56-5C2. The A340 received its formal go-ahead in June 1987.

Two versions are on offer, the 375-seat (standard) **A340-300** or the short-fuselage, extended-range **A340-200**, normally seating 263. The first A340 to fly was an A340-300, on 25 October 1991. The A340-200 followed on 1 April 1992. Both versions are built alongside the A330, at Toulouse. The flight decks of the A340 and A330 are virtually identical, with only a different number of throttles on the

Airbus has been successful winning a small but important VVIP customer base for the the A340. This A340-211 is operated by the Qatar Amiri Flight.

Airbus aircraft played an important part in the post-invasion re-equipment of Kuwait Airways. New types to enter service included four A340-313s, in 1995.

centre console. As a result, the FAA has allowed cross-cockpit crew qualification (between the A340, A330 and A320) for the first time ever.

The A340 was certified by the JAA on 22 December 1992 and the first A340-200 was handed over to Lufthansa on 2 February 1993. The first A340-300 was delivered to Air France on 26 February. A growth version of the A340-300, the **A340-300X**, with an increased maximum take-off weight of 606,250 lb (275000 kg) and a range of 8,400 miles (13519 km) was ordered by Singapore Airlines. The first example flew on 25 August 1995 and deliveries followed on 17 April 1996. This variant has since been renamed the **A340-300E**.

A follow-on extended range **A340-400** development was dropped in favour of the latest stretched 313-seat **A340-500** and 380-seat **A340-600** developments, launched in December 1997. The Trent 553-powered A340-500 will be the world's longest-ranged airliner with a design range of 8,500 nm (15742 km, 9781 miles). Launch customer is Egyptair and deliveries are scheduled to begin in 2002. The larger Trent 556-powered A340-600 is optimised for a reduced range of 7,500 nm (13890 km, 8,630 mile) and Virgin Atlantic will be the launch customer with deliveries beginning in 2002. By September 1999 total A340 orders stood at 270 with 163 delivered.

SPECIFICATION: Airbus A340-300
Powerplant: four 31,200-lb (138.8-kN) CFM International CFM56-5C2 turbofans
Accommodation: two (flight deck), maximum of 440 passengers (375 standard)
Dimensions: span 197 ft 8 in (60.3 m); height 54 ft 11 in (16.74 m); length 209 ft (63.7 m)
Weights: operating, empty 286,150 lb (129800 kg); maximum take-off 573,200 lb (260000 kg)
Performance: maximum operating speed Mach 0.86; maximum operating altitude 40,000 ft (1220 m); maximum range, with reserves and standard load 7,710 miles (12416 km)

Antonov An-2 (SAP Y-5)

The **Antonov An-2** 'Colt' flew for the first time on 31 August 1947 and production was initially undertaken in the Soviet Union, where several thousand were built. Subsequently, other assembly lines were established in China and Poland. The various factories completed somewhere in the region of 20,000 examples, making it one of the most numerous aircraft to be built since World War II.

The An-2's antiquated appearance tends to disguise its capabilities. The fuselage is an all-metal, stressed-skin, semi-monocoque structure and is quite robust, while the wing is a mix of ancient and modern, utilising an all-metal, two-spar structure but also incorporating fabric covering material to the rear of the front spar. Leading-edge slots on the upper wing and trailing-edge flaps on both upper and lower wings result in impressive STOL performance, and also help bestow docile handling qualities.

In addition to being easy to fly, the An-2 has also demonstrated a good degree of versatility, with suitably adapted versions being used for photographic survey, fire-fighting, weather research and casualty evacuation. The basic **An-2P** general-purpose transport can carry up to 2000 kg (4,519 lb). The provision of a generously-proportioned side door permits reasonably bulky loads to be carried or, alternatively, it can take up to 19 passengers in tip-up seats. The **An-2R** is an agricultural version fitted with fuselage hoppers and underwing spraybars, while the **An-2T** and **An-2TP** are passenger-configured for 12 occupants in standard seats.

The An-2 survives in large numbers in its native Poland, in a wide variety of roles. This particular example served as a sport parachute aircraft.

Power for the An-2 is usually provided by a PZL Kalisz ASz-621R nine-cylinder radial piston engine, but Antonov did develop and test a turboprop version. Known as the **An-3**, it was fitted with a 1,450-shp (1081-kW) Glushenkov TVD-20 engine and had a lengthened fuselage. The An-3 was available only as a modification of the An-2, with the conversion project centred upon a factory in Kiev. The An-2 survived in production at Poland's PZL's Mielec plant into the early 1990s, but today production has effectively ceased. However aircraft can still be built to order and unsold An-2s remain available.

Since 1970, approximately 300 aircraft have been built by China's Shijiazhuang Aircraft Plant (previously Huabei/Nanchang) as the **SAP Y-5N** (Yunshuji 5 – transport aircraft 5) with Chinese-built HS5 engines. The **Y-5B** is a dedicated agricultural version which first flew on 2 June 1989. It has been joined by the **Y-5B(K)** passenger version in 1993, the multipurpose **Y-5B(D)** in 1995, an the paradropping **Y-5C**, developed for the PLA, in 1996. This version has three distinctive winglets or 'tip sails' on the upper wingtips.

This recent-production Chinese-built Y-5 has been fitted with a large flat-glass window in the cabin to give its passengers a better view.

SPECIFICATION:
Antonov (PZL-Mielec) An-2
Powerplant: one 1,000-hp (746-kW) PZL Kalisz ASz-621R air-cooled, radial piston engine
Accommodation: two (flight deck), maximum of 19 passengers (seated)
Dimensions: span, upper 59 ft 7¼ in (18.18 m), lower 46 ft 8½ in (14.24 m); height, tail down 13 ft 2 in (4.01 m); length, tail down 40 ft 8¼ in (12.40 m)
Weights: empty 7,605 lb (3450 kg); maximum take-off 12,125 lb (5500 kg)
Performance: max level speed 160 mph (258 km/h); service ceiling 14,425 ft (4400 m); max range, with standard load 560 miles (900 km)

Antonov An-12 (Shaanxi Y-8)

Ukraine (China)
Four-engined rear-loading transport

Starting in 1955 Antonov led the way in transport aircraft design when it introduced the prototype of the twin-turboprop **An-8**, NATO codename 'Camp'. The An-8 had all the features of a modern tactical airlifter: a high-wing, rear-loading door with a 'beaver' tail, rough field landing gear and a ground-mapping radar. The An-8 was intended purely as a military transport, but only 100 were built. The type was widely believed to have disappeared from use in the 1970s, as larger and more capable aircraft took its place. However, during the 1990s several An-8s reappeared in the hands of the plethora of small cargo airliners that sprung up across the former Soviet Union.

The larger four-engined **An-12** made its maiden flight during 1958 and entered service the following year. Built alongside the commercial **An-10 Ukraina** at first, it was adapted with the military very much in mind. Compared with the An-10, the An-12 had a revised aft fuselage (with hardly any windows) with a rear cargo door. A rear gun turret was another sign of its military roots, though later civil versions did delete this feature. Several hundred examples of the basic **An-12BP 'Cub-A'** were obtained for service with the state airline, although Aeroflot's unique status resulted in these often being employed for military duties.

An-12 production continues in China (as the Y-8), where the Shaanxi Aircraft Company still produces small refinements to the basic design, like this Y-8C.

Bulgaria's Air Sofia operates a small fleet of six An-12BPs for ad-hoc cargo charter flights around Europe, Africa and the Middle East.

An-12s were exported to several air arms that traditionally looked to the Soviet Union as a source of military hardware. Such nations often operated aircraft in dual civil/military markings but most of these elderly An-12s have now been withdrawn. Substantial numbers of An-12s passed into service with the range of colourful (and ever-changing) new airlines set up throughout the former Soviet Union. The economic collapse of 1998 grounded many of these operators and called the commercial future of the An-12, in Russia and the CIS, into question.

The type's future is secure for it is still in production in the People's Republic of China, as the **Shaanxi Y-8** (Shaanxi Aircraft Company). Chinese 'licence'-production started at the Xian factory in 1969 and the first example flew on 25 December 1974. SAC undertook production the following year. Models include the **Y-8B**, a civilianised military transport; the fully-pressurised **Y-8C** (only a small forward cabin section of the An-12 was pressurised); the **Y-8D**, fitted with Collins avionics for export; and the somewhat specialised **Y-8F** 'goat transporter', with up to 350 livestock pens. Amazingly, the latest of these versions, the **Y-8C**, first flew as recently as 17 December 1990. By 1999 approximately 50 Y-8s were in airline service in China, and production continues at the rate of about five per annum.

SPECIFICATION:
Antonov An-12
Powerplant: four 3,495-hp (2942-kW) Ivchenko AI-20K turboprops
Accommodation: five (flight deck)
Dimensions: span 124 ft 8 in (38 m); height 34 ft 6½ in (10.53 m); length 108 ft 7¼ in (33.10 m)
Weights: empty 61,730 lb (28000 kg); maximum payload 44,090 lb (20000 kg); maximum take-off 134,480 lb (61000 kg)
Performance: maximum cruise speed 385 mph (620 km/h); service ceiling 34.120 ft (10400 m); maximum range, with max payload 900 miles (1450 km)

Antonov An-24/-26/-32 (Xian Y-7)
Twin-engined utility transports

Conceived in the late 1950s to replace Il-12s, Il-14s and Li-2s, the twin-turboprop **An-24 'Coke'** flew for the first time on 20 December 1959 and entered Aeroflot service in July 1962.

Approximately 1,100 were built by 1978, with the original 44-seat An-24 supplanted by the improved-performance 50-seat **An-24V**. Other variants included the **An-24TV** and **An-24RT** freighters, and the **An-24RV**. The latter had a Tumanskii RU-19-300 turbojet instead of the original TG-16 gas turbine auxiliary power unit, for better take-off performance.

Having received about 40 aircraft from the Soviet Union, China began licence-production of the An-24 as the **Xian Y-7**. A prototype flew in 1970 but the Y-7 did not enter service until 1986. Approximately 20 were built. The addition of winglets, new avionics and a three-man cockpit (replacing the five crew of the Y-7), resulted in the 52-seat **Y-7-100**, which flew in 1985. This became the standard production version with 65 delivered to Chinese operators by late 1998. Several other versions are under long-term development. These include the: **Y-7-200A**, a stretched 60-seat version with a Collins EFIS cockpit and PW127C turboprops. A prototype flew in December 1993; **Y-7-200B**, improved Y7-100 with Harbin WJ5E engines and four-blade props, EFIS cockpit and a redesigned wing without winglets. A prototype flew in November 1990; **Y-7E**, a hot-and-high version with more powerful APU, first flown in July 1994; and the cargo-carrying **Y-7H-500**, which is, in fact, a copy of the An-26 freighter.

Cubana still operates a handful of An-24RVs, configured for 48 passengers. The An-24RV has a turbojet booster fitted in the starboard nacelle.

Ongoing development in the USSR led to the **An-26 'Curl'** which made its first flight in 1968. This dedicated light tactical transport (**An-26A**) was fitted with a rear loading ramp and also had a booster engine as a standard feature. The improved **An-26B** can accommodate three standard freight pallets. Small numbers are in civilian service, and Antonov has also developed a water-bomber version.

Other members of the family comprise the **An-30 'Clank'** and the **An-32 'Cline'**. The former is optimised for the aerial survey role and is instantly recognisable by its glazed nose. About 130 were built, exclusively for military use.

The An-32 is also primarily a tactical transport derivative and was unveiled at the 1977 Paris air show. It is fitted with considerably more powerful engines driving larger propellers. Their revised clearance requirements necessitated fitting the engines in overwing nacelles, giving the 'Cline' a distinctive 'hunch-back' appearance. The **An-32B** is a dedicated flying hospital, while the **An-32P Firekiller** is a fire-fighting version with water tanks scabbed on to the fuselage side.

China's Xian Y-7 family is largely derived from the Antonov An-24. However, the Y-7H (as seen here) is based on the rear ramp-equipped An-26 freighter.

SPECIFICATION:
Antonov An-24RV
Powerplant: two 2,550-hp (1902-kW) Ivchenko AI-24A turboprops, plus one 1,985-lb (8.8-kN) RU19-300 auxiliary turbojet
Accommodation: three (flight deck), maximum of 50 passengers (44 standard)
Dimensions: span 95 ft 9½ in (29.20 m); height 27 ft 3½ in (8.32 m); length 77 ft 2½ in (23.53 m)
Weights: empty 29,320 lb (13300 kg); maximum take-off 46,300 lb (21000 kg)
Performance: cruising speed at 19,700 ft (6,000 m) 280 mph (450 km/h); service ceiling 29,525 ft (9000 m); range, with max payload and reserves 341 miles (550 km)

Antonov An-28 and An-38

The Antonov **An-28** 'Cash' made its initial flight in the USSR during September 1969. Production may have been undertaken in the USSR for Aeroflot, but responsibility for manufacture of the An-28 was transferred to PZL-Mielec of Poland in 1978. The first Polish-built example made its maiden flight in July 1984, with Polish certification following in February 1986. Production of the initial An-28 ended in the early 1990s, but PZL has gone on to offer several developments.

In 1992 the **An-28B1T** appeared, optimised for parachuting/air drops with a sliding rear door, which retracts under the fuselage. The **An-28PT**, which first flew in July 1993, boasted new PT6A-65B turboprops driving new five-blade Hartzell props, with Bendix/King avionics and colour weather radar. The An-28PT has since been renamed the **M-28 Skytruck**, by PZL. A temporary type certificate was granted to the M-28 in March 1994, followed by full certification in March 1996. The first deliveries were made in January 1996, to Latina de Aviación, Colombia and at least 20 aircraft are believed to have been produced since then.

PZL has developed a stretched version of the M-28, the **M-28 03/04 Skytruck Plus**. The 10th production An-28/M-28 airframe was used for ground tests during August 1997. A first flight was

The An-38 is intended to replace An-28s, Let 410s and even Yak-40s in Russian service. This is the prototype, but small numbers are now in service.

PZL-Mielec built the standard An-28, chiefly for Aeroflot, until 1984. Small numbers operate on the Polish civil register and with the air force.

expected in 1998. The **M-28 03** will have a fuselage stretched by 1.84 m (6 ft ½ in), a cabin ceiling raised by 25 cm (9¼ in) and an enlarged ventral cargo pannier. The **M-28 04** adds an upwards-opening freight door, in the aft starboard side, replacing the rear ramp of the M-28 03, and all previous aircraft.

Developments at Antonov's design centre in Kiev led to the joint Russo-Ukrainian **An-38** project, which culminated in a first flight of the prototype at the NAPO production plant in Novosibirsk on 22 June 1994. The An-38 is is fitted with two Allied Signal (Garrett) TPE-331-14GR turboprops driving five-blade Hartzell propellers. It can accommodate up to 27 passengers or 2500 kg (5,510 lb) of freight.

The basic aircraft, certified in April 1997, has been dubbed the **An-38-100**. Also on offer are the **An-38-200** with Omsk MKB TVD-20 engines (test flown on the third and fourth prototype) and the **An-38K**, with an upwards-hinging side cargo door in the rear port fuselage. The An-28-100 can also be outfitted for a range of patrol/surveillance/military transport mission, medevac, paradropping, and geophysical/photographic survey tasks. Antonov claims to have 180 orders from various Russian airlines, with export options on an additional 200 aircraft. The first (three) An-38-100s entered service with Vostok Airlines in 1998.

SPECIFICATION:
PZL-Mielec M-28 Skytruck
Powerplant: two 1,100-hp (820-kW) Pratt & Whitney Canada PT6A-65B turboprops
Accommodation: two (flight deck), maximum of 18 passengers
Dimensions: span 72 ft 4¼ in (22.06 m); height 16 ft 1 in (4.90 m); length 41 ft 7½ in (12.68 m)
Weights: empty, equipped 8,598 lb (3900 kg); maximum take-off 14,330 lb (6500 kg)
Performance: economical cruising speed at 9,850 ft (3,000 m) 168 mph (270 km/h); service ceiling 19,685 ft (6000 m); range, with max fuel reserves and payload 848 miles (1365 km)

Antonov An-72 and An-74

Like most Antonov transports the **An-72** has its roots in a military design, albeit a novel one. The An-72 was created with its engines mounted above the wing to take advantage of the 'Coanda' effect. This system, also known as upper surface blowing, uses the engine exhaust running directly over the wing surface to generate lift and impart impressive STOL (Short Take-Off and Landing) performance. The first of two prototypes flew on 31 August 1977 and eight pre-production aircraft, with enlarged wings and fuselage, followed as the **An-72A**. The type gained the NATO codename 'Coaler-A'.

The An-72 was intended as a military transport and has clamshell rear doors that can be opened in flight for air-dropping. Folding-seats can carry up to 68 passengers or 57 paratroops. Alternative loads include 24 stretchers, four containers or pallets. An APU is fitted in the port main gear fairing to provide ground power and cabin air conditioning.

The **An-72AT** 'Coaler-C' was a dedicated cargo version designed to carry a range of standard Russian-built containers and pallets. Antonov also developed the **An-72S** (Salon), a VIP version with a galley and divided cabin for 20 passengers. Military versions of the An-72 include the **An-72P**, a dedicated armed maritime patrol aircraft.

Antonov has chosen to concentrate current production efforts on the **An-74 'Coaler-B'**, which was originally simply a specialised version of the An-72, developed in the mid-1980s. The An-74 was intended to support Aeroflot's Polar Division, and

Antonov is putting increasing effort into marketing the current An-74 family. This is the demonstrator aircraft for the An-74TK-200 combi freighter.

Soviet military operations in the Arctic. The aircraft was capable of landing on ice floes, in all weather conditions, and featured strengthened landing gear and extensive de-icing equipment. Outwardly it was identical to the An-74 but for two blister windows on the port fuselage side.

Variants of the An-74 now on offer in conjunction with the Polyot Industrial Association production plant, Omsk, Russia, include: the **An-74-200**, increased payload freighter; **An-74-200D Salon**, business/VIP transport for 10/16 passengers. Can accommodate a car in rear fuselage; **An-74T-200**, primary freighter version with 10000-kg (22,045-lb) payload; **An-74TK-200**, primary convertible passenger/cargo aircraft, folding seats for up to 52. Combi layouts available. **An-74T-100**, as An-74T-200 but with extra navigator (crew of four); **An-74TK-100**, as An-74TK-200 but with extra navigator.

Production of the An-72/An-74 is believed to total approximately 200. Small numbers are operated by civilian firms and Antonov is emphasising the type's rough-field capabilities to oil gas and mineral exploration companies.

This an An-72AT, the all-cargo version of the original aircraft, designed for the Soviet military. Today's production is concentrated on the An-74.

SPECIFICATION:
Antonov An-74TK-200
Powerplant: two 14,330-lb (63.74-KN) ZMKB Progress/Ivchenko D-36 Srs 3A turbofans
Accommodation: three (flight deck, basic), maximum of 68 passengers
Dimensions: span 104 ft 7½ in (31.89 m); height 28 ft 4½ in (8.65 m); length 92 ft 1¼ in (28.07 m)
Weights: empty 48,105 lb (21820 kg); maximum take-off 80,468 lb (36500 kg)
Performance: cruising speed at 32,810 ft (10,000 m) 373 mph (600 km/h); service ceiling 22,300 ft (6800 m); range, with payload and reserves 1,615 miles (2600 km)

Antonov An-124 and An-225

When it first flew on 26 December 1982, the **An-124 Ruslan** (a giant of old Russian folk tales) became the world's largest production aircraft, dwarfing even the C-5 Galaxy. Developed to meet a joint Aeroflot and air forces requirement for a heavy strategic freighter, the An-124 ('**Condor**' to NATO) is similar to the C-5, although it has a conventional low-set tailplane rather than a T-tail. It has a rear loading ramp and an upward-hinging nose. The constant-section main hold has a titanium floor, and can be lightly pressurised. Winches and travelling cranes are provided, the latter with a lifting capacity of more than 20000 kg (44,000 lb). The upper cabin, seating 88 behind the wing carry-through, is fully pressurised. The aircraft can be made to kneel, giving the hold floor a downwards slope of up to 3.5°, to assist loading or unloading. The An-124 has a fully fly-by-wire control system. Despite its size, it is designed to operate from semi-prepared strips, including packed snow or even ice-covered swamps.

The basic Russian-certified civil freighter version is now referred to as the **An-124-100**. Production continues at the Aviastar factory, Ulyanovsk. A westernised version, the **An-124-100M**, with all-new avionics, is under development. The **An-124-102** will have a full EFIS cockpit, while the proposed **An-124-130** would be re-engined with General

The sole An-225 Mriya visited the Paris air show in 1989 carrying the Soviet Buran orbiter. It first flew in that piggyback configuration in May of that year.

The An-124 entered Russian military service in 1987. Since then several airlines, such as Volga-Dnepr, have begun to offer its services on the civil market.

Electric CF6 turbofans. A Rolls Royce re-engining proposal, from Air Foyle, exists also. A Stage 3/Chapter 3 hush-hit was introduced by ZMKB Progress in 1997.

Britain's Air Foyle manages commercial An-124 operations worldwide on behalf of the Antonov Design Bureau which operates six An-124-100s. Another British company, HeavyLift, has a joint venture with Russian specialist cargo operator Volga-Dnepr, which has a fleet of seven An-124-100s.

The **An-225 Mriya** (Dream), first flew on 21 December 1988, and is a derivative of the An-124 primarily intended for the carriage of outsized loads for the Soviet space programme. The fuselage is stretched by 8 m (26 ft 2 in), giving a corresponding increase in hold length (to 43 m/141 ft) and volume, but the rear loading ramp is deleted. The An-225 is designed to carry external 'piggyback' loads, for which two upper fuselage hardpoints have been provided. The tail unit has been completely redesigned, with increased span and endplate fins replacing the single centreline tailfin of the An-124. The aircraft has a new centre-section, with two further D-18T turbofans, bringing the total to six. It can carry payloads of up to 250000 kg (551,146 lb). Only one An-225 has been built (with another still uncompleted), and its current flight status is unknown.

SPECIFICATION: Antonov An-124-100
Powerplant: four 51,590-lb (229.5-kN) ZMKB Progress (formerly Lotarev) D-18T turbofans
Accommodation: six (flight deck), passenger cabin for 88 aft of flight deck
Dimensions: span 240 ft 5¼ in (73.30 m); height 69 ft 2 in (21.08 m); length 226 ft 8½ in (69.10 m)
Weights: operating, empty 385,800 lb (175000 kg); maximum payload 264,550 lb (120000 kg); maximum take-off 864,200 lb (392000 kg)
Performance: maximum cruising speed at 32,800 ft (10,000 m) 497 mph (800 km/h); maximum range, with maximum payload 3,480 miles (560000 km)

Avro Regional Jet 70, 85 and 100

Developed by Hawker Siddeley as the **HS 146**, the **British Aerospace 146** used four Textron Lycoming (now AlliedSignal) ALF502 turbofans and an efficient wing to achieve very low noise levels and outstanding field performance. Flying on 3 September 1981, the first aircraft was a short-body **BAe 146 Series 100**, able to carry 82-94 passengers in an 85-ft 11-in (26.19-m) fuselage. On 1 August 1982 came the first **Series 200**, stretched to 93 ft 10 in (28.60 m) to carry up to 112; the even longer (by 7 ft 10 in/2.38 m) **Series 300**, which first flew on 1 May 1987, could carry up to 128 in maximum density.

The launch customer was Dan-Air, which began operations on 27 May 1983. The first Series 200 went into service with Air Wisconsin in June 1983, this airline also being responsible for the first Series 300 service in December 1988.

Special variants of the 146 were the: **146-QT Quiet Trader** all-cargo aircraft with an upward-hinging side cargo door, which was purchased by TNT for overnight parcel deliveries; the **146-QC** which could be rapidly-reconfigured from passenger to cargo carriage; and the **Statesman**, fitted out for VIP transport. Production of the 146 ended in 1993, with 219 built – 216 of which are still in service

Using the three 146 variants as a solid basis, BAe relaunched the aircraft as the **Avro Regional Jetliner** (RJ) series in 1992, adding more powerful engines and digital avionics. The RJ family currently comprises the **RJ70**, **RJ85** and **RJ100**, based on the 146-100, 146-200 and 146-300 fuselage lengths

Aer Lingus Commuter operates a fleet of 110-seat BAe 146-300s (equivalent to the RJ100) on services around Ireland and to the UK.

respectively. The principal difference is the adoption of AlliedSignal LF507 turbofans in place of the ALF 502s of the 146. These offer full-authority digital engine control (FADEC), in addition to greater economy.

The first RJ85 (for Crossair) flew on 27 November 1992. Avro International Aerospace, established as a division of British Aerospace Regional Aircraft, delivered the 100th RJ, to Northwest Airlines, in January 1998. This was the 321st 146/RJ airframe to be built. Series production of the RJ70 has now ceased. By September 1999 RJ orders had reached 154 with 131 delivered. Sales and leasing of 146/RJs is conducted by British Aerospace Asset Management, which revitalised the market for the type during the 1990s.

Avro continues to offer the 120-seat **RJ115** – similar in size to the RJ100 but with greater fuel capacity and a redesigned cabin. In February 1999 BAe launched the **RJX** family. These aircraft will be powered by the all-new AlliedSignal AS977-1A turbofan (which can be retrofitted) and will feature many design refinements plus a new cockpit.

Malmo Aviation's BAe 146-200s (equivalent to the RJ85) were operated through a major leasing deal with British Aerospace Asset Management.

SPECIFICATION:
Avro RJ100
Powerplant: four 7,000-lb (31.14-kN) Textron-Lycoming LF 507 turbofans
Accommodation: two (flight deck), maximum of 128 passengers (100 standard)
Dimensions: span 86 ft (26.21 m); height 28 ft 2 in (8.59 m); length 101 ft 8¼ in (30.99 m)
Weights: operating, empty 55,915 lb (25362 kg); maximum take-off 97,500 lb (44225 kg)
Performance: maximum operating speed 351 mph (565 km/h); maximum range, with max payload 1,342 miles (2159 km)

BAC/Aerospatiale Concorde

The world's only successful SST (SuperSonic Transport) began life as a French project in 1957. Sud-Aviation, Dassault and Nord-Aviation, in association with Air France, answered a French government-inspired SST requirement, and their first design was a 70-passenger, delta-winged, Mach 2.2 airliner based on the SE.210 and dubbed **Super Caravelle**. At the same time in the UK, a similar airline/industry programme was underway, headed by the British Aircraft Corporation and Hawker Siddeley. Their design, the **BAC 223**, was a four-engined, 100-seat aircraft, but by the early 1960s both groups were coming closer and closer together. So much so, in fact, that on 29 November 1962 a historic Anglo-French supersonic aircraft agreement was signed, which uniquely featured a 'no-break clause' that made the resultant design virtually immune to vacillation or cancellation.

This design emerged as the **Concorde**, with no little effort expended to finding a name acceptable to both nationalities. A needle-nosed and slender fuselage (with only an 8-ft 8-in/2.68-m cabin) sat above a graceful, ogival, delta wing, under which were slung four Rolls-Royce/SNECMA Olympus afterburning turbojets. The aircraft's most distinctive feature is its unique 'droop snoot' nose, which can be lowered by up to 12.5° to improve crew visibility

British Airway's Concordes were the only aircraft to retain a 'British' feel when the airline rebranded itself with ethnic-styled designs.

Concorde has been cleared for service until 2030 after in-depth structural studies. Air France, however, intends to withdraw its aircraft before then.

for take-off and landing. Pre-production aircraft differed in detail, and all had shorter fuselages.

Concorde was assembled both at Filton and Toulouse, and the premier French **Concorde 101** was rolled out on 11 December 1967, flying on 2 March 1969. It was followed by the first British **Concorde 102** on 9 April. Air France had signed for five aircraft in May 1963, and subsequently 18 airlines made commitments for 80 aircraft. Firm orders came from British Airways and Air France for five (later seven) and four (later six), respectively, but all other interest lapsed. On 21 January 1976 both airlines placed the type into transatlantic service.

When British Airways was privatised in 1984, the UK government 'sold' its Concordes (entirely funded by the taxpayer) to the airline, with an eighth 'spares ship', for a mere £9.3 million. Air France now operates six aircraft (a seventh was scrapped in 1994). In the early 1990s some British Airways' aircraft suffered rudder failures and structural problems, but a major investigation was undertaken to iron out any more serious complications. Several international groups have studied the development of future supersonic airliners in the 1990s, but the **European Supersonic Research Programme** group (Aerospatiale, BAe and DASA) suspended its work in 1999, citing a lack of research funds and the uncertain market.

SPECIFICATION:
BAC (BAe)/Aerospatiale Concorde
Powerplant: four 38,050-lb (169.3-kN) Rolls-Royce/SNECMA Olympus 593 Mk 610 turbojets
Accommodation: three (flight deck), maximum of 144 passengers (standard 100)
Dimensions: span 83 ft 10 in (25.56 m); height 37 ft 5 in (11.40 m); length 203 ft 9 in (62.10 m)
Weights: operating, empty 173,500 lb (78700 kg); maximum take-off 408,000 lb (185065 kg)
Performance: maximum cruising speed, at 51,000 ft (15635 m) Mach 2.04 (1,345 mph; 2179 km/h); service ceiling 60,000 ft (18290 m); max range, with reserves 4,090 miles (6580 km)

BAC/ROMBAC One-Eleven Twin-engined short- to medium-range airliner

The **BAC One-Eleven** was a successful design that achieved considerable initial sales only to be left behind by developments of rival aircraft which the One-Eleven had beaten into service. When BAC was formed in 1960 by the conglomeration of Hunting, Vickers and others, it inherited the **Hunting 107** design that later formed the basis of the One-Eleven. British United Airways launched the project, ordering 10 80-seat aircraft in May 1961, and Aer Lingus was the first non-UK operator. While the first One-Eleven made its maiden flight on 20 August 1963, the flight test programme was hit when this aircraft was lost two months later. It entered an unrecoverable 'deep stall', a phenomenon unique to T-tailed designs and previously unknown.

The first production version, the 93-ft 6-in (28.4-m) 63/80-seat **One-Eleven 200**, was finally certified in April 1965 and won substantial orders in the US and Europe. A total of 58 was built. Next came the heavier, Spey Mk 511-engined **One-Eleven 300** that could accommodate 89 seats over a reduced operating range. Nine were built before this version was superseded by the **One-Eleven 400**. FAA regulations limiting American Airlines' two-crew operations to aircraft below 80,000 lb (36288 kg) led to the short-range Series 400, which was a Series 300 development with a restricted MTOW. After a first flight on 13 July 1965, 70 were built.

Inspired by a BEA requirement, the next variant was the stretched (by 13 ft 6 in/12.3 m) **One-Eleven 500**, which first flew on 30 June 1967. The delay in

The BAC One-Eleven Series 500 was a stretched 100-seat version. The bulk of aircraft surviving in commercial service today are One-Eleven 500s.

building this version meant that the DC-9-30 was already firmly established, and no Series 500s were sold in the US. Some aircraft, with the suffix 'DW' (Developed Wet), can use water boosting for extra power on take-off. Eighty-six were completed before this version, and the entire One-Eleven line, was transferred to Romania in the early 1980s. The last UK-built version, the **One-Eleven 475**, combined the more powerful engines of the Series 500 with the short fuselage of the Series 200. Twelve were built, including two side-loading freighters.

Romaero SA, based at Bucharest-Baneasa airport, obtained all BAe's (formerly BAC) One-Eleven tooling with the intention of building a further 22 **ROMBAC One-Eleven 500**s. Production proceeded slowly, with only nine completed (ending in 1988), albeit to a very high standard. Bournemouth-based European Aviation is now working with Florida's Quiet Technologies to develop a Stage 3-compliant hush kit for the One-Eleven. Existing hush-kits only meet Stage 2 noise reduction requirements. Of the 241 One-Elevens completed and delivered about 120 remain active in mid-1999.

Britain's European Aviation is now the largest One-Eleven operator, with a fleet of 16 One-Eleven 500s acquired largely from British Airways in 1993.

SPECIFICATION:
BAC (BAe) One-Eleven Series 500
Powerplant: two 12,500-lb (55.6-kN) Rolls-Royce Spey Mk 512DW turbofans
Accommodation: two (flight deck), maximum of 119 passengers (standard 99)
Dimensions: span 93 ft 6 in (28.50 m); height 24 ft 6 in (7.47 m); length 97 ft 4 in (29.67 m)
Weights: operating, empty 54,582 lb (24,758 kg); maximum take-off 104,500 lb (47400 kg)
Performance: maximum cruising speed, at 21,000 ft (6400 m) 541 mph (871 km/h); maximum cruising altitude 35,000 ft (10670 m); maximum range, with reserves 2,165 miles (3484 km)

Beech Model 99

During the early 1960s, the growth in commuter traffic prompted Beech to develop a twin-turboprop airliner based on its successful Queen Air executive twin. The resultant Beech **Model 99 Airliner** first flew in July 1965. Retaining the overall low-wing, swept-tail layout of the Queen Air, the Model 99 had a stretched fuselage allowing the aircraft to carry 15 passengers in addition to the two pilots. The Queen Air's three main cabin windows were increased to six. The lengthened nose had a hatch for the carriage of baggage, and there was a moveable internal bulkhead to allow the cabin to be rapidly reconfigured for the carriage of freight, passengers or a mixture. The seats were easily removable, and a cargo door was an option, installed forward of the standard passenger door, which incorporated an airstair. A large ventral baggage pannier was another option later seen on many aircraft. Full airways navigation equipment was standard, but the individual equipment could be varied to meet customer requirements. Anti-icing for the propeller blades was also standard, but pneumatic de-icing boots for the leading edges of the wings and tail unit were optional extras.

On 2 May 1968 the first production Model 99 was delivered to Commuter Airlines Inc. Production ran until the end of 1975, by which time a total of

Many operators opted to add the ventral freight/baggage 'speedpak', as seen on this C99. The Beech 99 could also be configured with an all-cargo cabin.

Pacific Coastal Airlines operates a network of feeder and bush services across British Columbia. This B99 served with them during the mid-1990s.

164 aircraft had been built for 64 customers. During this run, there were two improved versions, the **A99** and **B99**, which featured numerous improvements. Both variants were powered by the PT6A-27 680-shp (507-kW) engine in place of the original 550-shp (410-kW) PT6A-20.

Some four years after shutting the production line, Beech announced on 7 May 1979 that it would re-enter the feederliner market with an improved **C99 Commuter**, powered by the 715-shp (533-kW) PT6A-36. To speed the certification process, a B99 was bought back from Allegheny Commuter to serve as a prototype and was initially fitted with PT6A-34 engines. The first of the new-production aircraft took to the air on 20 June 1980, and heralded a minor revival of the type's fortunes, which also spurred the development of the larger Beech 1900 series.

Production of the C99 raised the total figure to 239, the final aircraft being manufactured in 1986. By this time, the 1900 was established as the company's main competitor in the commuter market, and many other manufacturers had produced highly popular designs (notably EMBRAER). Approximately 171 Beech 99s remain in service on passenger and cargo work, and many regard the type as the true pioneer of the commuter market.

SPECIFICATION:
Beechcraft B99 Airliner
Powerplant: two 680-hp (506-kW) Pratt & Whitney Canada PT6A-27 turboprops
Accommodation: two (flight deck), maximum of 15 passengers
Dimensions: span 45 ft 10½ in (14.00 m); height 14 ft 4¼ in (4.38 m); length 44 ft 6¾ in (13.58 m)
Weights: empty, equipped 5,872 lb (2663 kg); maximum take-off 10,900 lb (4944 kg)
Performance: maximum cruising speed at 12,000 ft (3650 m) 282 mph (454 km/h); service ceiling 26,313 ft (8020 m); maximum range, with reserves 838 miles (1348 km)

Beech (Raytheon) King Air and Super King Air

USA
Twin-turboprop business aircraft

Today's **King Air** family has a pedigree stretching back to the piston-engined **Model 65/80 Queen Air**, of 1958. Beech developed a turboprop-powered version of the Queen Air, but with PT6A-6 engines and a pressurised cabin. The production aircraft became the **Model 65-90 King Air** and the first example flew on 21 November 1963. A range of refined variants followed including the **A90, B90, C90, C90-1, C90A, E90** and the T-tailed **F90**. In 1969 came the **Model 100 King Air** family, stretched by 50 in (127 cm) to hold up to 15 seats. This version had six cabin windows, compared to the four introduced from the B90 onwards.

The first **Model 200 Super King Air** flew on 27 October 1972. It was based on the Model 100, but featured a T-tail, increased wing span, more fuel and improved pressurisation. The cabin was fitted with seven seats as standard. It was powered by two 850-hp (634-kW) PT6A-41 turboprops. A range of versions followed and these included the: **Model 200C**, rear cargo door; **Model 200T** survey/patrol version, wingtip fuel tanks; **Model A200**, 750-shp (559-kW) PT6A-38 engines – associated **A200C, A200CT** also; **Model B200**, 850-shp (634-kW) PT6A-42s – associated **B200C/T/CT** also.

On 8 February 1981 the Beech Aircraft Company became a subsidiary of the Raytheon company. That same year the **Model 300 Super King Air** made its first flight on 6 October. This was based on the B200 but powered by two 1,050-hp (783-kW) PT6A-60As driving four-bladed props. The Model

Distinctive features of the eight- to 11-seat Model 350 include its seven cabin windows, 2-ft (61-cm) high winglets and four-bladed Hartzell propellers.

300 also had an increased take-off weight and several airframe changes. The **Model 300LW** was certified to a higher maximum take-off weight for European tax reasons. Raytheon stretched the Model 300 by 34 in (86.4 cm) to produce the **Super King Air 350** (originally the Model **B300**). This new version has a longer wing with winglets.

Today Beech aircraft are built by the Raytheon Aircraft Company, a division of Raytheon, set up in 1994. From 1996 onwards the 'Super' title was deleted from all Model 200/300s. Current production includes the Collins Pro Line II EFIS-equipped **King Air C90B**, powered by two PT6A-21s driving four-bladed props. The **C90SE** (Special Edition) has three-bladed props and an Allied Signal CNI-5000 avionics package. The **C90B Jaguar Special Edition** has exterior styling and interior outfitting mirroring that of Jaguar cars. Model 200 production is concentrated on the B200/C/T/CT and **B200SE**, with Collins EFIS-84 avionics and three-bladed props. The Model 350 and cargo door-equipped Model **350C** also remain in production. Production of all civil King Air versions now exceeds 3,200.

The Model 200 serves civil, and military, operators around the world, chiefly as a VIP/executive aircraft or as a high-speed priority freight transport.

SPECIFICATION:
Beech Raytheon B200 King Air
Powerplant: two 850-hp (634-kW) Pratt & Whitney (Canada) PT6A-42 turboprops
Accommodation: two (flight deck), standard seating for seven passengers
Dimensions: span 54 ft 6 in (16.61 m); height 14 ft 10 in (4.52 m); length 43 ft 10 in (33.36 m)
Weights: empty, equipped 8,192 lb (3716 kg); maximum take-off 12,500 lb (5670 kg)
Performance: maximum cruising speed at 27,000 ft (8230 m) 330 mph (537 km/h); service ceiling 35,000 ft (10670 m); maximum range, with reserves 2,139 miles (3442 km)

Beech (Raytheon) 400

Twin-engined short- to medium-range business jet

The aircraft that is now a well-known product in the US business-jet market began life in Japan. Mitsubishi designed a small biz-jet in the mid-1970s with the aim of offering superb performance, low cabin noise and the roomiest cabin in its class. The resulting **MU-300 Diamond I** first flew in Japan on 29 August 1978, and was joined on flight test duties by the second on 13 December. Following completion of these trials, both aircraft were shipped to MAI, the US-based distributor for Mitsubishi aircraft, who reassembled the aircraft for FAA certification, beginning on 10 August 1979. After four aircraft had been delivered from Japan, they began to arrive as major sub-assemblies from the parent company, for final assembly by the US factory in Dallas.

FAA certification was received on 6 November 1981, and 65 Diamond Is were delivered before the **Diamond IA** was introduced in January 1984. This aircraft featured uprated engines, higher weight and better avionics, and a small number were added to the overall total. The **Diamond II** first flew in June 1984, a similar-looking aircraft but powered by JT15D-5s and with a revised interior.

In December 1985 Beech acquired the rights to the Diamond II, and MAI ceased to market the Diamond in March 1986. Renamed **Beechjet 400**,

The Beechjet 400A is the current production model and made its first flight on 22 September 1989 – the same year all Beech production moved to Wichita.

In 1998 Hainan Airlines became the first customer for the Beechjet in China. The airline uses its aircraft for pilot training and other transport tasks.

the design was assembled at Beech's Wichita factory from Mitsubishi-supplied kits. Two options for the Diamond II, namely a tailcone baggage compartment and an extended-range tank, were adopted as standard. The first Beech-assembled aircraft was rolled out on 19 May 1986. In 1989 all production moved to Beech, but the company continued to support earlier Diamond deliveries.

At the 1989 NBAA show, Beech announced an improved aircraft, the **Beechjet 400A**. While retaining the overall dimensions, the 400A introduced a larger cabin and a new-look 'glass' cockpit, with a Collins Pro Line 4 EFIS system, and an increased cruising altitude. The cabin usually accommodates eight, with fold-down tables between pairs of facing seats. This is the current version, of which over 240 had been sold by mid-1999, following 64 Beechjet 400s. Like all Beech aircraft, the Beechjet is today a product of the Raytheon Aircraft Company.

A massive order was received from the US Air Force for the **Beechjet 400T**, or **T-1A Jayhawk**, to fulfil a multi-engined trainer requirement (Tanker Transport Training System). A total of 180 were delivered between July 1991 and July 1997. Bringing the Beechjet's story full circle, nine similar aircraft have also been sold to the Japan Air Self Defense Force (as **T400**s).

SPECIFICATION:
Beechcraft Beechjet 400A
Powerplant: two 2,965-lb (13.19-kN) Pratt & Whitney Canada JT15D-5 turbofans
Accommodation: two (flight deck), maximum of eight passengers
Dimensions: span 43 ft 6 in (13.25 m); height 13 ft 11 in (4.24 m); length 48 ft 5 in (14.75 m)
Weights: operating, empty 10,625 lb (4819 kg); maximum take-off 16,100 lb (7303 kg)
Performance: maximum level speed at 27,000 ft (8230 m) 539 mph (867 km/h); service ceiling 43,400 ft (13230 m); maximum range, with reserves 1,948 miles (3135 km)

Beech (Raytheon) 1900

Design of the **Beechcraft 1900** commuter airliner was launched in 1979, with Beech beginning the fabrication of a trio of flying prototypes, a static test airframe and a pressure test specimen, during the course of 1981. Assembly of the these prototypes was completed in 1982, and the formal roll-out of the first aircraft was followed by a successful first flight on 3 September 1982.

Testing of the newest Beechcraft was carried through swiftly and culminated when FAA certification was achieved in November 1983 (including certification for single-pilot operations), by which time work was well in hand on an initial batch of production aircraft. The first major version to appear was the **Beech 1900C**, which found favour with a number of commuter operators in the USA. Deliveries began in February 1984 and 255 were completed. Aircraft built with a 'wet wing', incorporating 563-Imp gal (2559-litre) fuel tanks, are designated **Model 1900C-1**s. Beech also marketed a similar version that was specifically aimed at the business community. Known initially as the **King Air Exec-Liner** (later as the **Model 1900C/-1 Exec-Liner**), the first example was handed over to the General Telephone Company of Illinois during the summer of 1985. Fourteen are in use in the United States, Saudi Arabia and Zambia.

Not content with limiting itself to the civil market, Beech also supplied a modest quantity of transport and special missions aircraft, based on the Model 1900C, to military customers. These include the Egyptian air force, Republic of China air force and

As a small 19-seat turboprop, the Beech 1900D is now something of an anomaly in the commuter and regional aircraft marketplace – but it still survives.

the USAF Air National Guard, where its serves as the **C-12J** mission support aircraft.

Deliveries of the Model 1900C continued until 1991, when Beech (Raytheon) switched its production resources to the improved **Model 1900D**. Based on the 1900C, the newest variant entered service with Mesa Airlines during 1991, and is now the only current production variant. As with the preceeding Model 1900C, a VIP-orientated **Model 1900D Exec-Liner** was built in small numbers but it is no longer available.

Among the changes introduced in the 1900D are its increased-volume 'stand-up' cabin with a flat floor, winglets, finlets and rear fuselage strakes, bigger windows and a larger passenger door. New Pratt & Whitney Canada PT6A-67D turboprops are installed as standard, as is a Collins EFIS-84 cockpit. Bonded metal sub-assemblies for the aircraft are now built in China by the Xian Aircraft Company. Like all Beech aircraft the Model 1900 is now a product of the Raytheon Aircraft Company. It is one of the few 19-seat aircraft still in production and, by mid-1999, a total of 325 Model 1900Ds had been delivered.

The original Beech 1900Cs had an altogether more streamlined shape although, inside, passengers have to step over the main spar on the cabin floor.

SPECIFICATION: Beechcraft 1900D
Powerplant: two 1,279-hp (954-kW) Pratt & Whitney Canada PT6A-67D turboprops
Accommodation: two (flight deck), standard configuration for 19 passengers
Dimensions: span, over winglets 57 ft 11¾ in (17.67 m); height 15 ft 6 in (4.72 m); length 57 ft 10 in (17.63 m)
Weights: empty, typical 10,650 lb (4831 kg); maximum take-off 16,950 lb (7688 kg)
Performance: maximum cruising speed at 16,000 ft (4875 m) 326 mph (524 km/h); maximum service ceiling 33,000 ft (10058 m); maximum range, with 10 passengers and reserves 1,698 miles (2733 km)

Bell Model 212, 214 and 412

With the Model 205 'Huey' established as the world's leading assault and transport helicopter, Bell teamed with Pratt & Whitney of Canada in the late 1960s to develop a new version powered by the PT6T-3 Twin-Pac powerplant. This consisted of two turboshafts driving through a common gearbox and single drive shaft. With this powerplant, the **Model 212**, also known as the **Twin Two Twelve**, was developed for both civil and military markets. In the civil field, the type was of particular interest for gas/oilfield exploration work, where twin-engined safety was vital. Able to carry 14 passengers, the 212 was also available in a float-equipped version, which is certified for single-pilot IFR operation. The uprated PT6T-3B was introduced in 1980. About 900 Bell 212s have been built for military and civil customers to date. The type was also built under licence in Italy as the **Agusta-Bell AB 212**, but production has now switched wholly to the AB 412.

Using the airframe of the 212, Bell developed the **Model 214**, which was powered by a single Avco Lycoming T5508D turboshaft flat-rated at 2,250 shp (1678 kW) for take-off. A dedicated civil model was the **214B BigLifter**, which could carry 8,000 lb (3629 kg) on an external cargo hook, or specialised fire-fighting equipment. Internal accommodation remained at 14 passengers or a sizeable cargo load.

Bell's Model 212 has become an invaluable offshore support, transport and load-carrying helicopter that is in worldwide civil and military service.

For the first time on any production Bell helicopter, the Model 412 introduced a four-bladed main rotor. Italian AB 412s are built as the 'Gryphon'.

From the basic 214 came the **Model 214ST 'Supertrans'**, with a revised and lengthened airframe able to carry 17 passengers. Twin-engined power was restored using 1,625-shp (1212-kW) General Electric CT7-2 turboshafts, again driving through a common gearbox. Full IFR instrumentation was standard and, as with other models, weather radar was often fitted in a radome on the nose.

The chief current production aircraft is the **Model 412**. Announced in 1978, the first delivery to a civil customer took place on 18 January 1981. The 412 adds a four-bladed rotor system to the original 212 airframe. Versions include the: **Model 412SP** (Special Performance) with 55 per cent extra fuel capacity and increased maximum take-off weight; **Model 412HP**, certified in 1991 with uprated transmission; **Model 412EP** (Enhanced Performance), PT6T-3D engine and three-axis digital flight control system, now the standard production model. Indonesia's IPTN has a licence to build 100 aircraft as the **NBell 412**. Since 1981 Agusta has also been an important 412 builder, producing aircraft (largely for government customers) as the **AB 412** family. Since 1986 all Bell helicopter production has been undertaken in Mirabel, Quebec, by Bell Helicopter Textron Canada. Model 212/412 production moved there in 1988/89. Total production exceeds 430.

SPECIFICATION: Bell 412EP
Powerplant: two 1,800-hp (1342-kW) Pratt & Whitney Canada PT6T-3D Turbo Twin-Pac turboshafts
Accommodation: single pilot, maximum of 14 passengers
Dimensions: main rotor diameter 46 ft (14.02 m); height, tail rotor turning 15 ft (4.57 m); length, rotors turning 56 ft 2 in (17.12 m)
Weights: empty, standard 6,789 lb (3079 kg); maximum take-off 11,900 lb (5397 kg)
Performance: max cruising speed, at sea level 140 mph (226 km/h); hovering ceiling, in ground effect 10,200 ft (3110 m); maximum range, with no reserves 463 miles (745 km)

Boeing 707 and 720 Four-engined short-/medium- and long-range airliners

The design that established Boeing as 'plane maker to the world' is the **Model 707**. The first US jet transport to enter service, the 707 had its roots in the **Model 387-80** (or simply the **Dash 80**), which first flew on 15 July 1954. This one-off company funded demonstrator also gave rise to the military **Model 717 (C-135)** family.

Work began on a the civil aircraft, and in October 1955 Pan American Airways announced an order for 15. The first 707 proper flew on 20 December 1957. The initial production model was the marginally-transatlantic **707-100**, chiefly serving the US domestic market. Powered by four Pratt & Whitney JT3C turbojets, it could carry an absolute maximum of 189 passengers, with a more normal load of 137. This version led to the **707-100B** with more efficient JT-3D turbofans. A long-range, short-fuselage development, the **707-138B**, was produced solely for QANTAS. Only five **707-200s** were built for Braniff, with 'hot-and-high' JT4A turbojets. The final production version was the truly intercontinental stretched **707-300**. Powered by JT4As, this version first flew in January 1959, but soon became the **707-300B** with the substitution of JT3D turbofans. The **707-400** was a 707-300 with its JT4As replaced by Rolls-Royce Conway 508s.

The final 707 version was the cargo/passenger (Combi) **707-300C**, featuring a large cargo door in the forward port fuselage. Certified in 1963, 337 were built until 1979, when the last civil 707 (No. 938) was delivered to TAROM. Including military variants

This 707-321C is a former Pan American aircraft which is today one of two operated as a pure freighter by Aeroservicios Ecuatorianos (AECA).

of the design, such as the **E-3 Sentry**, 1,012 (916 civil) Model 707s were built, before the line closed in 1992. The ultimate civilian airframe was the unique **707-700**, a CFM56-powered prototype.

The **Model 720** was a short- to medium-range version intended for the US market, and it first flew on 23 November 1959. Similar to the 707-100, it had a fuselage of only 136 ft 2 in (41.5 m) – 8 ft 2 in (2.5 m) shorter – and seated 130 passengers. Sixty-five were completed, followed by 89 JT3D-powered **Model 720Bs**. Eleven 720s were converted also to 720B standard. The last airline operator was MEA, a handful of 720s survive as VIP transports and Pratt & Whitney Canada flies one as an engine test-bed. About 110 707s are still in service, chiefly as freighters. Several have been hush-kitted by Comtran (**Q707**) to avoid Stage 2/Chapter 2 noise regulations. Stage 3 hushkits are now available from both Burbank Aeronautical II and QTV, of the USA. Burbank also offers 707 winglets for retrofit. Ireland's Omega Air and Tracor of the USA have developed a JT8D-219 re-engining programme to meet the same noise reduction requirements.

This anonymous aircraft is one of two 707-3K1Cs, fitted with Comtran's Stage 2 hushkits, operated by Romania's TAROM for lease to other airlines.

SPECIFICATION: Boeing 707-320C
Powerplant: four 18,000-lb (80-kN) Pratt & Whitney JT3D-3B turbofans
Accommodation: three (flight deck), maximum of 219 passengers (standard 150)
Dimensions: span 145 ft 9 in (44.42 m); height 42 ft 5 in (12.93 m); length 152 ft 11 in (46.61 m)
Weights: (freighter) operating, empty 141,100 lb (64000 kg); maximum payload 88,900 lb (40324 kg); maximum take-off 333,600 lb (151315 kg)
Performance: maximum level speed 627 mph (1010 km/h); service ceiling 36,000 ft (10972 m); maximum range, with maximum payload and reserves 3625 miles (5835 km)

Boeing 717

What we know today as the **Boeing 717** actually began life at Long Beach as the **McDonnell Douglas MD-95**. The aircraft was announced by MDC in June 1994 after a long series of design studies for new 100-130-seat aircraft. The MD-95 was conceived as an MD-80 'shrink' (dubbed **MD-87-105**), powered by the MD-80's JT8D-200 engines, or perhaps Rolls-Royce Tays. The aircraft that emerged actually owed far more to the DC-9, using the wing and empennage of the DC-9-34, the enlarged fin of the MD-87 and new-technology BMW Rolls-Royce BR700 turbofans. It was intended to assemble the MD-95 in China as part of McDonnell Douglas's MD90-30 Trunkliner programme, but this deal was never signed and, after several changes of mind, production reverted to the line at Long Beach, California.

In August 1997 McDonnell Douglas merged with the Boeing Company, in what effect was a total take over. The historic family of Douglas airliners were rechristened as Boeings and, in January 1998, the MD-95 became the Model 717. This decision was greeted with surprise as Boeing had already devoted the Model 717 designation to the huge C-135 family. The production version became the **717-200**, with Boeing reserving the **717-100** designation for a possible future 85-seat version.

Major assemblies for the 717 come from foreign contractors including Alenia, KAL Aerospace, Hyundai, ShinMaywa, IAI and many others.

The first 717 for AirTran, one of the four aircraft dedicated to the flight test programme, was rolled out on 23 January 1999. It flew the following month.

The 717 is aimed at the 100-seat 'regional' market, over routes of 1,500 miles (2414 km). It faces competition from Boeing's own 737-600 and emerging designs such as the Avro RJX and Airbus A318. Two versions will be available – the basic gross weight (BGW) and high gross weight (HGW) 717.

McDonnell Douglas struggled to find a launch customer but finally announced an order for 50, with 50 options, from Florida's ValuJet (now known as AirTran Airlines), on 19 October 1995. By mid-1999 that figure had climbed to 115 firm orders and 100 options. Against this background of sluggish demand, suggestions grew that Boeing would terminate the programme – the only one of the former McDonnell Douglas airliners that it had elected to keep. Boeing maintains that it is committed to the 717 and is now, reportedly, studying the 85-seat **717-100X** and 130-seat **717-300X** concepts closely.

The first 717-200 was rolled out on 10 June 1998 and made its maiden flight on 2 September. Four aircraft were dedicated to the nine-month flight test programme. After joint US and European FAA/JAA certification AirTran took delivery of its first aircraft in September 1999. The first European customer is Bavaria International Aircraft Company, a leasing firm, which will deliver its first two aircraft to Greece's Olympic Aviation.

SPECIFICATION: Boeing 717-200
Powerplant: two 18,500-lb (82.3-kN) BMW Rolls-Royce BR 715 turbofans
Accommodation: two (flight deck), standard layout for 106 passengers
Dimensions: span 93 ft 5 in (28.47 m); height 29 ft 1 in (8.86 m); length 124 ft (37.80 m)
Weights: operating, empty (BGW) 69,830 lb (31675 kg), (HGW) 70,790 lb (32110 kg); maximum take-off (BGW) 114,000 lb (51710 kg), (HGW) 121,000 lb (54885 kg)
Performance: maximum level speed 504 mph (811 km/h); service ceiling 36,000 ft (10972 m); design range, with 106 passengers and reserves (BGW) 1,580 miles (2545 km)

Boeing 727

For many years, until finally overtaken by the 737, the **Boeing 727** was the world's 'favourite airliner', selling a total of 1,831 by the time production ended in 1984. Boeing's second jetliner was planned with three Allison-built Rolls-Royce Spey engines. When the launch order was received from Eastern Airlines for 40 727s, however, this had changed to a trio of Pratt & Whitney JT8Ds. The 727 was structurally very similar to the 707, but featured a more dramatically swept wing with many high-lift devices and a T-tail. The first 727 (which became the **727-100**) flew from Renton on 9 February 1963, with 131 orders including 12 from Lufthansa, the first overseas customer. Boeing stretched the design by 20 ft (6.09 m), producing the **727-200**. Engine power was later increased by the addition of JT8D-11 and -17 turbofans. The final major version was the **727-200 Advanced** of 1970, featuring JT8D-15, then JT8D-17 and -17R engines.

During the 1970s, Boeing proposed a further 18 ft 4 in (5.6 m) fuselage stretch to produce the **727-300**, but instead opted for a new design, the 757. Before production finally closed, Boeing developed a 727 freighter, the **727-200F**, 15 of which were built for Federal Express. Powered by JT8D-17A engines, this version has a strengthened cabin floor, a large freight door and, of course, no windows. The last of 1,260 727-200s was delivered to Allegheny Airlines on 30 November 1982. Approximately 1,370 727s were still in regular service in September-1999.

Iberia is Europe's last major Boeing 727 operator. However, its fleet of over 20 Advanced 727-256s is now due for replacement, by A319/320/321s.

Valsan, in association with Rohr, has refitted 727s with JT8D-217C or -219 engines, acoustically treating the centre nacelle (while removing the thrust reverser) to quieten the aircraft. Valsan also developed a winglet refit, which appeared on two Delta aircraft in late 1993. Since 1996 Valsan's re-engining programme has been in the hands of BFGoodrich, as the **Super 27**.

Dee Howard has re-engined 44 727-100s for UPS as the **727QF** (Quiet Freighter), by fitting Rolls-Royce Tay 651-54 turbofans, and a Collins EFIS cockpit. Dee Howard was unsuccessful in a bid to re-engine 150 Delta 727s and 737s with Tay 655s, but is now offering a BMW Rolls-Royce BR715/Tay 727 re-engining programme.

Federal Express Aviation Services has developed the only Stage 3 727 hush-kit. It has orders and options for more than 800 sets. Raisbeck and DuganAir offer Stage 3 compliance by modifying flap and slat settings and using reduced thrust to lower noise signature. DuganAir also offers the Quiet Wing System modification, adding Winglet Systems' winglets to the 727.

The addition of winglets to some 727s, such as this Super 27-modified 727-2M7 of the Bahrain Amiri Flight, boosts range and reduces fuel burn.

SPECIFICATION:
Boeing 727-200
Powerplant: three 15,500-lb (68.9-kN) Pratt & Whitney JT8D-15 turbofans
Accommodation: three (flight deck), maximum of 189 passengers (standard 145)
Dimensions: span 108 ft (32.92 m); height 34 ft (10.36 m); length 153 ft 2 in (46.69 m)
Weights: operating, empty 99,600 lb (45178 kg); maximum take-off 190,500 lb (86405 kg)
Performance: maximum operating speed Mach 0.90; service ceiling 42,000 ft (9144 m); maximum range, with reserves 2510 miles (4040 km)

Boeing 737-100 and -200 Twin-engined short- to medium-range airliners

When Boeing launched its 'baby', the **Model 737**, it seemed like the company was again playing 'catch-up', as the BAC One-Eleven and DC-9 were already on offer. Using the nose and fuselage cross-section of the 707/727, Boeing announced the design in November 1964 and worked hard to win its first orders, which came from Lufthansa. This was the first time Boeing had launched a design with no US customer and, initially, Lufthansa wanted only 10 aircraft. This first version became known as the **737-100** and made its maiden flight on 9 April 1967. Entering service in Germany in February 1968, only 30 were built (by 1969) before Boeing switched to the longer and heavier **737-200**, as required by United Airlines, which had ordered 40 and taken 30 options. The 737-200 first flew on 8 August 1967, entering United service in April 1968.

Boeing continued to aerodynamically refine the basic aircraft while adding thrust reversers and revising the flap design. Continued improvements to the wing leading edge, engine mounts, Krueger flaps, braking system and undercarriage led to the the **737-200 Advanced**, introduced from the 280th production example. A range of engine options became available over the 737's life, from the JT8D-9 to the -17, and the operating weight of the 737 increased accordingly. The 737-200 Advanced could

Since 1995 Lithuanian Airlines has operated two Advanced 737-2T4s, from its base Vilnius, on its European route network.

Irish low-fares airline Ryanair has a fleet of 21 Advanced 737-200s, including several in special advertising schemes such as this one for Jaguar cars.

also accommodate additional fuel tanks in the belly hold. Some aircraft were delivered with add-on rough-field landing gear for gravel strip operations, and 104 freighter versions, the **737-200C** and **QC** (Quick Change), were built between 1965 and 1985. Towards the end of its life, increased use of composites was made in the 'first-generation' 737. The last of 865 -200 Advanced aircraft was delivered to CAAC on 18 December 1987, bringing to a close the production run of 1,144 aircraft. Approximately 935 of these are still in service.

While Boeing's attention moved to subsequent CFM56-engined versions, other companies began to upgrade the older 737s, over 750 of which are still in use. Nordam, of Tulsa, Oklahoma, and AvAero of Florida have each developed an FAA-approved Stage 3/Chapter 3-compliant hush-kits for the 737-200.

The Nordam system was certified in June 1992 and early customers included Lufthansa, Air New Zealand and US Airways. The AvAero system was certified in August 1994 and the manufacturer claims that it is more efficient than the Nordam approach. Pratt & Whitney has also been working on a modification to the JT8D engine nacelle that will reduce radiated noise by 3dB. An EFIS cockpit upgrade is on offer from Rogerson Kratos who have developed a similar refit for FedEx's 727 fleet.

SPECIFICATION:
Boeing 737-200 Advanced
Powerplant: two 15,500-lb (68.9-kN) Pratt & Whitney JT8D-15 turbofans
Accommodation: two (flight deck), maximum of 130 passengers (standard 120)
Dimensions: span 93 ft (28.35 m); height 37 ft (11.28 m); length 96 ft 11 in (29.54 m)
Weights: operating, empty 60,507 lb (27445 kg); maximum take-off 115,500 lb (52390 kg)
Performance: maximum cruising speed 532 mph (856 km/h); service ceiling 33,000 ft (10060 m); maximum range, with reserves 2913 miles (4688 km)

Boeing 737-300, 737-400 and 737-500

After 17 years of building 737s, Boeing took the family into a new era with the introduction of the stretched, re-engined 128-seat **737-300**. Revealed in 1980, Boeing was already working on the 757 and 767, and a 'new-generation' short-haul airliner was an obvious next step. Launch customers were Southwest and USAir. The 737-300 is 109 ft 7 in (33.4 m) long, some 8 ft 8 in (2.68 m) longer than the 737-200. There is still 70 per cent airframe commonality between the two, but the -300 boasts colour weather radar, a digital flight management system and auto-throttle, all in a 'glass' EFIS cockpit. The most obvious difference is the CFM56-3B (or -3C) engines, with their distinctive flat-bottomed nacelles. The first 737-300 was rolled out on 17 January 1984 and made its maiden flight on 24 February. The type received FAA certification on 14 November 1984 after 1,300 flight-test hours. The first deliveries were made to USAir on 28 November 1984 and to Southwest Airlines on 30 November. Southwest was the first to place the 737-300 in to service, on its Dallas-Houston route, on 7 December.

Boeing next examined the market for a 150-seat design, potentially an all-new design, the **7-7**. In 1983 this became the **737-400**, but Boeing stated that it did not expect to build such an aircraft for several years. Finally, after much indecision, the 737-400 was launched, in 1986, with an order for 25 from Piedmont Airlines. The new aircraft was stretched by 10 ft (3.04 m) and has a tailskid to protect the longer fuselage from over-rotation on take-off.

This 737-33R of Air New Zealand wears a special scheme marking the 1999/2000 millennial America's Cup which will be held in Auckland.

The 737-400 also has two overwing exits in place of the 737-300's one. First flight occurred on 23 February 1988. FAA certification was obtained on 2 September and Piedmont (later absorbed by USAir, which became US Airways) placed its first 737-400 into service on 1 October 1988.

Boeing still planned a new short-fuselage 737 (the **737 Lite**), which was launched as the **737-500** in 1987, making its maiden flight on 30 June 1989. Braathens SAFE, of Norway, was the launch customer. The 737-500 measures 101 ft 9 in (31 m), almost exactly the same size as the 737-200. The first deliveries were made to Southwest on 28 February 1990 – the same day FAA certification was obtained.

By June 1999 737-300 orders stood at 1,108 with 1,096 delivered. 737-400 orders stood at 486 with 482 delivered, while 737-500 orders stood at 388, with all delivered. Boeing now refers to the these aircraft as the 737 'Classic'. While the Classic family is still available to customers, Boeing's attention has now moved on to the Next Generation 737s and the Classic line will probably close around the year 2000.

Aeroflot operates 10 737-4MOs acquired in 1998 through Sailplane Leasing. They are maintained on the Bermudan register and wear a non-standard scheme.

SPECIFICATION:
Boeing 737-400
Powerplant: two 22,000-lb (97.86-kN) CFM International CFM56-3C-1 turbofans
Accommodation: two (flight deck), maximum of 171 passengers (standard 146)
Dimensions: span 94 ft 4 in (28.88 m); height 36 ft 6 in (11.13 m); length 119 ft 7 in (36.45 m)
Weights: operating, empty 73,710 lb (33434 kg); maximum take-off 138,500 lb (62822 kg)
Performance: maximum cruising speed 564 mph (908 km/h); cruising altitude 35,000 ft (10668 m); maximum range, with reserves 3,105 miles (5000 km)

Boeing 737-600, 737-700, -800 and -900

USA
Twin-engined short- to medium-range airliners

Surprisingly quickly after the launch of the 737-500, Boeing announced that it was looking at further developments of the 737 family. In 1992 discussions began with IAE and Pratt & Whitney about developing new engines for the 737, as an alternative to the existing CFM56. Plans formalised around the **737-X** concept. This involved a fuselage stretch, new engines, a new wing and the incorporation of new avioncs and new technology generally.

In June 1993 the **Next Generation 737** was offered to customers, but without the choice of engines once envisaged. The sole powerplant would be the newly-developed CFM56-7. Three new aircraft were on offer; the 108-seat **737-600**, originally dubbed the **737-500X** and the same size as the 737-500; the 128-seat **737-700**, formerly the **737-300X** and comparable to the 737-300; and the 160-seat **737-800**, previously the **737-400X**.

The Next Generation 737 was launched on 17 November 1993 with an order for 63 737-300Xs from Southwest Airlines. Production was launched on 19 January 1994 when Southwest and Boeing signed a definitive contract for what had become the 737-700. The first was rolled out on 8 December 1996 and made its maiden flight on 9 February 1997. The type was certified on 7 November 1997 and deliveries began immediately afterwards.

Outwardly, there is little to distinguish the 737-700 from its predecessor the 737-300. All the Next Generation 737s have an enlarged fin and wing area.

Air Berlin was already a 737-400 operator when it took delivery of the first of its 14 CFM56-7 powered 737-800s, in July 1998.

Go-ahead for the stretched 737-800 was given on 5 September 1994. The it can carry up to 189 passengers, but with a typical load of 160 it outranges the 737-400 by 920 miles (1480 km). The launch customer was Hapag Lloyd which announced an order for 16 aircraft on 18 November 1994. The first 737-800 flew on 31 July 1997 and Hapag Lloyd accepted its first aircraft on 22 April 1998.

The third member of the family received its launch order from SAS on 14 March 1995, when the airline signed for 70 orders and options (to be split among -700s and -800s also). The type made its maiden flight on 22 January 1998 and the first 737-600 delivery occurred on 18 September.

By June 1999 737-600 orders stood at 113 with 20 delivered. 737-700 orders stood at 469 with 114 delivered and 737-800 orders stood at 519 with 118 delivered.

In November 1997 Alaska Airlines launched the **737-900**, which incorporates a further 8-ft 8-in (2.64-m) stretch over the 737-800 to carry a standard load of 177 passengers. The design was finalised in February 1999 and first deliveries are due in April 2001. Boeing has also developed the **Boeing Business Jet** (or **BBJ**) using the fuselage of the 737-700 with the strengthened wing (with optional winglets) and engines of the 737-800.

SPECIFICATION:
Boeing 737-700 (standard gross weight)
Powerplant: two 22,000-lb (97.9-kN) CFM International CFM56-7B turbofans
Accommodation: two (flight deck), maximum of 149 passengers (standard 128)
Dimensions: span 112 ft 7 in (34.31 m); height 41 ft 2 in (12.55 m); length 110 ft 4 in (33.63 m)
Weights: operating, empty 83,790 lb (38006 kg); maximum take-off 133,000 lb (60330 kg)
Performance: maximum operating Mach number 0.82; maximum cruising altitude 41,000 ft (12500 m); design range, with 126 passengers 1,824 miles (2935 km)

Boeing 747-100, -200 and -300 Four-engined long-range airliners

In 1965, combining work done for the USAF's CX-HLS competition (eventually won by the Lockheed C-5), with preliminary studies for a new high-capacity airliner, Boeing began planning a 'double-bubble'-fuselage aircraft with 10-abreast seating and a gross weight of approximately 530,000 lb (240400 kg). Pan American signed a letter of intent for 25 in December 1965. The **Model 747-100** was formally launched in 1966, followed by the heavier **747-100B**, an all-cargo **747-100F** and the Combi **747-100C**. Pratt & Whitney JT9D turbofans were chosen to power the type. The first aircraft was rolled out on 30 September 1968 at Boeing's new 43-acre (17.4-ha) facility at Paine Field, Seattle, and made its first flight on 9 February 1969. Pan Am operated the first revenue service between London and New York on 22 January 1970. In all 205 747-100s were completed, but before production had finished Boeing introduced a heavier (by some 10 per cent) development, the **747B**, or **747-200** with much improved payload/range capability. Certified in December 1970, the first of these entered service with KLM in February 1971.

The next version was the nose-loading **747-200F** freighter, which entered service with Lufthansa in April 1972. The **747-200(SCD)** is a freighter with a side cargo door. Also in 1972, Japan Airlines introduced the **747SR** (Short Range), identical to the 747-100 but restressed to carry 523 passengers over an increased number of flying cycles. In total, 384 747-200s of all versions were delivered.

Alitalia Cargo 747 freighter services are operated using aircraft leased from Atlas Air, as illustrated by this 747-2F6B(SF) now fitted with a side cargo door.

In June 1980 Boeing revealed the **747SUD** (Stretched Upper Deck). Essentially a -200 with the upper deck extended by 23 ft (7 m), it was renamed the **747-300** by the time of its maiden flight on 5 October 1982. Swissair was the launch customer, and the SUD modification could be, and was, applied retrospectively. A total of 81 were completed.

Between 1974 and 1977 Boeing undertook 24 conversions of 747-100s to -100F freighters, along with two Combis. In 1989 Boeing Wichita revived this earlier conversion work and now offers -100 and -200 all-cargo conversions. GATX/Airlog made five similar conversions between 1988 and 1991. In 1994 the line was revived and -200 to -200F and Combi to full freighter conversions have been undertaken. In 1996 the FAA effectively grounded all 10 existing GATX/Airlog conversions saying it had wrongly certified them using incorrect data.

Other freighter/Combi conversions are offered by HAECO/TAECO in Hong Kong – which has undertaken conversions for SAA, Atlas Air and Air China – and IAI's Bedek Division which has modified aircraft for Lufthansa.

South African Airways operates 747-200s, -300s, -400s SPs and dedicated -200F freighters. This 747-312 still wears special Olympic Team colours.

SPECIFICATION: Boeing 747-200B
Powerplant: four 52,500-lb (233.5-kN) General Electric CF6-50E2, or 53,110-lb (236.25-kN) Rolls-Royce RB211-524D4-B, or 54,750-lb (243.5-kN) Pratt & Whitney JT9D-7R4G2 turbofans
Accommodation: three (flight deck), maximum of 480 passengers (standard 365)
Dimensions: span 195 ft 8 in (59.64 m); height 63 ft 5 in (19.33 m); length 231 ft 10 in (70.66 m)
Weights: operating, empty 383,600 lb (173998 kg); maximum take-off 775,000 lb (351534 kg)
Performance: maximum level speed 610 mph (981 km/h); cruising altitude 45,000 ft (13715 m); maximum range, with 366 passengers 7,940 miles (12778 km)

Boeing 747SP

Soon after the launch of the 747 it became clear that some customers needed a similar aircraft capable of covering great distances, without the penalties of the 747's 'excessive' passenger capacity. As a result, in August 1973, Boeing announced that an extended-range, short-bodied development of the 747-100, the **747SP** (Special Performance), was underway. This new version had a rate of climb, cruising altitude and cruising speed all increased in comparison with the 747-100, and a range in excess of 6,904 miles (11112 km). The 747SP is 47 ft 1 in (14.35 m) shorter than the 747-100/-200, and has a fin extended by 5 ft (1.52 m), with a double-hinged rudder. The centre-section was redesigned to retain the trademark upper deck. The rear fuselage was radically 'pinched in' to reduce its width. This reduction in length necessitated the extension of the fin. The tailplanes were also lengthened by 10 ft (3 m).

The launch order came from Pan American, which ordered 10 in September 1973. The first SP, the 265th production 747, was rolled out on 19 May 1975 and first flew on 4 July. Pan Am put the type into service on its Los Angeles-Tokyo route on 25 April 1976. A total of 45 747SPs were built for customers such as Braniff, CAAC, China Airlines, Iran Air, Korean Air Lines, Pan Am, QANTAS, South African Airways, Syrian Arab Airlines and TWA, with

Syrianair still has the two 747SP-94s that it acquired in 1976 in everyday service on its Middle Eastern and European routes.

This 747SP-Z5 was the very last SP to come off the line and was delivered to the Abu Dhabi Amiri Flight (UAE government) in December 1989.

the last delivery coming in 1989. This was, in fact, a specially-ordered VIP aircraft, and the last true airline delivery occurred in 1982.

Subsequently, 747SPs have appeared in the colours of Alliance, American Airlines, Australia Asia, Air Mauritius, Cameroon Airlines, Corsair, Flitestar (Trek), Luxair, Mandarin Airlines and Namib Air. The largest operators were Pan Am and United Airlines – which took over Pan Am's 10 aircraft and its Pacific routes during the late 1980s. United began to retire its fleet in 1995. One ex-United aircraft has been modified to serve as NASA's **SOFIA** (Stratospheric Observatory For Infrared Astronomy) flying telescope. Today, the largest operators are Iran Air and South African Airways (four aircraft each).

Ten SPs are currently flown by government/royal owners; three in the UAE (Abu Dhabi and Dubai), two in Qatar, Saudi Arabia and Bahrain and one in Oman. One of the Omani aircraft (A40-SP) and one UAE aircraft (A6-ZSN) have been fitted with a satellite communications dome behind the main 'hump'. Another of the UAE aircraft (A6-SMR) has been fitted with a 'glass' EFIS cockpit and is thus unique among SPs. A VIP 747SP (YI-ALM) was also delivered to the government of Iraq, though it wore basic Iraqi Airways colours. Since 1991 this aircraft has remained stored at Tunisia.

SPECIFICATION: Boeing 747SP
Powerplant: four Pratt & Whitney JT9D-7A, or Rolls-Royce RB211-52B2/-524C2/-524D4 turbofans, rated between 46,250 lb (205.7 kN) and 53,110 lb (236.325 kN)
Accommodation: three (flight deck), maximum of 440 passengers (standard 276)
Dimensions: span 195 ft 8 in (59.64 m); height 65 ft 5 in (19.94 m); length 184 ft 9 in (56.31 m)
Weights: operating, empty 333,900 lb (151454 kg); maximum take-off 700,000 lb (317515 kg)
Performance: max speed 619 mph (996 km/h); service ceiling 45,100 ft (13745 m); max range, with 276 passengers 7,658 miles (12324 km)

Boeing 747-400

At the 1984 Farnborough air show, Boeing unveiled the '**Advanced 747-300**'. With its further increased wingspan and higher operating weight, the new 747 would be lighter than previous models, with much use of composite materials in its construction. Range would be extended and its EFIS cockpit could be managed by just two crew. The cockpit design is a major advance over previous 747s with two colour multi-function displays available to each pilot for their Honeywell/Sperry FMS (Flight Management System). To increase range, 6-ft (1.8-m) winglets and an additional tailfin fuel tank were added. Northwest Airlines became the launch customer with an order for 10 on 22 October 1985.

The first 747-400 was rolled out on 26 January 1988, and took to the air on 29 April. Certification with PW4056 engines came on 10 January 1989, followed by CF6-80C2Bs on 8 May and RB211-524Gs on 8 June 1989. Finally, the RB211-524H was added on 11 May 1990. That same month the 747-400 became the only basic 747 model on offer.

In February 1990 a freighter version, the **747-400F**, was launched. While this has all the improvements (including the winglets) of the -400, it possesses the short upper deck of the 747-200. The 747-400F can carry 244,000 lb (110676 kg) of cargo 4,950 miles (7970 km). Air France became the launch customer in September 1989. The first example flew on 7 May 1993 and, by June 1999, 49 had been ordered with 29 delivered. A Combi **747-400M** was launched in 1989, able to carry 266 passengers and 60,000 lb

British Airways currently has a massive fleet of 57 747-436s in service, though it has revised some future 747 orders in favour of the smaller 777.

(27215 kg) of freight above the floor. By June 1999 21 had been ordered and delivered.

In October 1990 Boeing began development of the **747-400D** (Domestic) in association with Japan Air Lines and All Nippon Airways. Like the 747-200SR, the 747-400D is a high-capacity transport intended for the Japanese domestic market. It has no winglets, five additional windows in the upper deck and a total of 566 seats. Certified in October 1991, a total of 19 have been delivered. By June 1999 standard 747-400 sales had reached 434 with 383 delivered.

A **747-400 PIP** (Performance Improvement Package) evolved in 1993, making aerodynamic and structural changes to increase range to 8,000 nm (14816 km; 9,206 miles). In December 1997 the **747-400IGW** (Increased Gross Weight) became available, adding one or two fuel tanks in the hold and pushing take-off weight up to 910,825 lb (413,140 kg). Two increased capacity designs, the **747-500X** and **747-600X** were shelved in 1997. Instead, Boeing is developing the **747-400X** (**747-400ER**) which will have more fuel, extended range and would provide the baseline airframe for any future 747 stretch.

The 747-400F – such as this Asiana Cargo example – retains the distinctive winglets of the -400 but not the extended upper deck of the passenger model.

SPECIFICATION: Boeing 747-400
Powerplant: four General Electric CF6-80C2B1F/ C2B1F1/C2B7F, or Pratt & Whitney PW4056/ 60/62, or Rolls-Royce RB211-524G/H turbofans, rated between 56,750 lb (252.4 kN) and 62,000 lb (275.8 kN)
Accommodation: two (flight deck), maximum of 568 passengers (standard 390)
Dimensions: span 211 ft 5 in (64.44 m); height 63 ft 8 in (19.41 m); length 231 ft 10 in (70.66 m)
Weights: operating, empty 402,900 lb (182754 kg); maximum take-off 870,000 lb (394625 kg)
Performance: max level speed 612 mph (984 km/h); service ceiling 45,000 ft (13716 m); max range, with 420 passengers 8,314 miles (13398 km)

Boeing 757

By the mid-1970s the end of sales of the Model 727, Boeing's best seller, was in sight. A replacement was a priority and a stretched, rewinged and re-engined 727 was considered before Boeing, after much dialogue with the airlines, settled on the 190/200-seat **7N7** ('N' for narrow). Bearing a marked resemblance to the 727, this aircraft received the go-ahead, after firm orders for 40 from British Airways and Eastern Airlines, in 1979.

Later that year, however, the appearance of the new type, now named the **Model 757**, was completely revised, emerging far more similar to the 767 that was in parallel development. Finding themselves with two new airliners at once, Boeing set out to make the two designs as compatible to design, manufacture and operate as possible – transforming the 757 into its current shape. A prototype was rolled out on 13 January 1982 and made its maiden flight on 19 February. For the first time, Rolls-Royce engines had been chosen as a launch powerplant, and the airframe and RB211 engine combination was certified by January 1983. Eastern placed their aircraft into service first, on 1 January 1983, followed by British Airways on 9 February.

In 1984 PW2037 engines were flown on the 757, as Delta Airlines had specified the more efficient engines for its aircraft. Rolls-Royce developed

The 757-200PF has no windows or passenger doors, a new crew entry door, a large cargo door in the port forward fuselage and a 9g cargo restraint system.

The state colours of Arizona adorn this America West 757-2S7, named **City of Phoenix** *– Phoenix is the airline's home town.*

correspondingly improved versions of the RB211. In 1985 the **757-200(ER)** (Extended Range) was certified for EROPS with Rolls-Royce engines, followed by Pratt & Whitney-powered 757s in 1990.

In 1985 a UPS order launched the **757-200PF** (Package Freighter). The 757-200PF first flew on 11 August 1987, and the first delivery took place on 16 September. A total of 78 -200PFs, of 80 ordered, have been delivered. A second cargo version, the Combi **757-200C** (now the **757-200M**), was launched with an order from Royal Nepal Airways in 1986. Featuring the same cargo door as the PF, the 757-200C retains standard seats and cabin fittings and can carry 164 passengers plus freight pallets in the forward fuselage. To date only one 757-200M has been delivered, to Nepal, on 15 September 1988.

It was not until 1996 that Boeing launched the first major 757 development, the **757-300**. Stretched by 23 ft 4 in (7.13 m) it boosts passenger capacity by 20 per cent and cargo capacity by 50 per cent. Maximum seating is 289, with a standard layout for 240. The launch customer was Condor, which placed an order for 12 (later 13) on 12 September 1996. The first delivery was made on 10 March 1999 and 757-300 orders currently stand at 17. By August 1999 total 757 orders stood at a total of 872 with 754 delivered.

SPECIFICATION: Boeing 757-200

Powerplant: two 37,400-lb (166.4-kN) Rolls-Royce 535C, or 38,200-lb (170-kN) Pratt & Whitney PW2037, or 40,100-lb (178.4-kN) Rolls-Royce 535E4, or 41,700-lb (185.5-kN) Pratt & Whitney PW2040 turbofans

Accommodation: two (flight deck), maximum of 239 passengers (standard 178)

Dimensions: span 124 ft 10 in (38.05 m); height 44 ft 6 in (13.56 m); length 155 ft 3 in (47.32 m)

Weights: operating, empty 126,060 lb (57180 kg); maximum take-off 250,000 lb (113395 kg)

Performance: max operating speed Mach 0.80; service ceiling 40,000 ft (12192 m); max range, with 186 passengers 4,603 miles (7408 km)

Boeing 767

Both the 757 and the **Model 767** can trace their roots back to Boeing's 7X7 designs of the mid-1970s. At one stage, Boeing considered a tri-jet long-range **7X7LR**, which it planned to develop with Italian and Japanese partners. The design matured until finally allocated its 767 title in 1978. Three versions were planned, the first and smallest as a direct competitor to the A310. This initial 180/190-seat **767-100** was never built. Instead, the mid-range, 200/210-seat, 159-ft 2-in (48.51-m) **767-200** was launched in 1978, with orders for 30 from United Airlines.

The first 767 was rolled out on 4 August 1981 and flew on 26 September; the type was certified in July 1982, with PW JT9Ds. United put its 767-200s into service on the Denver-Chicago route on 19 August 1982. The first development was the higher MTOW **767-200ER** (Extended Range). Only Air Canada and El Al acquired this early version, which offered little improvement over the basic 767-200. A new series -200ER, with increased fuel capacity, flew on 30 May 1984, with initial deliveries made to Ethiopian Airlines. The 767-200ER later gained higher-rated CF6-80C2 and PW4052 engines.

Orders from Japan Air Lines launched the stretched 269-seat **767-300**, which first flew on 30 January 1986. The 767-300 is structurally similar to the 767-200, but lengthened by 21 ft 1 in (6.43 m). Boeing again offered a **767-300ER**, from 1987 onwards, with a higher MTOW and extra fuel. American Airlines was the first to order this version, with an initial purchase of 15. Variations of this

This 767-322ER of United Airlines is decorated with the various colours of United's partners in the Star Alliance international airline partnership.

long-range model followed, almost customer-by-customer, as different engines and increased gross weights became available. Several 767/engine combinations have been qualified for ETOPS, although these are not necessarily all 767-200ER/-300ERs. By June 1999 deliveries (and sales) for the baseline 767 variants stood at: 767-200, 128; 767-200ER, 101 (111); 767-300, 100 (107); 767-300ER, 392 (433).

UPS launched the **767-300F**, a freighter version similar to the 757-200PF, with an order for 30 (with 30 options) in January 1993. First flight for this version, with a payload/range of 90,000 lb (40823 kg) over 4,000 nm (7408 km; 4,603 miles) took place on 20 June 1995. The first delivery occurred on 12 October. Asiana was the next customer and current orders stand at 32 with 29 delivered.

Boeing is now beginning flight tests of the stretched 261/305-seat **767-400ER**. The -400ER is stretched by 21 ft (6.4 m), compared to the -300, and can be powered by CF6-8002 or PW4000 engines. Launch customer was Delta Air Lines, which ordered 21 on 20 March 1997. The first 767-400ER was rolled out on 26 August 1999.

Uzbekistan Airways operates a wide mix of Western and Soviet-era airliners – including two 767-33PERs – from its main bases at Tashkent and Samarkand.

SPECIFICATION:
Boeing 767-300ER
Powerplant: two 56,750-lb (252.4-kN) Pratt & Whitney PW4056, or 60,000-lb (266.9-kN) General Electric CF6-80C2B4 or Pratt & Whitney PW4060 turbofans
Accommodation: two (flight deck), maximum of 290 passengers (standard 250)
Dimensions: span 156 ft 1 in (47.57 m); height 52 ft (15.85 m); length 180 ft 3 in (54.94 m)
Weights: operating, empty 179,400 lb (81374 kg); maximum take-off 400,000 lb (181437 kg)
Performance: cruising speed Mach 0.80; service ceiling 40,000 ft (12192 m); maximum range with reserves 6,978 miles (11230 km)

Boeing 777

Throughout its history, Boeing has been faced with make-or-break decisions to develop a new type that will dictate the future of the company. The Model 707 and 747 are two such examples, and it is fair to say that they have now been joined by the **Model 777** as a milestone in the Boeing story.

Boeing's first fully fly-by-wire airliner began life as the **7J7** in the early 1980s. It later became the **767-X** as airlines requested a design that fitted in between the 767-300 and 747-400. The final configuration was revealed in 1989 and formally launched, as the **777-200**, in October 1990 with an order for 34 (and 34 options), from United Airlines. While the 777 retains the appearance of an enlarged 767, it is a fundamentally new aircraft with many unique design features, materials and manufacturing techniques.

Three versions are currently available. The baseline **777-200** (once known as the '**A Market**' or **777-200A**) is aimed at the US transcontinental market, carrying 249 passengers over a range of 4,200 nm (7773 km, 4,830 miles). The **777-200ER**, has a range of 7,380 nm (13658 km, 8,487 miles) with 305 passengers and a maximum take-off weight of 632,500 lb (286902 kg). It has also had a succession of names. Until 1998 it was the **777-200IGW** (Increased Gross Weight). Before that it was the **777-200B** and (initially) the '**B Market**' 777.

British Airway's first batch of 777-236ERs were all GE-90-powered. It second batch will have Trent 895 engines and a higher take-off weight yet again.

Egyptair's 777-266ERs, delivered in 1997, are all powered by PW4090 engines. This is the latest and most powerful development of the PW4000 engine.

On 9 April 1994 the first 777, a 777-200, was rolled out at the Everett plant and made its maiden flight on 12 June 1994. After FAA/JAA certification on 19 April 1995. The first 777 service was inaugurated by United Airlines on 7 June 1995. British Airways undertook the first service with a GE90-powered 777-200 on 17 November 1995. The first Trent 800-powered 777 for Cathay Pacific flew on 26 May. The first (GE90-powered) 777-200IGW flew on 7 October 1996 and was delivered to British Airways on 6 February 1997.

The third current 777 version is the stretched **777-300**, 20 per cent larger than the -200 and capable of carrying between 368 and 450 passengers. The 777-300 is extended by 33 ft 3 in (10.15 m) to give a fuselage length of 242 ft 4 in (73.88 m). The first 777-300 flew on 16 October 1997 (Trent engines) followed by another on 4 February 1998 (PW4000) engines. The first delivery was made to Cathay Pacific on 29 May 1998.

Boeing is now studying two very-long range developments, the **777-200X** and **777-300X** which will be powered solely by the GE90 engine. The new 777s will have increased operating weights and a design range (in the case of the -200X) of over 9,942 miles (16000 km). By August 1999 total 777 orders had reached 429 with 227 delivered.

SPECIFICATION:
Boeing 777-200
Powerplant: two Rolls-Royce Trent 877, or Pratt & Whitney PW4074 or General Electric GE90-75B turbofans rated between 74,000 lb (329 kN) and 77,000 lb (342 kN) each
Accommodation: two (flight deck), maximum of 440 passengers (standard 375)
Dimensions: span 199 ft 11 in (60.93 m); height 60 ft 6 in (18.44 m); length 205 ft 11½ in (62.78 m)
Weights: operating, empty 306,800 lb (139160 kg); maximum take-off 545,000 lb (247210 kg)
Performance: max cruising speed Mach 0.87; service ceiling 43,100 ft (13136 m); maximum range, with reserves 5,929 miles (9537 km)

Boeing Vertol Model 234

Studies for what became the **Chinook** began in the 1950s and coalesced around a US Army requirement for a new battlefield transport helicopter. Boeing's proposal, the **Boeing Vertol Model 114**, was developed from the tandem rotor helicopter designs of the Vertol Aircraft Corporation in the early 1950s – such as the **Model 107 (H-46 Sea Knight)**. In 1960 Boeing took over Vertol (establishing Boeing Vertol) and maintained its design approach with the Model 114. The US Army signed a contract for five pre-production **YHC-1B** aircraft in 1959, which were redesigned as **YCH-47A**s and named Chinook (a native American word for a Arctic wind). The first aircraft made its maiden flight on 21 September 1961 and deliveries of production standard **CH-47A**s began in December 1972.

The Chinook was intended as a military heavylift helicopter. However, the potential crossover into commercial operations was not lost on Boeing Vertol and so, in 1978, it announced a wholly civil version of the military model.

This aircraft, the **Model 234** was developed along two lines. The **Model 234LR** was a dual passenger/ freight Combi model, while the **Model 234UT** was a utility version for specialised tasks such as logging and heavy construction. Provision for extra fuel tanks was made in the side 'pods' and in the main cabin, in the case of the Model 234UT. The fuselage 'pods' also provide flotation augmentation in the event of an emergency water landing. The Chinook is designed to remain upright in stormy seas with

Model 234UT Chinooks did not have the external 'pods' of the Model 234LR passenger aircraft and instead carried fuel in internal tanks.

waves up to 30-ft (9.15-m) in height. The aircraft were also fitted with weather radar, dual-four -axis automatic flight control system and a comprehensive de-icing system

British Airways Helicopters launched the Model 234LR programme in November 1978 with an initial order for three aircraft to operate oil rig support missions in the North Sea. In this long-range transport role the Chinook can carry up to 44 passengers. The Combi aircraft can carry a mix of 16 passengers and 16,000 lb (7258 kg) of freight. The first Model 234LR flew on 19 August 1980 and entered service in July 1981. The 234UT was certified in 1982. In May 1985 a new version, the **Model 234ER** (Extended Range), was certified, capable of carrying 17 passengers over 874 nm (1621 km, 1,008 miles). Boeing also developed the **Model 234MLR** (Multi-purpose Long Range), similar to the LR but with internal fuel tanks. Production of the commercial Chinooks was suspended in the early 1990s, but since 1997 Boeing Helicopters has been negotiating to restart the line in China with the Harbin Aircraft Manufacturing Company.

This Model 234LR shows off the fuel-carrying sponsons that are common to virtually all Chinooks. It is also fitted with a nose-mounted weather radar.

SPECIFICATION:
Boeing Helicopters Model 234LR
Powerplant: two Textron Lycoming AL 5512 turboshafts, rated at 4,074-shp (3039 kW), maximum continuous
Accommodation: two (flight deck), maximum of 44 passengers (standard 36)
Dimensions: rotor diameter 60 ft (18.29 m); height 18 ft 11½ in (5.78 m); length 52 ft 1 in (15.87 m)
Weights: operating, empty 25,900 lb (11748 kg); maximum take-off 48,500 lb (22000 kg)
Performance: max cruising speed 167 mph (269 km/h), at 2,000 ft (600 m); operational ceiling 15,000 ft (4575 m); maximum range, with reserves 610 miles (982 km)

Bombardier Global Express

Development of the **Global Express** long-range executive jet was announced at the 1991 NBAA show and formally launched on 20 December 1993. The aircraft was a originally a Canadair design, drawing on that company's experience with the **Regional Jet** and associated **Regional Jet Special Edition (SE)**. The SE was a 19-seat corporate version of the Regional Jet airliner, produced to a special order from TAG Aeronautics, which was seeking an aircraft capable of flying non-stop London-Jeddah with three crew and five passengers. The first SE was delivered in 1995 and to date Canadair has produced six examples.

These paved the way for the Global Express, an ultra-long range business jet aimed at sectors up to 6,500 nm (12030 km, 7475 miles), and intended to compete head-to-head with the Gulfstream V. Though Canadair remains the design authority and builds some of the airframe assemblies, the Global Express (or **GX**) is marketed as a Bombardier aircraft – Bombardier Inc. (now the Bombardier Aerospace Group) having owned Canadair since 1986. As a result it has been allocated the designation **BL901**.

The eight- to 19-seat Global Express combines the fuselage cross-section of a Challenger, with the cabin length of a Regional Jet and an all-new supercritical wing, featuring leading-edge slats and

This is the third Global Express pre-production aircraft, seen unpainted while still involved in company flight tests during 1998.

Bombardier puts the market for extra-long range business jets at between 500 and 800 aircraft, over 15 years. It hopes to win 50 per cent of those orders.

winglets. The advanced cockpit is built around a Honeywell Primus 2000XP EFIS system. The GX uses a fly-by-wire control system, with a sidestick controller for the pilots and is optimised for both high-speed and short-field operations.

Japan's Mitsubishi Heavy Industries is a key partner in the programme, developing and manufacturing the wing and fuselage centre-section. Short Brothers designed and builds the forward fuselage, horizontal stabiliser, engine nacelles and other composite components. De Havilland Canada supplies the rear fuselage, engine pylons, vertical stabiliser and also undertakes final assembly at its Downsview plant.

The prototype was rolled out on 26 August 1996 and first flew on 13 October. Four aircraft were dedicated to the flight test programme, the last of these taking to the air on 8 September 1997. Bombardier had hoped for certification in early 1998 and to deliver 20 aircraft during that year. Several hitches in the test programme saw that schedule pushed back by over a year. The GX did not achieve FAA certification until 13 November 1998 and JAA certification until 7 May 1999. The first customer delivery was finally made on 8 July 1999, to Toyota. According to Bombardier firm orders for the Global Express stand at 104 by July 1999.

SPECIFICATION:
Bombardier BL901 Global Express
Powerplant: two 16,490-lb (65.3-kN) BMW Rolls-Royce BR710A2-20 turbofans
Accommodation: two (flight deck), up to 19 passengers, 12 as standard
Dimensions: span 93 ft 6 in (28.50 m), over winglets; height 24 ft 10 in (7.57 m); length, overall 99 ft 5 in (30.30 m)
Weights: operating, empty 48,800 lb (22135 kg); maximum take-off 93,500 lb (42410 kg)
Performance: max level speed, above FL.310 Mach 0.90; max operating altitude 51,000 ft (15545 m); max range, with 8 passengers and reserves 7,710 miles (12408 km)

Britten-Norman BN-2

John Britten and Desmond Norman's **Islander** design began life in April 1964. The two held a 25 per cent stake in Cameroon Air Transport and the Islander was produced to fulfil its requirements and those of other airlines operating in 'austere' environments. The maiden flight occurred on 13 June 1965. Testing resulted in a switch from Rolls-Royce Continental IO-360-Bs to Avco Lycoming 0-540 piston engines. With this revised powerplant and a slight increase in wingspan, a **BN-2** production prototype first flew on 20 August 1966 and 23 were built to this standard. In June 1969 production moved on to the improved **BN-2A** and 890 were built until 1989. In addition to production at Bembridge, licence agreements were also reached with Romaero of Romania (first flight 4 August 1969, 500 built) and PADC of the Philippines (47).

The **BN-2B** made its debut in 1979, at about the same time that the company was acquired by Switzerland's Pilatus, becoming Pilatus Britten Norman. The BN-2B offered an increased landing weight, changes in cabin design and a choice of powerplants. **The BN-2B-26** was fitted with Continental O-540s, while the **BN-2B-20** had more powerful IO-540s – both with a three-bladed prop. A total of 153 were built before production ended in 1997 – though the type is still on offer to customers.

Britain's Aurigny Air Services was the first Trilander operator and it flies its aircraft – including cartoon character G-JOEY – to the Channel Islands.

Aspiring Air of Wanaka, New Zealand, which operates two BN-2B-26s is typical of the many small Islander operators around the world.

Two extra seats were added to the long-nosed **BN-2S**, but the next major development came on 6 April 1977 when turboprops were added. Initial Lycoming LTP 101s were changed to Allison 250-B17Cs for the production **BN-2T Turbine Islander**, which flew in that form on 2 August 1980. BN-2T deliveries have now reached 64.

Perhaps the most distinctive variant of the Islander was the **BN-2A Mk III Trislander**. First flown on 11 September 1970, this had a lengthened fuselage for up to 17 passengers and a third engine mounted in the much-modified tail assembly. Production was launched soon after and versions included: the increased MTOW **BN-2A Mk III-1**; long-nosed **Mk III-2**; and auto feather-capable **Mk III-3**. The last of 73 UK-built Trislanders was delivered in September 1984. Another 12 were also built as the **Tri-Commutair** in the USA by the International Aviation Corp. In May 1999 the Trislander was unexpectedly revived by an order for three aircraft from China Northern Airlines, to be delivered by November 2001.

Britten Norman is now owned by Biofarm Inc.. of the UK and in January 1999 it bought up Romaero's manufacturing and overhaul facility at Banaesa. Romaero will now supply components and sub-assemblies to the Bembridge plant in the UK.

SPECIFICATION:
Britten-Norman BN-2T Turbine Islander
Powerplant: two 400-hp (298-kW) Allison 250-B17C turboprops
Accommodation: two (flight deck) and up to 10 in cabin
Dimensions: span 49 ft (14.94 m); height 13 ft 8¾ in (4.18 m); length 35 ft 7¾ in (10.86 m)
Weights: empty, equipped 4,040 lb (1832 kg); maximum take-off 7,000 lb (3175 kg)
Performance: maximum cruising speed 196 mph (315 km/h) at 10,000 ft (3050 m); service ceiling 23,000 ft (7010 m); range with maximum fuel and reserves 679 miles (1093 km)

Canadair CL-215 and CL-415

The need to protect Canada's substantial forests from fire prompted the development of a purpose-built fire-fighting aircraft in the mid-1960s. After a symposium on the subject was held in Ottawa, in 1963, Canadair began to develop an amphibian that could scoop up water without lengthy periods spent reloading on the ground. The provincial government of Quebec, and France's Sécurité Civile organisation, approached Canadair and placed the launch orders for what became the **CL-215**.

While the Canadian company had no previous experience in building such an aircraft, it developed a simple yet rugged design, proofed against salt water corrosion and of considerable bulk. Its single-step hull hides a fully retractable nosewheel, while the main gear folds into fuselage recesses beneath the high wing. For its main fire-fighting role, the CL-215 can carry 1,200 Imp gal (5455 litres) of water, or retardant, in two tanks. Lake or sea water can be scooped up through two retractable inlets under the hull while the aircraft skims across the surface, before taking off once more. It takes just under one second to release the entire load and, as Canada is privileged to have so much inland water, the CL-215 can make a drop on a given target approximately every 10 minutes. Most, though not all, customers operate the CL-215 in this way.

With a first flight on 23 October 1967, 125 CL-215s were built before production ended in 1990. Current operators include the governments of eight Canadian provinces along with France,

The CL-415 is a new-build turboprop-powered fire-fighter, renamed to make it distinct from re-engined versions of the piston-powered CL-215.

Greece, Italy, Spain, Thailand (SAR version for navy), Venezuela and Croatia. On 8 June 1989 a Quebec aircraft, fitted with Pratt & Whitney Canada PW123AF turboprops in place of the original Pratt & Whitney R-2800 radial piston engines, made its maiden flight. This re-engined version, the **CL-215T**, is now available to any existing CL-215 customer, and Spain ordered 15 conversion kits, delivered by the end of 1993.

On the production line, Canadair introduced the **CL-415** in 1991. Intended as a turboprop from the outset, the CL-415 has winglets and finlets for added control at high power settings. It also possess a much refined structure and a Honeywell EFIS cockpit. The first example flew on 6 December 1993 and Quebec was again the launch customer. The CL-415 is capable of skimming 1,350 Imp gal (6137 litres) of water in 12 seconds while flying over a lake, even with waves of 2½ ft (0.76 m). The first of Quebec's eight aircraft was delivered in December 1994 and these have been followed by 12 for France, six for Italy and one for Croatia. Production stood at 34 by early 1999.

The piston-engined CL-215 is still an impressive and capable fire-fighting aircraft, though many operators have opted for the turboprop upgrade.

SPECIFICATION:
Canadair CL-415
Powerplant: two 2,380-hp (1775-kW) Pratt & Whitney Canada PW123AF turboprops
Accommodation: two (flight deck)
Dimensions: span 93 ft 11 in (28.63 m); height 29 ft 5½ in (8.98 m); length 65 ft ½ in (19.82 m)
Weights: operating, empty 27,190 lb (12333 kg); disposable payload 13,500 lb (6123 kg); maximum take-off, water 37,850 lb (17168 kg)
Performance: maximum cruising speed 234 mph (376 km/h); take-off distance, water 2,670 ft (814 m); scooping distance, at sea level 4,240 ft (1293 m)

Canadair Challenger

The aircraft that evolved into the **Challenger** began as Bill Lear's (of Learjet fame) proposed **LearStar 600**. A deal was struck in April 1976 under which Canadair secured exclusive rights covering the design, manufacture and marketing process. Further development soon resulted in important changes being made and the aircraft was renamed **Canadair Challenger** in March 1977.

Three pre-production examples were produced for development work and the first of these made its maiden flight on 8 November 1978, with the initial production aircraft following suit on 21 September 1979. Canadian certification of the Avco Lycoming-ALF502L-2-powered **Challenger 600** (**CL600**) was achieved in August 1980 and production continued until 1983 when it was replaced by the improved **Challenger 601** (**CL601**). This version, which made its maiden flight on 17 September 1982, was powered by General Electric CF34s and fitted with winglets. Eighty-five CL600s were built and 78 have been refitted with winglets, to be referred to as the **CL600S**. The initial CF34-powered aircraft, 66 of which were delivered between May 1983 and May 1987, were re-designated **CL601-1A** when the further improved **CL601-3A** was introduced.

The CL601-3A first flew on 28 September 1986. It boasted CF34-3A engines and a Collins Pro Line 4

The Challenger 601-3A was the main production variant in the late 1980s and early 1990s. It was the first Challenger to introduce an EFIS cockpit.

The Challenger 604 is the current sole production variant. It boats the longest range and the best performance of any of the Challenger line.

EFIS cockpit, and 134 were delivered between May 1987 and October 1993. The extended-range **CL601-3A/ER** (later simply the **601-3R**) first flew on 8 November 1988 and became available in March 1989. In this version the tail fairing was replaced with a conformal fuel tank, which extended the fuselage length by 1 ft 6 in (46 cm). CF-34-3A1 engines were also added and earlier-production aircraft could be brought up to this standard. When production ceased in 1996 59 new-build aircraft had been delivered along with 92 modification kits.

Canadair became part of the Bombardier Group in 1986 (since 1996 the Bombardier Aerospace Group) and is now producing the **Challenger 604**. This latest Challenger is powered by two new CF34-3B engines, and is optimised to cruise at Mach 0.74 over ranges of up to 4,077 nm (7500 km, 4691 miles). A prototype was modified from a CL601-3R (the new aircraft has the engineering designation CL600-2B16) and first flew on 18 September 1994, powered by CF-34-3A engines. It flew again with production-standard powerplants on 17 March 1995. The Challenger 604 was certified by the FAA on 2 November 1995 and the first was delivered in January 1996. By June 1999 production stood at 104, giving a grand a total of 448 Challengers of all versions.

SPECIFICATION:
Canadair Challenger 604
Powerplant: two 9,220 (41-kN) General Electric CF34-3A turbofans (with APR)
Accommodation: two (flight deck), up to 19 passengers
Dimensions: span 64 ft 4 in (19.61 m), over winglets; height 20 ft 8 in (6.30 m); length 68 ft 5 in (20.85 m)
Weights: operating, empty 26,630 lb (12079 kg); maximum take-off 47,600 lb (21591 kg)
Performance: max cruising speed 548 mph (882 km/h); max operating altitude 41,000 ft (12500 m); max range, with 5 passengers and reserves 4,691 miles (7550 km)

Canadair Regional Jet

The purchase of Canadair by the Bombardier Group in 1986 provided the impetus and funding to develop an oft-discussed airline version of the Challenger. This was launched in 1987 as the **Regional Jet**. The name was modified to **Canadair RJ** and now has been further abbreviated to **CRJ**.

The design added two 'plugs' to the CL601 fuselage, stretching it by 20 ft (6.10 m), and included a much-modified wing and wingbox. By the late 1980s the Regional Jet (in its definitive form) became a 50-seat aircraft and a firm launch order for 13 (with 12 options) was signed on 15 May 1990 by DLT.

The first RJ flew on 10 May 1991 and three prototypes undertook the flight test programme, leading to Canadian certification in July 1992. Deliveries began to Lufthansa Cityline (formerly DLT) on 19 October 1992, and final European JAA and US FAA certification was granted on 21 January 1993. The original 50-seat, 1,128-mile (1816-km) range aircraft was the **Regional Jet 100**. It was available alongside the **Regional Jet 100ER** (Extended Range) which had additional fuel boosting its range to 1,865 miles (3002 km). First customer for the ER was Lauda Air. In March 1994 Canadair introduced the **RJ100LR** (Long Range) combining the extra fuel of the ER with a higher take-off weight, further increasing range by 345 nm (397 miles,

Cincinnati-based Comair is a Delta Connection operator and the US CRJ launch customer. It put its first aircraft into revenue service on 1 June 1993.

Mesa Airlines operates a fleet of CRJ200ERs from its bases at Phoenix and Albuquerque on its own behalf and on services for America West and US Airways.

638 km). A 30-seat executive version, the **Corporate JetLiner** was also developed and first of these was delivered to the Xerox Corp in 1993. Six have been built to date. An extended-range corporate version, the **Special Edition**, was also launched in 1995 (see **Bombardier Global Express** entry).

The RJ100 was replaced by the **CRJ200** as the standard production version in 1996 and the first delivery was made to Tyrolean Airways on 15 January. The CRJ200 is powered by improved CF34-3B1 engines and so can cruise higher, further and faster than the RJ100, with a 50-passenger load. **CRJ200ER** and **CRJ200LR** versions are also available. The latter has a maximum range of 2,307 miles (3713 km). Three hot-and -high versions – the **CRJ-200B**, **CRJ-200BER** and **CRJ-200BLR** – have been developed. In June 1999 CRJ100/200 orders stood at 551, with 238 options and 313 delivered.

On 27 May 1999 the prototype of the 70-seat **CRJ700** made its maiden flight. The CRJ700 (previously the **CRJ-X**) was launched in 1997 and the first customer will be Brit Air (in February 2001). The CRJ700 has been stretched by a further 20 ft (6.10 m) and is powered by the CF34-8. Orders for the CRJ700 stand at 96. Bombardier is now working towards the launch of the all-new 90-/110-seat **BRJ-X** in early 2000 with first deliveries in 2003.

SPECIFICATION:
Canadair Regional Jet Series 200
Powerplant: two 9,220-lb (41-kN) General Electric CF34-3B1 turbofans
Accommodation: two (flight deck), up to 52 passengers
Dimensions: span, over winglets 69 ft 7 in (21.21 m); height 20 ft 8 in (6.30 m); length 87 ft 10 in (26.77 m)
Weights: operating empty 29,180 lb (13236 kg); maximum take-off 47,450 lb (21523 kg)
Performance: maximum operating speed Mach 0.85; maximum operating altitude 41,000 ft (12500 m); maximum range, with maximum payload and reserves 1,110 miles (1787 km)

CASA 212 and CN.235

Developed for a Spanish air force requirement, the **CASA C.212 Aviocar** first flew on 26 March 1971. The initial **C.212-100** began to enter service in the late spring of 1974, but was supplanted by the **C.212-200** in 1979. This new version introduced more powerful Garrett (now AlliedSignal) TPE331-10 turboprops and an increased MTOW. Further redesign in the 1980s led to the **C.212-300**, which was certified in December 1987. With a longer, pointed nose and distinctive winglets, the -300 is available as the 23/26-seat **C.212-300 Airliner** and **C.212-300 Utility**. In June 1997 CASA launched the **C.212-400**, with 1,100-hp (820-kW) TPE331-12RJ engines and equipped with an EFIS cockpit. By early 1999 approximately 440 C.212s of all versions have been delivered.

Since 1976 the C.212 has also been built by IPTN in Indonesia as the **NC.212**. Strangely, Series 300s built by IPTN are known as **NC.212-200**s.

Experience with the C.212 and the relationship that existed between CASA and IPTN resulted in the formation of the Airtech company to develop a larger 45-seat twin-turboprop, the **Airtech CN.235**. Design work was launched in January 1980 on a 50-50 basis, and each production centre (at Seville and Bandung) completed one prototype. CASA's flew first, on 11 November 1983, with IPTN's following on 30 December 1983. CASA is responsible for the wing centre-section, centre and forward fuselages, while IPTN builds the rear fuselage, tail section and outer wing.

The CASA C.212 Aviocar – this example is a C.212-200 – has had a long life, its latest incarnation being the advanced EFIS-equipped C.212-400.

Delivery of the first production examples got under way in late 1986, with Merpati Nusantara being the first customer to accept an Indonesian-built machine, while CASA's initial example went to the Royal Saudi Air Force in February 1987. Each manufacturer built 15 **CN.235-10**s with CT7-7A engines, before moving on to the CT7-9C-powered **CN.235-100**. In March 1992 the current production version, the **CN.235-200**, was introduced, featuring a higher operating weight, refined rudder and tail, reduced field-length requirements and improved (almost doubled) range. A quick-change cargo/passenger version, the **CN.235-200QC**, was certified in 1992 also.

The CN.235 was intended as a dual use military transport and civil airliner, but military orders have far outstripped those to airlines. Sales have been limited to a handful of customers in Spain (Binter Canarias, Binter Mediterraneo) and Indonesia (Mandala Airlines, Merpati Nusantara). Only Austral of Argentina lay outside this customer set and it no longer operates the two CN.235-200s it received in 1993. By 1999 approximately 30 CN.235s were in airline service.

The CN.235s once operated by Binter Canarias are now all in the hands of sister airline Binter Mediterraneo, which operates from Malaga.

SPECIFICATION:
CASA C.212 Series 300 Airliner
Powerplant: two 900-hp (671-kW) AlliedSignal TPE331-10R-513C turboprops
Accommodation: two (flight deck), maximum of 26 passengers
Dimensions: span 66 ft 6½ in (20.28 in); height 21 ft 7¾ in (6.60 m); length 52 ft 11¾ in (16.15 m)
Weights: empty 8,333 lb (3780 kg); maximum take-off 16,975 lb (7700 kg)
Performance: maximum cruising speed 220 mph (354 km/h); service ceiling 26,000 ft (7925 m); maximum range, with 25 passengers and reserves 273 miles (440km)

Cessna Model 208 Caravan I
Single-engined STOL utility transport

Cessna's **Model 208 Caravan I** is the ultimate expression of the famous manufacturer's family of single-engined, high-wing aircraft designs. Its size and load-carrying ability sets it in a class of its own and takes it into a realm previously occupied by larger and more expensive twin-engined aircraft. The Model 208 evolved as Cessna's ultimate 'bush-plane – a 10-seat design aimed at replacing the thousands of (piston-engined) DHC Beavers, Otters and other smaller Cessna aircraft in service around the world. Preliminary work began in 1981 and among their objectives the designers listed: a 62-in (157-cm) wide cabin, permitting three-abreast seating; a 50 x 49-in (1.27 x 1.24-m) main cargo door, split horizontally; three additional access doors for cargo and passengers.

The prototype Model 208 made its first flight on 9 December 1982. The Caravan has a fixed tricycle undercarriage (the cabin floor is approximately 6-ft/ 1.82-m above the ground), a tall squared-off fin with a large leading-edge fillet, a strut-braced wing, and a 600-hp (447-kW) Pratt & Whitney PT6A-114 turboprop driving a three-bladed McCauley prop. The long wing is fitted with spoiler-ailerons to improve roll control and long span wing flaps to keep stalling speed down to the remarkable level of just 61 kt (112 km/h, 70 mph).

Production of the original Caravan I, seen here, has now ceased after it was replaced in 1988 by the more powerful Model 208-675 Caravan.

The Cessna Grand Caravan is a 14-seat version of the basic Model 208, developed from the stretched Model 208B Super Cargomaster.

Sixty one examples of the basic Model 208 were sold before the type achieved phenomenal sales success at the hands of Federal Express (FedEx) – ordering 177 of a specially developed version, the **Model 208A Cargomaster**. The Cargomaster is tailored for all-freight operations and has no cabin windows, no starboard rear door, a taller tail and an underfuselage cargo pannier. The Cargomaster is fitted with extended exhausts to deflect their hot gases wide of the pannier. So successful was the Cargomaster that FedEx ordered the **Model 208B Super Cargomaster**, which has a 4-ft (1.22-m) fuselage stretch. Deliveries began in 1986 and to date over 400 have been built. From the Super Cargomaster, Cessna has developed the **Model 208B Grand Caravan** a similarly stretched version, with windows and a 14-seat cabin. In 1998 the basic 208 was replaced by the **Model 208-675**, with a 675-hp (503-KW) PT6A-114A engine.

On 30 April 1998 the Soloy Corporation flew the prototype of its **Pathfinder 21** variant of the Model 208B. This aircraft is powered by two PT6D-114A turboprops driving a single prop. The fuselage has been stretched 2 m (6.56 ft) more than the Model 208B and a large faired-in cargo pannier has ben added under the fuselage floor. Total Model 208 Caravan sales had reached 1,000 by early 1999.

SPECIFICATION:
Cessna Model 208B Caravan I
Powerplant: one 675-shp (503-kW) Pratt & Whitney Canada PT6A-114A turboprop
Accommodation: one (flight deck), up to 14 passengers
Dimensions: span 51 ft 1 in (15.88 m); height 14 ft (4.27 m); length 37 ft 7 in (11.46 m)
Weights: empty, equipped 3,800 lb (31724 kg); maximum take-off 8,000 lb (3629 kg)
Performance: maximum operating speed 202 mph (325 km/h); maximum operating altitude 20,000 ft (6100 m); maximum range, with maximum fuel 1,484 miles (2389 km)

Cessna 500 Citation I,
500 Citation II and Citation Bravo

USA

Twin-engined business jets

Having been a brand leader in supplying propeller-driven aircraft to the business community for many years, Cessna lagged behind its competitors when it came to introducing a jet-powered design. It was not until 15 September 1969 that the prototype of a new executive jet known as the **Fanjet 500** made its first flight. Like most contemporary designs the Cessna aircraft utilised pod-mounted engines attached to each side of the rear fuselage. Subsequently renamed as the **Citation**, deliveries of this Pratt & Whitney JT15D-1A turbofan-powered machine began just before the end of 1971, and it very quickly met with success. Refinement of the basic design next led to the **Model 500 Citation I** and **Model 501** (certified for single-pilot operation). A total of 691 Citation Is had been built when production ended in 1985.

By then the stretched **Model 550 Citation II** (and **Model 551**) had been available for a number of years, following its maiden flight in prototype form on 31 January 1977. Apart from having a longer fuselage, this also embodied an increase in wingspan and more powerful JT15D-4 turbofan engines. Further improvements, most notably to the wing structure, culminated in the **Citation S550 S/II** that became the basic production model in 1984, by which time more than 500 examples of all types had been built. A total of 733 Citation IIs – including 15 **Model 552 T-47A**s for the US Navy – were built until 1996 when it was replaced by an improved version of the basic 550 design.

Developed from the best-selling Model 500, the Cessna Citation II remained in production for almost 20 years and its successor is still in demand.

This came in the shape of the improved **Model 550 Citation Bravo**, which was announced at the Farnborough air show in September 1994. The new Bravo was based on the Citation II airframe, but featured new technology Pratt & Whitney Canada PW530A turbofans (with thrust reversers as standard), trailing link undercarriage design, a modified wing design, a Honeywell Primus EFIS cockpit (with more legroom for the pilots) and all new interior design and cabin fittings. The Citation Bravo offers a startling improvement in performance over earlier Citation IIs. For example the new aircraft can climb to 41,000 ft (12,500) 41 minutes earlier than a Citation II, has a faster cruising speed and overall range extended by 250 nm (463 km, 288 miles) – while still carrying six passengers.

The first of the new breed Citation Bravos (a modified Model 550) made its maiden flight on 25 April 1995 and the first production aircraft flew in mid-1996. After type FAA type certification in January 1997 the first aircraft was delivered to a US customer on 25 February 1997. By early 1999 Citation Bravo production had reached 70.

The Cessna Model 500 Citation I was a pioneering design for the company, and one from which the huge family of Cessna business jets is derived.

SPECIFICATION:
Cessna Model 550 Citation Bravo
Powerplant: two 2,885-lb (12.83-kN) Pratt & Whitney Canada PW530A turbofans
Accommodation: two (flight deck), up to 10 passengers (seven standard)
Dimensions: span 52 ft 2 in (15.90 m); height 15 ft (4.75 m); length 47 ft 2½ in (14.39 m)
Weights: empty 8,750 lb (3969 kg); maximum take-off 14,800 lb (6713 kg)
Performance: maximum operating speed, at FL280 Mach 0.70; maximum operating altitude 45,000 ft (13715 m); maximum range, with maximum fuel 2,186 miles (3518 km)

Cessna 525 CitationJet, CJ1 and CJ2

To replace the Citation I, its 'entry-level' business jet, Cessna began work on a completely new design that would not only be the baby of its Citation family but attract a new level of customer – one who had not previously considered acquiring a business jet. The resultant **Model 525 CitationJet**, was announced at the 1989 NBAA convention, four years after Citation I production had ceased. Cessna took 50 orders for the CitationJet at its launch and by the time of the first delivery, production was sold out for 18 months. The new aircraft was the smallest jet Cessna had ever built, some 10¾ in (27 cm) shorter than the Citation I. Despite the reduction in length, the new aircraft had a roomier cabin, as the cabin floor had been dropped adding 5 in (13 cm) of head-room for its standard load of five passengers.

An entirely new supercritical laminar-flow wing was designed, with single-slotted flaps. The cockpit was built around a Honeywell SPZ-5000 two-screen EFIS system, with a three-axis digital autopilot/flight director. A pair of the innovative new Williams-Rolls FJ 44 small turbofans were chosen to power the CitationJet, but perhaps its most distinctive aspect was the high T-tail – a design feature not seen on any of the smaller Cessna Citations to date.

The original CitationJet revolutionised the market – becoming the first of a new breed of small business jets. The Model 525 is being replaced by the CJ1/CJ2.

This is the prototype of Cessna's CJ2, the latest incarnation of the CitationJet family. The CJ2 is a stretched version of the highly popular Model 525.

The CitationJet's FJ44 engines were first flown on a Citation I testbed in April 1990. The CitationJet prototype made its maiden flight a year later on 21 April 1991. The second (pre-production) prototype flew on 20 November 1991. The CitationJet was awarded FAA certification on 16 October 1992 and this included approval for essential single-pilot operations (one of the CitationJet's most important selling points). On 30 March 1993 the first aircraft was handed over and Cessna anticipated a market for 1,000 aircraft over the next 10 years. The 100th example was rolled out on 8 March 1995 and by June 1999 a total of 326 aircraft had been delivered.

By mid-1999 Cessna was working towards the certification of two new developments of the basic Model 525. The rechristened **CJ1** will replace the CitationJet as the entry-level Citation. It is fitted with an all-new Rockwell Collins Pro Line 21 avionics suite and has a 200-lb (91-kg) increase in take-off weight. A demonstrator will fly later in 1999 and certification is expected before the end of the year. The CJ1 will be joined by the **CJ2**, a stretched CitationJet again fitted with the Pro Line 21 avionics and more powerful FJ-44-2C engines. The CJ2 prototype made its maiden flight on 26 April 1992. Certification is anticipated for mid-2000 with deliveries beginning early the following year.

SPECIFICATION:
Cessna Model 525 CitationJet
Powerplant: two 1,900-lb (8.45-kN) Williams-Rolls FJ44 turbofans
Accommodation: two (flight deck), five passengers
Dimensions: span 46 ft 9 in (14.25 m); height 13 ft 9 in (4.19 m); length 42 ft 7 in (12.98 m)
Weights: empty 6,453 lb (2927 kg); maximum take-off 10,400 lb (4717 kg)
Performance: maximum operating speed, at FL310 Mach 0.70; maximum operating altitude 41,000 ft (12500 m); maximum range, with maximum fuel 1,708 miles (2750 km)

Cessna 560 Citation V Ultra and 561XL Citation Excel

Cessna felt that there was still considerable room for growth in the original straight-wing Citation II airframe and further development resulted in the **Model 560 Citation V**. This incorporated a fuselage stretch over the basic aircraft resulting in a full eight-seat cabin and an extra (seventh) window. The cabin itself was restyled and improved with a new enclosed toilet/vanity area and passenger baggage compartments located to outside the main cabin.

The engineering prototype made its first flight in August 1987, and the new Citation was officially launched at the NBAA convention later that year. A pre-production prototype followed in early 1988 and FAA type certification came on 9 December 1988. The first customer deliveries began in April 1989.

A total of 260 Citation Vs were delivered before Cessna introduced an improved version, the **Citation V Ultra**, in 1994. The Ultra featured a digital autopilot and a Honeywell Primus II EFIS cockpit. It was fitted with improved JT15D-5D engines for better payload and performance. The new Citation V received its FAA certification in June 994 and the first aircraft was handed over on 26 July 1995 to Korean Air Lines. By June 1999 deliveries of the Citation Ultra had reached 280. Cessna is now developing the follow-in **Citation Ultra Encore** with a heated leading-edge, trailing link gear, and improved PW535A engines.

The Spanish air force took delivery of two SLAR-equipped Citation Vs, designated **TR.20**. The US Customs Service operates five modified **OT-47B**

The Citation V Ultra retains the slender lines of the Citation II but with a stretched fuselage and significant improvements under the skin.

aircraft – again based on the Citation V – for anti-smuggling surveillance and pursuit. These are fitted with an AN/APG-66 radar in the nose and an under-fuselage Northrop Grumman WF-360 FLIR.

In January 1996 the US Army selected the Citation Ultra for its C-XX medium-range transport requirement. The new version is known as the **UC-35A** and the Army is expected to order 35 aircraft over a five-year period. The first UC-35As were delivered in 1996 and by June 1999 12 had entered service.

In 1994 Cessna announced the **561XL Citation Exel**, a new design that combined the wing and tail surfaces of the Ultra with a shortened version of the Citation X fuselage – providing a 10-seat cabin with stand-up head room. The Excel is powered by two 3,785-lb (16.84-kN) Pratt & Whitney Canada PW545A turbofans. The prototype flew on 29 February 1996 and the Excel made its debut at the NBAA convention in November that year. The first production aircraft was rolled out on 21 November 1997. Deliveries commenced after FAA certification in April 1998. By June 1999 40 Excels had been completed with orders exceeding the 200 mark.

The Citation Exel is the most dramatic evolution of the original Citation II and is radically different even from the Citation V – from which it is derived.

SPECIFICATION:
Cessna Model 560 Citation Ultra
Powerplant: two 3,045-lb (13.55-kN) Pratt & Whitney Canada JT15D-5D turbofans
Accommodation: two (flight deck), up to eight passengers
Dimensions: span 52 ft 2½ in (15.90 m); height 15 ft (4.57 m); length 48 ft 10¾ in (14.90 m)
Weights: empty 9,250 lb (4196 kg); maximum take-off 16,300 lb (7393 kg)
Performance: maximum operating speed at FL 290, Mach 0.755; maximum operating altitude 45,000 ft (13715 m); maximum range, with maximum fuel 2,255 miles (3630 km)

Cessna 650 Citation III, VI and VII Twin-engined business jets

All the early Citation designs had been aimed at what could fairly be called the lower, less expensive and less sophisticated end of the business jet market – an obvious extension of Cessna's philosophy for its piston-engined aircraft. A radical redesign effort undertaken in the latter half of the 1970s gave birth to a very different-looking member of Citation family, shortly before the end of the decade. This was the **Model 650 Citation III**, which took to the skies for its first flight on 30 May 1979 and which launched the Citation into a new world of speed and performance. The Citation III was the first of the 'next-generation' Citations.

Gone was the familiar straight-winged layout, abandoned in favour of a slightly swept, supercritical wing of increased span. At the same time, the fuselage was significantly longer, with space for two crew and up to 13 passengers, while the fin was also greatly altered to a much more sharply swept configuration capped by a T-tail.

Customer deliveries started in spring 1983, with the 100th example being handed over just three years later. Production would eventually continue until 1992, by which time 187 Citation IIIs had been completed. At that time the Citation II was replaced on the production line by the developed **Citation VI** and **Citation VII** (both retaining the Model 650

The Cessna VI was a follow-on development of the Citation III, but the more powerful engines of the Citation VII saw it loose its edge in the market.

The Citation III has spawned two new Model 650s, which are outwardly identical: the light-weight Citation VI and the better performing Citation VII.

designation). The derivatives were very similar – both were six- to nine-seat jets, simplified and optimised for lower-cost operations.

The Citation VI used the Citation III airframe but powered by two 3,650-lb (16.24-kN) Garret (now AlliedSignal) TFE731-3B-100S turbofans and fitted with a new Honeywell SPZ-8000 avionics suite. The Citation VII was essentially similar but came with more powerful TFE731-4R-2S engines for improved 'hot-and-high' performance.

Cessna made public its plans to switch production to these models in 1990 and their development proceeded simultaneously. The first Citation VI was rolled out on 2 January 1991 and first deliveries took place in 1992. The first Citation VII was delivered in April 1992, to golfer Arnold Palmer – a loyal Citation owner and (almost) the traditional launch customer for new versions.

Production of the Citation VI ceased in May 1995, after 37 had been built, including two for navaid calibration acquired by China's Civil Aviation Administration. The Citation VII remains available and in late 1995 Cessna introduced the **Magnum Edition** version, with a choice of Universal UNS-1CP or Honeywell NZ-2000 flight management systems. By mid-1999 Citation VII production stood at a total of 110 aircraft.

SPECIFICATION:
Cessna Model 650 Citation VI
Powerplant: two 3,650-lb (16.24-kN) Garrett TFE731-3B-100S turbofans
Accommodation: two (flight deck), six passengers
Dimensions: span 53 ft 6 in (16.31 m); height 16 ft 9½ in (5.12 m); length 55 ft 5½ in (16.90 m)
Weights: empty, standard 11,811 lb (5357kg); maximum take-off 22,000 lb (9979 kg)
Performance: maximum operating speed 320 mph (515 km/h); maximum operating altitude 43,000 ft (13106 m); maximum range, with reserves 2,701miles (4348 km)

Cessna 750 Citation X

With an eye on capturing a substantial share of the long-range, high-speed, biz-jet market (an entirely new one for the Citation family) Cessna developed the **Model 750 Citation X**. The new aircraft, the largest jet ever built by Cessna, is optimised for a high operating Mach number over transcontinental and transatlantic ranges. This translates into speeds of Mach 0.9 over a range of approximately 3,800 miles (6115 km).

The Citation X is powered by a pair of FADEC-equipped Allison AE3007C turbofans (previously known as the GMA3007) sitting high above the rear fuselage. The cabin can carry up to 12 passengers, with a flight deck crew of two. The cockpit is fitted with a Honeywell Primus 2000 five-screen EFIS system. The wing is sharply swept-back to 37°, with 3° dihedral and faired into the fuselage by a large streamlined wingbox. All the control surfaces, spoilers, speedbrakes and flaps are made from weight-saving composite materials. The large T-tail features a one-piece all-moving tailplane and a two-piece rudder. The trailing-link construction landing gear has powered anti-skid carbon brakes for each of its twin-wheel boogies. The twin-wheel nose gear is hydraulically-steered.

The Citation X was launched by Cessna in October 1990 and the new Allison engines were test flown on a modified Citation VII in August 1992. The first flight of the Citation X prototype came on 21 December 1993. Two pre-production aircraft were used for the flight test programme.

The Citation X is the largest and most powerful Citation ever built. Its curved and purposeful design is optimised for long-range high speed cruising.

The first of these made its maiden flight on 27 September 1994 followed by the second example on 11 January 1995. Like all Citations, the Citation X is built at Cessna's Wichita facility, in Kansas. Cessna's single-engined aircraft are now built at a new plant in Independence, Kansas. Since 1992 Cessna has been a wholly-owned subsidiary of Textron Inc..

The Citation X test programme took in some 3,000 flight hours before winning FAA type certification on 3 June 1996. In recognition of the effort devoted to the new aircraft, and the advances made during its development, Cessna was awarded the prestigious Collier Trophy for aeronautical achievement, by the US National Aeronautic Association in February 1997.

The first Cessna Citation X was handed over to its high-profile launch customer, Arnold Palmer, in July 1996. Other prestigious customers include General Motors, Honeywell and the Williams Companies. On 19 September 1997 a Citation X became the 2,500th Citation jet to be built. By July 1999 Cessna had delivered 100 Citation Xs.

The Citation X is steadily winning orders and has taken Cessna firmly out of the realm of small corporate jets and into the big league.

SPECIFICATION:
Cessna Model 750 Citation X
Powerplant: two 6,400-lb (28.47-kN) Allison AE3007C turbofans
Accommodation: two (flight deck), up to 12 passengers
Dimensions: span 63 ft 11 in (19.48 m); height 18 ft 11 in (5.77 m); length 72 ft 2 in (22.00 m)
Weights: empty, equipped 21,400 lb (9707 kg); maximum take-off 35,700 lb (16193 kg)
Performance: maximum operating speed Mach 0.92; maximum operating altitude 51,000 ft (15545 m); maximum range, with maximum fuel 3,740 miles (6019 km)

Convair 240 to 580

USA
Twin-piston and turboprop airliners and freighters

The noble family of '**Convairliners**' was a product of the Consolidated Vultee company – universally known as Convair – which was established in 1943 through the merger of the Consolidated Aircraft Company and Vultee Aircraft Inc.. In the post-war world of the 1940s Convair was one of many manufacturers looking to develop a DC-3 replacement. It came up with the **Model 110** – an unpressurised, 30-seat, low-wing, all-metal aircraft with a tricycle undercarriage, powered by Pratt & Whiteny R-1830-65 piston engines. This single prototype gave birth to the **Model 240 Convairliner** (or **CV 240**), a larger 40-seat, pressurised version powered by two 2400-hp (179-kW) R-2800-CA3 Double Wasp engines. The Model 240 first flew on 16 March 1947. Pan Am placed an initial order for 100 and it entered service with major airlines around the world.

Production of the 340 ended in 1950 after 177 had been built. Competition from the rival Martin 4-0-4 encouraged Convair to develop the **CV 340**. This new version had a fuselage stretched by 4 ft 6 in (1.4 m) and could carry up to 44 passengers. It had a longer wing, 2,400-hp (1790-kW) R-2800-CB16 engines and a redesigned port-side cabin door. The prototype flew on 5 October 1951. United and Braniff were the launch customers and the first aircraft was handed over in March 1952.

This Convair 340 operated by Trans Dominican Airways was typical of the early-model piston-powered Convairs that soldiered on into the 1990s

Belgium's European Air Transport is the last European Convair operator. Its fleet of nine CV 580s operate overnight delivery services for DHL.

In 1955, after 205 had been built, the Model 340 was supplanted by the **CV 440 Cosmopolitan**. This aircraft had rectangular engine exhaust which cut down noise, a higher take-off weight. A longer radar nose was refitted to most aircraft. The 52-seat Metropolitan was especially popular among European airlines and 171 were built by the time production ended in 1958.

By the late 1950s Convair was looking to move to turboprop power for the Convairliners. It experimented with the Rolls-Royce Dart 542-4, which resulted in the **CV 600** (a re-engined CV 240, 33 built) and the **CV 640** (a re-engined CV340/440, 27 built). However, the definitive turboprop powerplant for the Convairs became the Allison 501-D13D. Fitting these engines to existing Convairliners transformed them into the **CV 580** and a total of 155 were produced by Pac-Aero at Burbank. By 1999 about 25 CV 600/640s and 126 CV 580s remain in service around the world.

Convair produced a wide range of military versions of the Convairliner family US Air Force under the **T-29** and **C-131** designations. In all 391 military variants were built.

Canada's Kelowna Flightcraft has developed a dramatically stretched version of the CV 580, the **CV 5800** freighter, with three produced so far.

SPECIFICATION:
Convair CV 580
Powerplant: two 3,750-hp (2798-kW) Allison 501-D13D turboprop engines
Accommodation: two (flight deck), up to 52 passengers
Dimensions: span 105 ft 4 in (32.11 m); height 22 ft 8 in (8.59 m); length 81 ft 6 in (24.84 m)
Weights: empty, operating 30,275 lb (13733 kg); maximum take-off 58,156 lb (26379 kg)
Performance: maximum cruising speed 289 mph (465 km/h); maximum range 1950 miles (3138 km/h)

Curtiss C-46 Commando

Originally conceived as a 36-seat passenger airliner and flown for the first time on 26 March 1940, the **Curtiss-Wright CW-20** very quickly attracted the attention of the US Army Air Corps, which was searching for a new general-purpose transport. As a consequence, a specialised military freighter version with the basic designation **C-46 Commando** was ordered into production, and this began to enter service in the summer of 1942. At the time of its introduction, it was the largest and heaviest twin-engined aircraft in USAAC service and it proved of particular value in the Pacific theatre of war, playing a key role in the movement of men and materiel throughout this region. Nowhere was this more apparent than in operations 'over the hump' of the eastern Himalayas between India and China, where the C-46's superior performance at high altitude clearly gave it the edge over the Douglas C-47 Skytrain. In general, though, it was less popular than the immortal 'Dak', by virtue of its poor single-engined performance characteristics.

Major variants in USAAC service were the **C-46A**, **C-46D**, **C-46E** and **C-46F**, while a much smaller number were also used by the US Marine Corps as the **R5C-1**. By the time production ended, successive orders for the improved versions eventually resulted in some 3,180 Commandos being built. Many war-surplus examples were eventually passed on to friendly nations in South East Asia and Latin America, with some of these continuing in use until well into the 1980s.

Canada's Buffalo Airways has a 1945-vintage C-46D and a 1944-vintage C-46F in service alongside the rest of its veteran fleet of propliners.

In the closing stages of World War II, Curtiss-Wright again began considering a commercial version. Given the company designation **CW-20E**, it was to be a 36-seater. Design was launched during 1944 and construction of a mock-up generated considerable interest, resulting in at least two major US airlines placing contracts by the end of 1944. At a later date, the ready availability of war surplus aircraft meant that a large number of redundant Commandos were disposed of to civil operators.

The type proved popular for hauling cargo through harsh terrain, where the type's good load, sturdy structure and low-speed handling made it ideal for operating from semi-prepared strips. Many carried meat in South America, and a few got into the hands of drug smugglers. A modest number of these veteran machines are still active around the world, though their numbers declined rapidly during the late 1990s. Many long-term operators have been forced to withdraw their C-46s due to the spiralling cost of fuel and spares. However about 20 Commandos are still active in Bolivia, Colombia, Canada and the United States.

Along with a handful of others, Alaska-based Everts Air Fuel still flies the C-46. Everts operates five Commandos as freighters and fuel tankers.

SPECIFICATION:
Curtiss C-46 Commando
Powerplant: two 2,000-hp (1492-kW) Pratt & Whitney R-2800-51 radial piston engines
Accommodation: two (flight deck)
Dimensions: span 108 ft (32.31 m); height 21 ft 9 in (6.62 m); length 76 ft 4 in (23.26 m)
Weights: empty 30,000 lb (13608 kg); maximum take-off 45,000 lb (20412 kg)
Performance: maximum speed 270 mph (435 km/h); service ceiling 24,500 ft (7470 m); maximum range 3,150 miles (5069 km/h)

Dassault Falcon 10 and 100

Perhaps confusingly, the Dassault **Falcon 10** actually appeared after the Mystère 20/Falcon 20 was well-established in production. Following the success of the Falcon 20, Dassault turned its attention to building a smaller, complementary business jet. The new aircraft emerged as a scaled down Falcon 20, but with more rakish lines. This was the sleek seven- to nine-seat Falcon 10, which originally known as the **Mini-Falcon** and as the **Mystère-Falcon 10** in its early years.

An initial prototype was built, powered by General Electric CJ610 turbojets and with these powerplants the Falcon 10 made its maiden flight on 1 December 1970. Changes were made to the wing incidence, dihedral and sweepback and six months after the maiden flight the modified Falcon 10 set a closed circuit speed record, for its class, of over 930 km/h (578 mph). A second prototype with the definitive Garrett TFE731-2 turbofans flew on 15 October 1971. French type certification was granted on 11 September 1973 and FAA certification followed 11 days later. Customer deliveries started shortly before the end of the year.

The Falcon 10 was built without sub-types, although the French navy acquired six modified special mission aircraft (some with ventral radars) as **Falcon 10MER**s.

Appearing some years after the Falcon 20, the Falcon 10 (or 'Mini-Falcon') is a super-sleek seven- to nine-seat bizjet, which led to the Falcon 100.

The Falcon 10 proved very popular in its native France, particularly with leasing and charter operators. This example was flown by Euralair.

Dassault turned out Falcon 10s at a rate of approximately two per month, with final assembly taking place at Istres. The fuselages were built by Potez and other components were supplied by SOGERMA, SOCEA, SOCATA and Latécoère. CASA of Spain built the wings while tail units and nose assemblies came from IAM in Italy.

Production continued until 1985, when 192 (including the three prototypes) had been built. At that point changes were introduced on the line. From the 193rd aircraft onwards a heated and pressurised rear baggage compartment was added but more significant improvements appeared on the 202nd production aircraft. From then on the aircraft was certified for operation at higher weights (maximum take-off weight grew by 225 kg/496 lb), a fourth cabin window was added in the starboard fuselage (opposite the door) and the cockpit was upgraded with a five-screen Collins EFIS 85 system.

This improved Falcon 10 became known as the **Falcon 100**. A total of 37 Falcon 100s were built, including one (the 183rd Falcon 10) which fell outside the production sequence. Total Falcon 10/100 production reached 227 when the last Falcon 100 was handed over by Dassault to a Mexican customer in September 1990. In 1999 210 remain in service worldwide.

SPECIFICATION:
Dassault Falcon 100
Powerplant: two 3,230-lb (14.40-kN) Garrett TFE731-2 turbofans
Accommodation: two (flight deck), maximum of nine passengers (seven standard)
Dimensions: span 42 ft 11 in (13.08 m); height 15 ft 11½ in (4.61 m); length 40 ft 11 in (12.47 m)
Weights: empty, equipped 10,760 lb (4880 kg); maximum take-off 18,740 lb (8500 kg)
Performance: maximum operating Mach number 0.87; maximum range, with reserves and four passengers 2,210 miles (3560 km)

Dassault Falcon 20 and 200

Dassault's **Falcon 20** was one of a crop of twin-engined executive jets that appeared during the early 1960s. The eight- to 10-seat business jet was designed in association with Sud Aviation (later Aerospatiale) and construction of a prototype began in 1962. Sud Aviation supplied the wings and tail, while Dassault was responsible for the fuselage and final assembly, A prototype, originally dubbed the **Mystère XX**, first flew 4 May 1963 powered by two 3,300-lb (14.6 kN) Pratt & Whitney JT12A-8 turbojets. These were replaced by General Electric CF700 turbofans in the final production form and the re-engined prototype flew on 10 July 1964.

The Falcon 20 was launched with an unprecedented order for 54 (with 106 options) from the Business Jets Division of Pan American Airways. These aircraft were marketed in the USA as the **Fan Jet Falcon** – though the **Mystère 20** name was retained in France and elsewhere. The first production aircraft flew on 1 January 1965. French and US certification was awarded on 9 June 1965.

The baseline model was the **Falcon 20C**. It was followed by the **Falcon 20D** (with extra fuel and CF700-2D turbofans), **Falcon 20E** (with increased weights, modified rudder and starter/generator) and the **Falcon 20F** (with extra fuel and full leading-edge slats). The **Falcon 20G** was a specialised maritime surveillance version (named Gardian/Guardian). Dassault has never acknowledged designations such as 'Da.20', and commonly referred to its Falcon 20 family as Mystères.

Dassault built several versions of the 10/12-seat Falcon 20, with a variety of engines. All were referred to by the manufacturer as the Mystère 20.

Production of the original Falcon 20 terminated in 1983, with 485 (including the prototype) of all versions built, following the introduction of the improved **Falcon 200** in 1981. At the time of its debut, the Falcon 200 was known as the **Falcon 20H**, and the difference between it an its predecessors was the addition of new Garrett ATF-3-6-2C turbofans in place of the original CF700s. Other, less visible variations involved the provision of a larger integral fuel tank in the aft fuselage, redesigned wingroot fairing and automatic slats and other systems changes.

The first Falcon 200 made its maiden flight on 30 April 1980. Thirty-one Falcon 200s were built until production closed in 1988 – bringing the total of Falcon 20/200s built to 516. In April 1989, Garrett (now AlliedSignal), in association with Dassault, began offering TFE731-5AR turbofan refits, in Falcon 900 nacelles with thrust reversers, to existing Falcons under the 'Dash-5' programme. Modified, aircraft become known as **Falcon 20C-5, Falcon 20D-5** etc. The prototype conversion flew on 7 October 1988 and was certified on 15 March 1989. By June 1999 a total of 453 Falcon 20/200s were in service.

This Falcon 20E, the 307th production example, is still in regular service today, as are most of the Falcon 20s and all but one of the Falcon 200s.

SPECIFICATION:
Dassault Falcon 20
Powerplant: two 5,200-lb (23.13-kN) Garrett ATF3-6A-4C turbofans
Accommodation: two (flight deck), maximum of 12 passengers (nine standard)
Dimensions: span 53 ft 6½ in (16.32 m); height 17 ft 5 in (5.32 m); length 56 ft 3 in (17.15 m)
Weights: empty, equipped 18,190 lb (8250 kg); maximum take-off 32,000 lb (14515 kg)
Performance: maximum speed 402 mph (648 km/h); service ceiling 45,000 ft (13715 m); maximum range, with reserves 2,890 miles (4650 km/h)

Dassault Falcon 50

After the Falcon 20, the logical next step for Dassault was to introduce a longer-range member of the Falcon family, capable of flying transcontinental or transatlantic distances. It chose to develop a three-engined jet, using the fuselage cross-section of the Falcon 20/200, but with an entirely new area-ruled fuselage, more internal fuel and a supercritical wing. The resultant aircraft was the **Falcon 50** (**Mystère 50**). It still used many Falcon 20/200 components but had a striking new centreline engine with a completely redesigned rear fuselage and tail section. The Falcon 50 was powered by three 3,700-lb (16.5-kN) Garrett TFE731-3 turbofans and had a cantilever wing with compound leading-edge sweepback. It could carry up to 12 passengers. Unlike earlier Falcons, the Falcon 50 (from the fourth airframe onwards) was assembled at Dassault's main Marignac plant. The fuselage and tail units were built by Aerospatiale and the engine cowlings were supplied by Hurel-Dubois.

The first prototype flew on 7 November 1976, followed by a second example on 18 February 1978. French DGAC type certification was awarded on 17 February 1979, followed by FAA type approval on 7 March. Deliveries commenced in July 1979 and the Falcon 50 became popular with private and government customers alike. The French air

The Falcon 50EX is a re-engined version of the original aircraft which boasts much-improved performance and all new digital avionics.

Dassault's first intercontinental biz-jet design was the Falcon 50 of 1976. It remained in production until 1995, when replaced by the new Falcon 50EX.

force took delivery of five aircraft using them as Presidential transports, and several other nations adopted Falcon 50s as head of state aircraft also. A total of 250 Falcon 50s were built and by June 1999 all but two of these were still in service.

In April 1995 Dassault announced the successor to the Falcon 50, the improved **Falcon 50EX**. This is an extended-range version, powered by more economical TFE731-40 engines. The cockpit is equipped with a Collins Pro Line 4 EFIS system (similar to that fitted to the Falcon 2000 and retrofittable to Falcon 50s). The EX was faster than the original aircraft, with maximum cruise speed increased from Mach 0.75 to 0.80. Maximum range was increased by 200 nm (370 km, 230 miles) and time-to-climb figures are all substantially reduced.

The first Falcon 50EX flew on 10 April 1996 and the new avionics suite was developed in parallel, on a Falcon 50 testbed. Full FAA approval was granted on 20 December 1996, after the first production-standard Falcon 50EX had flown in October. The type made its public debut at the 1996 NBAA convention and the first customer delivery (to Volkswagen) took place in February 1997. Dassault estimates a market for between 150 and 200 Falcon 50EXs and by June 1999 a total of 32 had been completed.

SPECIFICATION:
Dassault Falcon 50EX
Powerplant: three 3,700-lb (16.46-kN) AlliedSignal TFE731-40 turbofans
Accommodation: two (flight deck), maximum of 19 passengers (standard nine)
Dimensions: span 61 ft 10½ in (18.86 m); height 22 ft 10¾ in (6.98 m); length 60 ft 9¼ in (18.52 m)
Weights: empty, equipped 21,170 lb (9603 kg); maximum take-off 39700 lb (18007 kg)
Performance: maximum operating speed Mach 0.86; maximum cruising altitude 49,000 ft (14935 m); maximum range, with reserves and eight passengers 3,757 miles (6046 km)

Dassault Falcon 900

Less than four years after the first Falcon 50 was handed over, Dassault announced that it was to proceed with development of a new longer-range business jet, the **Falcon 900**. News of this programme was made public at the 1983 Paris air show, and the prototype was rolled out less than a year later, on 18 May 1984. In the event, this did not make its maiden flight until 21 September, and it was joined in the flight test effort by a second prototype on 30 August 1985. French and US type certification was obtained in March 1986.

In general, the Falcon 900 bears a strong family resemblance to the Falcon 50, although the fuselage is redesigned as a 'wide-body'. This gives the cabin almost twice the volume of the Falcon 50 (and 12 windows), and can carry up to 19 passengers. It also has slightly greater range, with the transatlantic capability of the Falcon 900 being demonstrated in fine style in September 1985 when the second aircraft made a non-stop flight of 4,954 miles (7973 km) from Paris to Little Rock, Arkansas, in order to appear at the NBAA show. In June 1988 a Falcon 900 became the 1,000th Dassault Falcon executive jet to be delivered.

Since 1992 Dassault has been offering its customers the improved **Falcon 900B**. Full-scale production of the 900B started with airframe No. 105, though seven of the 104 Falcon 900s built have since been modified to 900B standard. The new aircraft featured 4,750-lb (21.13-kN) TFE731-5BR-1C turbofans, (limited) rough-field capability,

The Falcon 900EX has the longest reach of any Falcon jet yet developed. Two additional internal fuel tanks allow it to out-range its predecessors.

improved landing aids, a higher cruising altitude (39,000 ft/11855 m) and increased range (4,600 miles/7402 km). The Falcon 900B was certified by the end of 1991 and by June 1999 82 (including conversions) had been produced.

In October 1994 Dassault launched a further improved version, the **Falcon 900EX**. The EX has more powerful TFE731-60 turbofans and an increased fuel load enabling it to fly 4,500 nm (8513 km, 5290 miles) non-stop at Mach 0.80. It is also equipped with a Honeywell Primus 2000 EFIS cockpit, INS, GPS, Satcom and even a Flight Dynamics HGS-2850 HUD. The prototype was rolled out on 13 March 1995 and first flew on 1 June. On 24 September 1995 the prototype flew from Luton (UK) to Las Vegas, a distance of 4,700 nm (8704km, 5,409 miles), in 11 hours and 40 minutes. FAA certification was awarded on 19 July 1996 and the first delivery occurred on 1 November 1996, to Anheuser-Busch. By June 1999 a total of 38 Falcon 900EXs had been delivered. Dassault is now offering customers the **Falcon 900C**, a 900B airframe with the advanced avionics of the Falcon 900EX.

Although the Falcon 900 resembles the Falcon 50, it is a much larger aircraft, with a reprofiled fuselage, advanced avionics and more powerful engines.

SPECIFICATION:
Dassault Falcon 900
Powerplant: three 4,500-lb (20-kN) Garrett TFE731-5AR-1C turbofans
Accommodation: two (flight deck), maximum of 19 passengers
Dimensions: span 63 ft 5 in (19.33 m); height 24 ft 9¼ in (7.55 m); length 66 ft 3¾ in (20.21 m)
Weights: empty, equipped 22,575 lb (10240 kg); maximum take-off 45,500 lb (20640 kg)
Performance: maximum operating speed Mach 0.87; maximum cruising altitude 51,000 ft (15550 m); maximum range, with reserves and eight passengers 4,491 miles (7227 km)

Dassault Falcon 2000

Intended as a follow-on to the highly successful Falcon 20/200 series, the latest addition to the expanding family of Dassault business jets was announced as the **Falcon X** at the 1989 Paris air show and launched as the **Falcon 2000** in October 1990. Four months later, in February 1991, Alenia entered the project as a partner, taking 25 per cent of the risk and bearing responsibility for manufacture of the aft fuselage and the engine nacelles.

Although it is a twin-engined aircraft, many of the Falcon 2000's physical characteristics echo those of the Falcon 900. For example, it shares the same fuselage cross-section, although it is 6 ft 6 in (1.98 m) shorter – almost exactly two-thirds the length of the three-engined aircraft, in fact. Strangely, its 134 cu ft (3.79 m³) baggage compartment is actually larger than the Falcon 900's. In addition, the Falcon 2000 uses the same basic wing structure as the Falcon 900, albeit in slightly modified form, since it has a revised leading-edge and lacks the inboard slats of the larger aircraft. The cockpit features a Collins Pro Line 4 EFIS system and a Honeywell FMZ-2000 flight management system. It can also be fitted with a Flight Dynamics HGS-2850 head-up display. In July 1997 the Falcon 2000 became the first business jet to be certified for full Cat IIIa operations using a HUD. Today about half the aircraft delivered are fitted with this system.

The wide-bodied Falcon 2000 began life as the Falcon X in 1989, and the prototype was rolled out in its definitive form in early 1993.

While nominally a Falcon 20/200 replacement, the Falcon 2000 is a much larger aircraft, essentially a twin-engined Falcon 900.

The Falcon 2000 has transcontinental rather than transatlantic capability, and is aimed at the 3,000 nm (5552 km, 3,450 miles) range bracket. Power is supplied by two General Electric/Garrett (now Allied Signal) CFE738 turbofan engines. The dedicated Falcon 2000 prototype flew for the first time on 4 March 1993. Roll-out of the second example took place at Bordeaux in December 1993. This aircraft was earmarked for use as a company demonstrator after completion of powerplant test work. The second Falcon 2000 to fly got airborne on 10 May 1994, and was actually the third aircraft built. In July 1994 this aircraft was ferried to Dassault's Falcon Jet Centre in Little Rock, Arkansas, to act as the US demonstrator. On its transatlantic journey it set two world speed records.

JAA type certification was awarded on 30 November 1994, by which time five aircraft had flown. The first Falcon 2000 was handed over to a (South African) customer on 16 February 1995. The Falcon 2000 is certified to Stage 3 noise levels and is one of the few business jets allowed to operate into London's City Airport, for example. By June 1999 75 aircraft were in service around the world. The most important customer is fractional ownership company NetJets which has ordered 51 Falcon 2000s for its international network.

SPECIFICATION:
Dassault Falcon 2000
Powerplant: two 5,918-lb (26.33-kN) GE/AlliedSignal CFE738-1-1B turbofans
Accommodation: two (flight deck), maximum of 19 passengers (standard 8)
Dimensions: span 63 ft 5 in (19.33 m); height 23 ft 2 in (7.06 m); length 66 ft 4½ in (20.23m)
Weights: empty, equipped 20.735 lb (9405 kg); maximum take-off 35,800 lb (16238 kg)
Performance: maximum operating speed Mach 0.87; maximum cruising altitude 47,000 ft (14330 m); maximum range, with reserves and eight passengers 3,596 miles (5788 km)

de Havilland Canada DHC-6

Building on experience gained with earlier short take-off and landing (STOL) aircraft such as the **DHC-2 Beaver**, **DHC-3 Otter** and **DHC-4 Caribou**, de Havilland Canada began work on a new design in 1964, aiming this firmly at the large market that existed for a 20-seater that possessed good field performance characteristics. The result was the **DHC-6 Twin Otter**, and construction of a batch of five aircraft started in November 1964.

Powered by 579-hp (432-kW) PT6A-6 engines, the first of these machines made its maiden flight on 20 May 1965, and the flight test programme culminated in type certification in the early summer of 1966. Not long after, the initial production example was delivered to Ontario's Department of Lands and Forests in July, with this **DHC-6-100** aircraft being fitted with PT6A-20 powerplants in place of the PT6A-6 that was used by the first four Twin Otters. The main benefit arising from this change was reliability, though the later version of the engine still possessed an identical power rating.

By the time that production was terminated in December 1988, a total of 844 Twin Otters had been completed for civil and military operators worldwide. Three basic models were eventually built, with the Series 100 leading the way. Just over 100 had been produced when the improved **DHC-6-200** made its debut. This had increased luggage capacity in an extended nose section, and some 115 were completed before the **DHC-6-300** version was introduced from the 231st example to

The four highly-distinctive DHC-6-310 Twin Otters of the British Antarctic Survey operate from Rothera Base, on the polar ice cap.

roll from the Downsview factory. This eventually became by far the most numerous derivative and deliveries got under way in the spring of 1969. A development of this was the **DHC-6-300S**, fitted with upper wing spoilers and other STOL improvements, six of which undertook test operations in the mid-1970s. Military utility DHC-6s were designated **DHC-6-300M** or **DHC-6-300MR**.

The main differences between the final production model and its predecessors centred around extra power and greater payload/range capability. In the case of the former, this stemmed from replacement of the PT6A-20 by the PT6A-27 version of Pratt & Whitney Canada's successful turboprop. This in turn allowed the take-off weight to be increased by some 2,000 lb (907 kg), which resulted in worthwhile payload benefits. In addition to the land-based Twin Otters, all three basic versions were available as floatplanes.

The last Twin Otter was delivered on 30 December 1998. By September 1999 approximately 623 remained in service, with the oldest aircraft expected to go on and reach 50,000 flying hours

All float-plane versions of the Twin Otter retained the shorter, rounded nose of the early-production landplanes, for improved handling on water.

SPECIFICATION:
DHC-6-300 Twin Otter
Type: twin-engined STOL transport
Powerplant: two 620-hp (462-kW) Pratt & Whitney Canada PT6A-27 turboprops
Accommodation: two (flight deck), maximum of 20 passengers
Dimensions: span 65 ft (19.81 m); height 19 ft 6 in (5.94 m); length 51 ft 9 in (19.77 m)
Weights: operating empty 7,415 lb (3363 kg); maximum take-off 12,500 lb (5670 kg)
Performance: maximum cruising speed 210 mph (338 km/h); service ceiling 26,700 ft (8140 m); maximum range, with reserves 805 miles (1297 km)

de Havilland Canada DHC-7

Having achieving considerable success with its previous STOL designs, de Havilland Canada began work on a much larger four-engined STOL airliner that would provide capacity and comfort to operators who regularly operated from very short fields. Customers would include airlines or agencies flying from austere locations in mountainous or jungle terrains, and regular airlines flying from small city or local airports.

With aid from the Canadian government, de Havilland Canada began work on two **DHC-7 Dash 7** prototypes in 1972, the first of which flew on 27 March 1975. The layout drew heavily on that of the **DHC-5 Buffalo** military tactical transport, featuring a high-set wing with large double-slotted flaps, four sets of spoilers and small ailerons. The four Pratt & Whitney PT6A-50 turboprops drove slow-turning four-bladed propellers, providing high power, low noise levels and a measure of slipstream blowing for the flaps. The tail surfaces were mounted high on the large upswept fin, keeping the tailplane well away from the engine exhaust blast. The tricycle undercarriage tucked neatly away into the forward fuselage and inboard engine nacelles.

Internally, the Dash 7 is routinely configured for 46-50 passengers in 2+2 seating, and is flown by a flight crew of two. Access to the main cabin is via a

The exotically-named Paradise Island Airways operates seven Dash 7s on services to the Caribbean from Ft Lauderdale and Miami airports.

Plymouth-based Brymon European (now owned by British Airways as Brymon Airways) operates an all-de Havilland fleet that includes five DHC-7s.

port-side door just aft of the wing, which features an integral airstair. Baggage is accommodated at the rear of the cabin, the compartment served by a starboard-side door. The toilet and galley facilities are also located at the back.

Rocky Mountain Airways was the first recipient of a Dash 7, acquiring its initial aircraft on 3 February 1978. The primary customers for the Dash 7 were US feeder airlines, though aircraft entered service around the world. For example, the Dash 7 was initially the only type allowed to land at London's City Airport.

Production began with the **Dash 7 Series 100** and **Series 101** – the latter being a freighter version with an upward-hinging cargo door on the port side of the forward fuselage. These were followed in 1986 by the **Series 150** and **151**, featuring higher weights and greater fuel capacity. A specialist variant was the **Dash 7 IR Ranger**, a specialised ice reconnaissance variant for the Canadian government that had an observation blister behind the flight deck and a side-mounted surveillance radar.

Production ended in 1988 with 114 aircraft built, following the take-over of DHC by Boeing, which decided to concentrate on Dash 8 manufacture. The de Havilland name was revived when it was taken over by the Bombardier Group in 1992. By late 1999 about 103 Dash 7s were still in service.

SPECIFICATION:

de Havilland Canada DHC-7 Series 150
Powerplant: four 1,120-shp (835-kW) Pratt & Whitney Canada PT6A-50 turboprops
Accommodation: two (flight deck), standard layout for 50 passengers
Dimensions: span 93 ft (28.35 m); length 80 ft 6 in (24.54 m); height 26 ft 2 in (7.98 m)
Weights: empty 27,480 lb (12465 kg); maximum take-off 47,000 lb (21319 kg)
Performance: maximum cruising speed 266 mph (428 km/h); service ceiling 21,000 ft (6400 m); range with 50 passengers and typical reserves 1,313 miles (2112 km)

de Havilland (Canada) DHC-8

Twin-turboprop advanced STOL airliner

Increasing demand for 30/40-seat regional aircraft in the late 1970s encouraged de Havilland Canada to build a follow-on to the DHC-7. The twin-engined **DHC-8 Dash 8**, was a scaled-down version of its predecessor with a similar high-wing and T-tail. In keeping with tradition the design was optimised for good STOL performance. The prototype **DHC-8-100** made its maiden flight on 20 June 1983 and the first production aircraft entered revenue-earning service with Canada's NorOntair on 19 December 1984.

The initial Series 100, powered by two 1,800-hp (1342-kW) PW120 turboprops, was supplemented by the larger **DHC-8-300**, which first flew on 15 May 1987. Time Air accepted the initial aircraft on 27 February 1989. The Series 300 was stretched by 11 ft 3 in (3.43 m) to seat 50-56 passengers. It also featured uprated PW123s. The **DHC-8-100A** and **DHC-8-300A** were powered by the improved PW120A and PW123A engine (with the same rating). The first -100A was delivered to Pennsylvania Airlines in July 1990 while the first -300A was handed over to Tyrolean Airways in 1991.

The **DHC-8-100B**, introduced in 1992, has two 2,150-hp (1603-kW) PW121s for better airfield and climb performance. The optional 43,000-lb (19505-kg) gross weight of the -300A is standard on the subsequent **DHC-8-300B**, which also incorporated more powerful 2,500-hp (1865-kW) PW123Bs. The latest evolution of the -300 came in the form of 1994's **DHC-8-300E**, and improved hot-and-high variant powered by PW123E turboprops.

In February 1996 Great China Airlines became the launch customer for the dramatically stretched Dash 8Q Series 400 (now simply the Q400).

In March 1992, Bombardier Aerospace, which had acquired de Havilland Canada from Boeing that year, announced the **de Havilland Dash 8 Series 200** (dropping the Canada title) a development of the -100 with improved speed and payload capability. It uses the same airframe, powered by PW123C engines. Deliveries began in April 1995. The design was further improved with the introduction of the PW123D-powered **Dash 8 Series 200B**.

Bombardier announced a major development in June 1995, unveiling the super-stretched **Dash 8Q Series 400**. With a fuselage extended by 22 ft 5 in (6.83 m) this aircraft can seat up to 78 passengers. It is powered by 5,071-shp (3781-kW) PW150A turboprops, has an EFIS cockpit and is also fitted with a new Noise and Vibration Suppression (NVS) system that makes the cabin quiet and vibration-free. The NVS is now available on any production Dash 8 and Bombardier has rechristened these aircraft **Q100, Q200**, etc. (Q=Quiet). The first **Q400** flew on 31 January 1998 and type certification was awarded in June 1999. A total of 590 Dash 8s had been ordered by June 1999, with 522 in service.

From its bases at London and Thunder Bay, Air Ontario flies a fleet of DHC 8-100s and -300s (as seen here) on regional and feeder services for Air Canada.

SPECIFICATION:
de Havilland DHC-8-300B
Powerplant: two 2,500-hp (1865-kW) Pratt & Whitney PW123B turboprops
Accommodation: two (flight deck), with a maximum of 56 passengers
Dimensions: span 90 ft (27.43 m); height 24 ft 7 in (7.49 m); length 84 ft 3 in (25.68 m)
Weights: operating empty 25,836 lb (11719 kg); maximum take-off 43,000 lb (19504 kg)
Performance: maximum cruising speed 328 mph (528 km/h); service ceiling 25,000 ft (7620 m); range with 50 passengers and standard fuel 1,010 miles (1626 km)

Douglas DC-3

The illustrious line of Douglas commercial transports began in 1932, when TWA announced that it needed an aircraft similar to the Boeing 247 (the airline asked for a 12-seat, three-engined design) more quickly than Boeing could provide it. Donald W. Douglas produced the **DC-1**, which first flew on 1 July 1933, followed by the refined **DC-2**, which was chiefly bought by US domestic airlines. All these were eclipsed by the immortal **DC-3** (originally the 14-berth **DST** – Douglas Sleeper Transport) which first flew on 17 December 1935. In its 24-seat 'day' version, this all-metal aircraft, powered by a pair of ultra-reliable Pratt & Whitney radial piston engines, revolutionised air transport.

The type is perhaps best known by its World War II appellation of **C-47** (**Skytrain** in the US, but **Dakota** to the RAF). Eisenhower ranked its as one of the five weapons crucial to Allied success and by 1945 10,692 had been built, in addition to over 2,000 unlicensed **Lisunov Li-2** copies in the USSR. The availability of such a quantity of aircraft at the war's end, in addition to its established reputation and ease of operation, ensured that the DC-3 (known everywhere, even now in the US, as the Dakota or 'Dak') would become the classic airliner design and an irreplaceable asset to companies around the world.

Oshkosh-based Basler Aviation is offering turbine conversions for the DC-3 by adding Pratt & Whitney PT6A-67R engines and stretching the fuselage.

The number of mainstream DC-3s operators is declining but the aircraft still remains in everyday service around the world.

Many manufacturers have sought to find a 'DC-3 replacement', but it has long been mooted that the only replacement for a DC-3 is another DC-3. To this end several type conversions have been produced over the years. Today two major modifications are on offer, both adding turboprops as an alternative to the ageing piston powerplants. In the United States, Basler Turbo Conversions Inc. (based at Oshkosh, Winsconsin) will refit and re-engine an aircraft with 1,220-hp (910-kW) Pratt & Whitney Canada PT6A-67R turboprops, stretching the fuselage by 8 ft 4 in (2.54 m) to counteract the resultant change in the centre of gravity. Christened the **Basler T-67**, over 35 aircraft had been delivered by June 1999, primarily to military customers, in Central and Southern America and Africa.

In South Africa, conversions are undertaken by Professional Aviation, who use 1,424-shp (1062-kW) PT6A-65ARs to produce the **Jet Prop DC-3 AMI**. These aircraft, which are zero-timed and stretched by 3 ft 4in (1.02 m), can seat up to 40 and are refitted with new hydraulics, electrics and avionics. The programme began in 1991, with the South African Air Force as its first customer. Hundreds of original DC-3/C-47s survive in commercial service around the world, chiefly as freighters, although there are many in passenger service also.

SPECIFICATION:
Douglas C-47 (typical post-war conversion)
Powerplant: two 1,200-hp (895-kW) Pratt & Whitney R-1830-S1C3G Twin Wasp radial piston engines
Accommodation: two (flight deck), with a maximum of 24 passengers
Dimensions: span 95 ft 11½ in (5.17 m); height 6 ft 11½ in (5.17 m); length 64 ft 5½ in (19.65 m)
Weights: empty 16,865 lb (7650 kg); maximum take-off 25,200 lb (11430 kg)
Performance: maximum cruising speed 230 mph (370 km/h); service ceiling 23,200 ft (7070 m); maximum range, with maximum payload 2,125 miles (3420 km)

Douglas DC-4, DC-6 and DC-7

Even before the DC-3 had flown, Douglas was discussing a larger, more advanced development with US airlines. This resulted in the **DC-4E** (four-engined) of 1936. An almost complete redesign led to the definitive **DC-4**, which first flew on 14 February 1942. As the US was embroiled in war by then, the aircraft rapidly became a military transport, the **C-54 Skymaster**. Like the DC-3, the C-54 established a solid reputation as a long-range transport and by 1945 over 1,000 C-54s and 79 new-build DC-4s were available for commercial service. The basic 62-ft 6-in (19.05-m) long aircraft could carry 44 passengers, although high-density seating versions could increase this to a staggering 86. The search for greater capacity and range lead to the stretched **DC-6**, which could comfortably accommodate 52. The DC-6 first flew on 15 February 1946 (as the military-designated **XC-112A**) and entered airline service with American Airlines on 29 June of that year. The basic DC-6 was supplemented by the stretched (by 5 ft/1.52 m) **DC-6A** that featured two freight doors on the port side, no windows and a restressed floor. A similarly improved passenger version was dubbed **DC-6B**. Military versions were christened **C-118**, but the last civil DC-6 version built was the passenger/freight-convertible **DC-6C**. A total of 704 aircraft was built for all customers.

The last and perhaps greatest of Douglas' classic 'propliners' was the **DC-7**. Prompted by American Airlines, Douglas designed a rival for the Lockheed Super Constellation, scaling up the DC-6B by 3 ft 4 in

A life-sized cardboard cut-out of Marilyn Monroe rides in the third window from the rear on every flight by 'Tanker 152', a DC-4 fire-bomber of ARDCO.

(1.02 m) and adding new 3,250-hp (2470-kW) Wright R-3350 Turbo Compound piston engines driving four-bladed props (as opposed to the DC-6's three). The **DC-7B** came next, offering optional saddle fuel tanks on the rear of the engine nacelles. The ultimate development was the long-range **DC-7C**, the 'Seven Seas', which could carry 107 passengers in style over 4,605 miles (7411 km). Its fuselage was further stretched to 112 ft 3 in (34.21 m), and 120 were built from a total of 457 DC-7s.

Many of these 'Douglas Dinosaurs' survive today. These include: the DC-4 tankers of Aero Flite and Aero Union in the USA; DC-6 freighters of Atlantic Airlines in the UK; fire-fighting DC-6s of Canada's Conair; DC-6 freighters of Aerosol, Air Colombia, ASUR and Transoceanica in Colombia; DC-6s of Bolivia's Air Beni and Fri Reyes and more fire-bombing tankers operated in the United States by ARDCO (DC-4s) and Central Air Service (DC-4s).

Several **Aviation Traders ATL.98 Carvairs** (a bulbous-nosed, UK-developed car freighter DC-4 conversion) survive in the USA, but none are currently active.

The Americas remain a haven for the big Douglases, with aircraft in regular service in the snows of Alaska or the tropics of Bolivia.

SPECIFICATION:
Douglas DC-6B
Powerplant: four 2,500-hp (1864-kW) Pratt & Whitney R-2800-CB17 Double Wasp 18-cylinder two-row air-cooled radial piston engines
Accommodation: three (flight deck)
Dimensions: span 117 ft 6 in (35.81 m); height 29 ft 3 in (8.92 m); length 105 ft 7 in (32.18 m)
Weights: empty 62,000 lb (28123 kg); maximum payload 24,565 lb (11143 kg); maximum take-off 107,000 lb (48534 kg)
Performance: maximum cruising speed 316 mph (509 km/h); service ceiling 21,700 ft (6615 m); maximum range, with maximum payload 1,900 miles (3058 km)

EMBRAER EMB-110 Bandeirante

Brazil
Twin-turboprop light transport

*A*lthough initially designed to meet a Brazilian air force requirement for a multi-role transport, the 19-seat **Bandeirante** (Pioneer) was to play a key role in the foundation of Brazil's aerospace industry and the development of the country's internal air transport network. The first of three prototypes, built by the Institute for Research and Development, made its first flight on 26 October 1968. This led to the establishment of EMBRAER in August 1969 to handle production of the new aircraft at São Jose dos Campos, near São Paulo. The first production Bandeirante flew on 9 August 1972 and was delivered to the air force in January 1973.

Production started with the **C-95** for the Brazilian air force. This type shared the line with the initial commercial model, designated **EMB-110C**, which entered service with Transbrasil on 16 April 1973. The 110C provided accommodation for 15 passengers and was powered by two Pratt & Whitney PT6A-27 turboprops. It was operated by local airlines and gave way to the improved **EMB-110P** with higher gross weight for 18 passengers, first sold to TABA of Brazil in 1976. The major civil versions were the **EMB-110P1** and **EMB-110P2**, the last-named based on a military cargo version with a fuselage lengthened by a 85-cm (9-in) plug. The former had quick-change facilities and a cargo door for all-

The Bandeirante still provides sterling service to smaller airlines around the world such as Finland's Skaergardsflyg, which operates two.

This late-production (1987 vintage) EMBRAER EMB-110P1A is seen wearing Brazilian test marks prior to its delivery to Angola.

freight or mixed operation, while the P2, first flown on 3 May 1977, became the front-line commuter model with accommodation for up to 21 passengers. Powerplant was two 750-shp (559-kW) Pratt & Whitney Canada PT6A-34 turboprops.

In 1981, new **P1/41** and **P2/42** versions were introduced to meet US FAR Pt 41 certification for a maximum gross weight of 5900 kg (13,101 lb). First delivery of a P1/41 was made to PBA of Boston, in spring 1981. The updated **EMB-110P1A** and **P2A** incorporated several interior improvements and 10° tailplane dihedral, reducing vibration. The first two P1As entered service with PBA in December 1983. Also available from 1983 were the **P1A/41** and **P2A/41**, which replaced the P1/41 and P2/41 models.

The designation **EMB-110E(J)** referred to a seven-seat executive transport version of the Bandeirante. Another civil variant was the **EMB-110S1**, a geophysical survey version with additional wingtip tanks similar to those of the **EMB-111**, a maritime patrol version. Development work in the 1980s on a projected pressurised Bandeirante, the **EMB-110P3**, was discontinued in favour of the larger Brasilia. A total of 499 Bandeirantes of all versions (plus three prototypes) was built by the time the last aircraft was delivered to the Brasilian air force in February 1991.

SPECIFICATION:
EMBRAER EMB-110P2A
Powerplant: two 750-hp (559-kW) Pratt & Whitney PT6A-34 turboprops
Accommodation: two (flight deck), maximum of 21 passengers (standard 19)
Dimensions: span 50 ft 3 in (15.33 m); height 16 ft 2 in (4.92 m); length 49 ft 6 in (15.10 m)
Weights: operating empty 7,751 lb (3516 kg); maximum ramp 12,566 lb (5700 kg)
Performance: maximum cruising speed 257 mph (413 km/h); service ceiling 22,500 ft (6860 m); maximum range with maximum fuel and reserves 1,244 miles (2010 km)

EMBRAER EMB-120 Brasilia

The **EMB-120 Brasilia** grew out of a number of projects based on a pressurised Bandeirante development and an increasing need for a larger 30-plus-seat aircraft. EMBRAER officially launched the new aircraft in September 1979. A twin-engined, low-wing design with a circular fuselage and a T-tail, the prototype EMB-120 made its initial flight on 27 July 1983 and received its Brazilian certification on 10 May 1985, followed by FAA type approval on 9 July 1985. The first customer, Atlantic Southeast Airlines of the USA, put the Brasilia into revenue service in October 1985, having taken ceremonial delivery of the second prototype at the Paris air show on 1 June 1985.

Initial production EMB-120s were powered by two 1,590-hp (1185-kW) Pratt & Whitney PW115 engines and had a maximum take-off weight of 10800 lb (23,810 kg). The **EMB-120RT** (Reduced Take-off) introduced more powerful 1,800-hp (1342-kW) PW118s, in early 1986, to improve performance at a higher gross weight of 11500 lb (25,353 kg). Maximum cruising speed was also increased and most aircraft have now been brought up to this standard. An 18-seat corporate model was handed over to United Technologies in the same year. Late in 1987, a hot-and-high version became available. This had improved PW118A engines which maintain maximum output up to a temperature of ISA+15° at sea level. Empty weight was also reduced by 858 lb (390 kg) through increased use of composites. The first customer was Skywest Airlines.

Founded in 1979, ASA (Atlantic Southwest Airways) is part of the Delta Connection network and operates from Atlanta, Georgia.

In 1992 the increased-weight, extended range **EMB-120ER** appeared. The first customer for this version was Utah-based Skywest. Earlier models can be brought up to ER standard with a simple retrofit. The **EMB-120ER Advanced**, available from 1993, is now the standard production variant. It incorporates interchangeable leading edges on flying surfaces, improved flaps, new seals to cut interior noise, increased cargo capacity, and a number of cabin improvements. Range has been extended through an increase in allowable take-off weight. EMBRAER has also developed a passive noise and vibration reduction system for the cabin.

Three cargo versions are still available. These include: the all-freight **EMB-120C**, based on the ER with a 4000-kg (8,818-lb) payload; **EMB-120 Combi**, a mixed configuration version capable of carrying 19 passengers a 1100-kg (2,425-lb) of cargo; and the **EMB-120QC** (Quick-Change) convertible in 40 minutes to all-freight or all-seating configuration. By June 1999 EMBRAER had delivered a total of 350 Brasilias and the type is currently in service with 32 operators in 13 countries.

Brasilian airline PENTA – Pena Transportes Aéreos – operates three EMB-120s alongside a larger fleer of Bandeirantes and Cessna Grand Caravans.

SPECIFICATION:
EMBRAER EMB-120ER Brasilia Advanced
Powerplant: two 1,800-hp (1342-kW) Pratt & Whitney PW118 or 118A turboprops
Accommodation: two (flight deck), maximum of 30 passengers
Dimensions: span 64 ft 10½ in (19.78 m); height 20 ft 10 in (6.35 m); length 65 ft 7½ in (20 m)
Weights: empty equipped 15,763 lb (7150 kg); maximum take-off 26,433 lb (11990 kg)
Performance: maximum operating speed 313 mph (504 km/h); service ceiling PW118As, 32,000 ft (9750 m); maximum range, with maximum fuel 1,874 miles (3017 km)

EMBRAER ERJ-145 and ERJ-135

The EMB-110 and EMB-120 were solid and popular designs, but few predicted that EMBRAER would go on to develop a family of jet airliners that would almost revolutionise the industry. To achieve this EMBRAER first took the fuselage of the Brasilia, stretched it and added two turbofans. This design, announced in 1989, went through major revisions – at first the engines were above the wing, later they were below – before it emerged in its current form, in 1991, as the **EMB-145**.

The aircraft has an all-new wing (with a supercritical section) and a fuselage with the same cross-section as the EMB-120. The EMB-145 is powered by a pair of Allison AE3007 turbofans, a new-generation engine derived from the T406 of the V-22 Osprey. After several false starts the first true launch order, for four aircraft, was signed with Australia's Flight-West airlines, in February 1994. EMBRAER also claimed to hold 136 letters of intent for the aircraft. A more substantial order came from Continental Express in September 1996, which signed for 25 aircraft. The first EMB-145 was officially rolled out at the San Jose dos Campos plant on 18 August 1995 – but by then it had already made its first flight on 11 August. A 13-month flight test programme involving three pre-production aircraft led to FAA certification on 16 December 1996. The first delivery

The ERJ-135 is powered by AE3007A-3 engines and is 11 ft 6 in (3.53 m) shorter than the ERJ-145. Its flight test programme lasted from July 1998 to May 1999.

City Airline of Sweden is the type of customer that EMBRAER tempted into the jet market with the ERJ-145's ease of operation and low costs.

was made to Continental Express on 19 December 1996. The first delivery to a European customer was to Regional Airways of France, in May 1997. After a slow start, sales of the EMB-145 began to accelerate as airlines began to line up for the new 50-seat jets. In October 1997 the EMB-145 was renamed the **Regional Jet 145**, or **ERJ-145**, to reflect its new market status. The basic version has become the **ERJ-145ER** with the introduction of the **ERJ-145LR** (Long Range), powered by more powerful AE3007A1s and fitted with extra fuel. By September 1999 EMBRAER had won 293 ERJ-145 orders, with 288 options, and 132 delivered.

To complement the ERJ-145 EMBRAER launched the smaller 37-seat **ERJ-135**, in September 1997. The first aircraft was rolled out on 12 May 1998 and flew on 4 July. Brasilian certification was awarded in June 1999. The first deliveries will be made to Continental Express in July 1999. ERJ-135 orders and options stand at 139 and 180, respectively.

In June 1999, at the Paris air show EMBRAER formally launched the all-new 70-seat **ERJ-170** and 100-seat **ERJ-190** families, on the back of a major order for 60 aircraft plus 100 options from Crossair. The ERJ-170 is expected to fly in October 2001 and deliveries will begin in December 2002. ERJ-190 deliveries are slated for 2004.

SPECIFICATION:
EMBRAER Regional Jet 145ER (ERJ-145ER)
Powerplant: two 7,040-lb (31.3-kN) Allison AE3007A turbofans
Accommodation: two (flight deck), standard layout for 50 passengers
Dimensions: span 69 ft 5 in (20.04 m); height 22 ft 1¾ in (6.75 m); length 98 ft (29.87 m)
Weights: empty equipped 24,586 lb (11152 kg); maximum take-off 45,415 lb (20600 kg)
Performance: maximum cruising speed Mach 0.78; Cruising altitude 35,000 ft (10668 m) maximum range, with 37 passengers 1,600 miles (2574 km)

Eurocopter Puma, Super Puma

This helicopter family was initially developed by Sud-Aviation (later to become Aerospatiale) to a 1962 French Army requirement for a medium transport helicopter. With development funds from the government, Sud-Aviation was able to proceed quickly, having already worked on a similar model, and the first of two prototypes, powered by twin 1,300-shp (970-kW) Turboméca Turmo IIIC4s, flew on 15 April 1965. The **SA 330 Puma** featured a fully-articulated main rotor with four aluminium blades and a five-bladed anti-torque tail rotor, and was capable of carrying up to 18 passengers. Initial customers were the French army and the UK Royal Air Force, the former taking delivery of the first production model in September 1968.

The **SA 330F** civil version, powered by the 1,290-shp (962-kW) Turmo IVA, flew for the first time in September 1969, and was superseded from 1976 by the **SA 330J**. Main differences were more powerful 1,580-shp (1177-kW) Turmo IVCs, composite main rotors and increased MTOW. Between 1970 and 1984, Aerospatiale sold 126 civil models. Design of a derivative, the **AS 332 Super Puma**, commenced in 1974, initially by refitting a Puma with two Turboméca Makila turboshafts and an uprated transmission as the **AS 331**. This modified experimental helicopter flew on 5 September 1977 and, after further changes to improve performance, led to the first flight of the AS 332 on 13 September 1978. Noticeable external differences include a lengthened nose, increased wheelbase,

Since 1983, Aberdeen-based Bond Helicopters has flown its fleet of suitably-registered AS 332L2 Super Pumas on oil rig support missions.

new landing gear and a ventral fin. The civil version, with seating for two crew and 19 passengers and two 1,877-shp (1400-kW) Makila 1A1 turboshaft engines, was given the suffix C. It was certificated on 24 April 1981, and this was followed on 2 December by the certification of the **AS 332L1 Super Puma Mk I**. This version differed in having a cabin lengthened by 2 ft 6 in (0.76 m) to provide seating for up to 24.

The **AS 332L2 Super Puma Mk II**, first flown on 6 February 1987, introduced new main and tail rotors and an uprated transmission, without changing the Makila 1A1 powerplants. The rear fuselage was lengthened by 1 ft 6 in (0.45 m) to accommodate an extra row of seats. The cockpit is fitted with a EFIS system and the Mk II uses a four-axis automatic flight control system with a built-in health and usage monitoring systems (HUMS). Present production (undertaken by Eurocopter France) includes the AS 332L2 and **AS 332L2 VIP** – fitted out for between eight and 15 passengers or with two four-seat lounges. The first AS 332L2 delivery to a commercial customer came in August 1993.

The original AS 330 Puma, such as this radar-equipped AS 330J, also found favour with oil support companies such as PHI of the United States.

SPECIFICATION:
Eurocopter (Aerospatiale) AS 332L2
Powerplant: two 1,654-shp (1,236-kW) Turboméca Makila 1A2 turboshafts
Accommodation: two (flight deck), maximum of 24 passengers
Dimensions: main rotor diameter 53 ft 1½ in (16.20 m); height 16 ft 4 in (4.97m); length, rotors folded 55 ft ½ in (16.78 m)
Weights: empty 10,331 lb (4660 kg), maximum take-off 20,502 lb (9300 kg)
Performance: maximum cruising speed 172 mph (277 km/h); service ceiling 16,995 ft (5180 m); maximum range, no reserves 927 miles (1491 km)

Fairchild Merlin, Metro

The **Metro** had its origins in an eight-passenger corporate aircraft by Swearingen Aircraft, based at San Antonio, Texas. A rebuilt Beech Queen Air with a pressurised fuselage and two Lycoming piston engines became the **Merlin I**, but this was shelved in favour of the **SA-26T Merlin IIA**, which was the first production aircraft to fly on 13 April 1965. At the same time, the company began construction of a pressurised commuter aircraft, known as the **SA-226TC Metro**, which made its maiden flight on 26 August 1969 and received certification in June 1970. The first Metro was powered by two Garrett AiResearch TPE331s and it could carry up to 20 passengers. Gross weight was restricted to 12,500 lb (5670 kg) to comply with US regulations for commuter aircraft. Production continued when Swearingen was taken over by Fairchild Industries in November 1971, but it delayed entry into service until 1973.

In parallel, the company produced the **SA-226T Merlin III** with increased seating for 11 passengers, and several external changes. Further changes led to the **Merlin IIIA**, powered by two 840-shp (626-kW) TPE331-3U-303Gs, and the **Merlin IIIB**. The original Metro was followed in 1974 by the **Metro II**, which introduced larger 'squared' cabin windows and an optional rocket unit for improved hot-and-high performance. When the MTOW restriction was lifted,

In production in one form or another for 30 years the Fairchild Metro/Merlin family has proved a popular one, particularly in the United States.

The popular Metro/Merlin family has remained a steady seller, particularly in the US, where it serves a niche market with little competition.

Fairchild next produced the **Metro IIA**, in 1980, at a gross weight of 13,100 lb (5944 kg). The equivalent 12-seat corporate transport versions of these two models were the **SA-226AT Merlin IV** and the **SA-226AT Merlin IVA**.

Further significant changes, including an increase in wingspan and more powerful 1,000-hp (745-kW) TPE331-11U-601G turboprops, resulted in the **SA-227AC Metro III**, which was certificated on 23 June 1980. For airlines that preferred to standardise on Pratt & Whitney engines, Fairchild produced the **Metro IIIA**. This model, with the 1,100-hp (820-kW) PT6A-45R engine and minor upgrades, first flew on 31 December 1981. The improved **SA-227CC** and **SA-227DC**, powered by TPE331-11U-621G/-701G engines were certified in June 1990 and these are the only current production versions, now built as the **Metro 23** by Fairchild Aircraft Inc.

The **Merlin 23** (originally **SA-227AT Merlin IVC**) is the corporate version and the **Merlin 23E** has an EFIS cockpit. The **Expediter I** was an all-cargo version of the Metro III with a rear cargo door, reinforced floor and a payload of 5,000 lb (2268 kg). It was replaced, in 1991, by the **Expediter 23** with an increased MTOW and greater payload capacity. By June 1999 approximately 610 Metro and Expediters had been delivered along with 500 Merlins.

SPECIFICATION: Fairchild Metro 23
Powerplant: two 1,000-hp (745-kW) AlliedSignal (Garrett) TPE331-12UA-701G turboprops
Accommodation: two (flight deck), with a maximum of 19 passengers
Dimensions: span 58 ft 1 in (17.70 m); height 16 ft 8 in (5.08 m); length 59 ft (18.09 m)
Weights: operating, empty 8,675 lb (3935 kg); maximum ramp 16,600 lb (7532 kg)
Performance: maximum cruising speed 331 mph (534 km/h); service ceiling 25,150 ft (7666 m); range with maximum payload and typical reserves 900 miles (1450 km)

Fairchild-Dornier Do 228

Dornier began studies of a new commuter airliner based on the Do 28 in the late 1970s. The new larger aircraft, originally known as the **Do 28E**, would make use of Dornier's advanced wing designs – known as Tragsflugels Neuer Technologie (TNT). The final **Do 228** design was launched at the start of the 1980s, and two versions were available from the outset. The 15- to 18-seat **Do 228-100** prototype, powered by two 715-hp (533-kW) Garrett TPE331-5 turboprops, was the first to fly on 28 March 1981 followed by the **Do 228-200** on on 9 May. This version, powered by more powerful TPE331-5As was stretched by 5 ft (1.52 m) and could carry up to 19/20 passengers. German type certification was awarded on 18 December 1981 and the first delivery was made to A/S Norving on 3 March 1982.

An agreement for production in India was concluded in 1983 with the Kanpur Division of Hindustan Aeronautics. Manufacture of the **HAL 228** began with assembly of major component parts supplied by Dornier, but later aircraft have incorporated a much greater indigenous contribution. In the early 1990s Dornier also entered negotiations with China to start up a second licence production line by 1996-97, but these talks came to nothing.

Dornier built just 13 Do 228-100s and 19 -200s before replacing them with improved models. The **Do 228-101**, **Do 228-201** were essentially identical to the original models, but introduced a reinforced fuselage structure and different mainwheel tyres to permit a maximum take-off weight of 13,184 lb

Druk Air is the Kingdom of Bhutan's sole airline, and it selected the Do 228 as the ideal type for STOL operations in its mountainous home.

(5980 kg). Both versions entered production in 1984, but demand for the short fuselage Do 228 fell away and only 22 -101s were built. The -201 was more successful and 53 were built. It was followed by the **Do 228-202** (38 built) with yet more fuel and a MTOW of 13,668 lb (6200 kg), the **Do 228-202K** (24 built) fitted with the underfuselage strakes of the Do 228-212 and the **Do 228-202F** (5 built), a cargo conversion with double doors in the cabin. The final production version was the **Do 228-212** (65 built) which featured a 14,110-lb (6400-kg) MTOW, uprated TPE331-10 engines, ventral rear fuselage strakes, new avionics, a strengthened undercarriage and improved brakes.

In June 1996 Fairchild Aerospace took an 80 per cent stake in Dornier, with the remainder held by Daimler-Benz Aerospace. Fairchild-Dornier is now in charge of all Dornier production and operations. Do 228 manufacture ceased in Germany with the roll-out of the 238th production aircraft in 1994 (this aircraft was delivered to Air Guadeloupe in 1997). Production of civil and military versions continues in India with over 50 delivered to date.

The Dornier Do 228 won a reputation as an excellently engineered aircraft, but one which was expensive to acquire and operate.

SPECIFICATION:
Dornier Do 228-200
Powerplant: two 715-hp (533-kW) AlliedSignal (Garrett) TPE331-5-252D turboprops
Accommodation: two (flight deck), maximum of 19 passengers
Dimensions: span 55 ft 8 in (16.97 m); height 15 ft 11½ in (4.86 m); length 54 ft 4 in (16.56 m)
Weights: operating empty 7,820 lb (3547 kg); maximum take-off 12,566 lb (5700 kg)
Performance: maximum cruising speed 265 mph (428 km/h); service ceiling 28,000 ft (8535 m); maximum range, with reserves 1,680 miles (2704 km)

Fairchild Aerospace Do 328/JET

From the Do 228, Dornier moved on with a more advanced development using the wing technology of the 228 in a larger aircraft with a much wider 'stand-up' cabin. The new aircraft, the T-tailed 33-seat **Do 328** was optimised for high-speed and 'near-jet' performance in terms of point-to-point block times. It was powered by two Pratt & Whitney PW119B turboprops. The aircraft is assembled at Dornier's Oberpfaffenhofen plant but fuselage shells are built by OGMA in Portugal then shipped to Aermacchi in Italy for completion.

The programme was launched in August 1988 and the first aircraft flew on 6 December 1991. Launch customer was Horizon Air, which ordered 35 (with 25 options). The second pre-production Do 328 flew on 4 June 1992 and it was joined by a third on 20 October. European JAA certification was awarded on 15 October 1993 and US FAA approval was obtained on 10 November. The first **Do 328-100** (the first production variant), was handed over to Air Engiadina on 21 October 1993.

A total of 35 Do 328-100s were built before the improved **Do 328-110** was introduced, with a larger tail, improved flaps, spoilers, wider props and an increased maximum take-off weight. As a result maximum range was pushed beyond the 1,000 nm (1850 km, 1150 miles) mark. A further developed

Sales of the Do 328 were slow but its transformation into the Do 328JET has proved to be a masterstroke, spawning a whole new family of aircraft.

Switzerland's Air Engiadina was the European launch customer for the Do 328. Its early model aircraft have now been brought up to -110 standard.

version the **Do 328-120** became available in March 1996. This had several airframe changes to improve short-field performance and PW119C engines. A total of 26 Do 328-110s and five -120s were built.

In 1997, the decision was made to abandon the turboprop design for a radical re-engining with Pratt & Whitney PW306B turbofans. This was the **Do 328JET** (originally **Do 328-300**) which first flew on 20 January 1998. Dornier's acquisition by Fairchild in 1996 acted as the spur for this change of direction and all new aircraft are now marketed and sold under the aegis of Fairchild Aerospace. Final assembly remains in Germany, but wing production is being moved to San Antonio.

The Do 328JET launch customer was Skyways Airlines which took delivery of its first aircraft in August 1999. A business jet version of the 328JET, the **Envoy 3** is now available. A stretched 42/44-seat version, the **Do 428JET**, is under development and will enter service in August 2002. Fairchild-Dornier plan to develop a whole family of regional jets – the 55-seat **528JET**, the 70-seat **728JET** and the 95/105-seat **928JET** – on the back of a huge order for 120 aircraft won in 1998 from Lufthansa Cityline. The 528JET and 728JET will be powered by General Electric CF34s and will enter service in 2003 and 2004, respectively.

SPECIFICATION:
Fairchild Aerospace Do 328JET
Powerplant: two 6,050-lb (26.9-kW) Pratt & Whitney PW306B turbofans
Accommodation: two (flight deck), maximum of 34 passengers (32 standard)
Dimensions: span 68 ft 10 in (20.98 m); height 23 ft 8½ in (7.23 m); length 69 ft 9¼ in (21.28 m)
Weights: operating empty 20,282 lb (9200 kg); maximum take-off 33,047 lb (14990 kg)
Performance: maximum cruising speed 460 mph (741 km/h); service ceiling 31,000 ft (9450 m); design range, with 32 passengers 1035 miles (1666 km)

Fokker F27 and FH227

At the beginning of the 1950s, many aircraft manufacturers began searching for a successor to the ubiquitous Douglas DC-3. Some are still trying, but one of the most accomplished of the earlier designs was Fokker's **F27 Friendship**. The F27 began life with the Dutch firm as the 32-seat **P.275** in 1950. Taking advantage of the newly-developed Rolls-Royce Dart turboprop, and matching two with a modified, circular, high-winged fuselage, the **F27 Mk 100** emerged in its final form in 1953. At this point Fokker chose the F27's upbeat name and entered into licence-production with Fairchild. The first Dutch-built aircraft flew on 24 November 1954, from Schipol, followed by a **Fairchild F27**, from Hagerstown, Maryland, on 12 April 1958.

Strangely, the first aircraft to enter airline service was a US-built one. West Coast Airways placed its first (modified 40-seat) F27 into service on 27 November 1958, while Aer Lingus followed with Dutch aircraft on 15 December. With uprated Dart Mk 532 engines, Fokker next flew the **F27 Mk 200** (**Fairchild F27A**) on 20 September 1962. This was followed by the **F27 Mk 300 Combiplane** (**F27B**), a passenger/freight version with a reinforced floor and large cargo door forward in the port fuselage. Fokker alone built the **F27 Mk 400** (chiefly as the **Troopship** for the Dutch air force), which combined a freight door with further uprated engines.

The next major development came in the form of the stretched **F27 Mk 500**, seating between 52 and 60 (and 15 featuring freight doors on either side).

Air Tanzania has two F27-600RF combi aircraft in service. The African airline is typical of the many operators who still value the F27's dependability.

This inspired Fairchild to come up with its own 'long' version. By 1966 the US manufacturer had become **Fairchild-Hiller**, and 79 of its **FH227** were eventually completed. Fairchild also built the corporate **F27F**, and higher-powered **F27J** and **F27M**. The final production version was Fokker's **F27 Mk 600**, which combined the short fuselage of the Mk 200 with the reinforced cabin and cargo door of the Mk 300/400 combiplanes. This was a true quick-change version with a roller floor, enabling the interior to be rapidly reconfigured.

Several military transport versions (with an 'M' suffix to the sub-type) and dedicated maritime patrol versions were built, but production of the F27 ended in favour of the Fokker 50 in June 1986. A total of 581 Dutch aircraft had been built, with a further 108 (29 F27s) completed in the United States, with sales to 168 customers in 63 countries. By 1999 a sizeable proportion of these were still in use around the world, with as many as 444 still in regular service. The type has retained its market value and secondhand F27s are still much in demand, particularly as freighters.

FH227s, like this Belgian example, found their way to Europe. The last major user was France's TAT, which has now withdrawn its aircraft from use.

SPECIFICATION:
Fokker F27 Mk 500 Friendship
Powerplant: two 2,210-shp (1648-kW) Rolls-Royce Dart Mk 552 turboprops
Accommodation: two (flight deck), maximum of 60 passengers
Dimensions: span 95 ft 1¾ in (29.00 m); height 28 ft 7½ in (8.71 m); length 82 ft 2¼ in (25.06 m)
Weights: operating empty 28,000 lb (12700 kg); maximum take-off 45,900 lb (20820 kg)
Performance: normal cruising speed 298 mph (480 km/h); service ceiling 29,500 ft (8990 m); range with 52 passengers and reserves 1,082 miles (1741 km)

Fokker F28 Fellowship

The success of the Fokker F27 convinced the Dutch firm that there was a market for a comparable, jet-powered, 32-seat design with a range of approximately 575 miles (926 km). As with the F27, Dutch governmental backing was sought, and Fokker also entered into a contract with Germany's VFW and HFB to build the rear fuselage and tail sections. Shorts, in Northern Ireland, was later selected to build the wings. In keeping with the precedent set by the F27, the new design was named **F28 Fellowship**. Rolls-Royce Spey Mk 555 turbofans were chosen as the sole powerplant. The F28 was launched with an order from LTU in November 1965, but by the time the first example had flown, on 9 May 1967, this was the only firm interest shown in the new airliner.

Norway's Braathens SAFE next placed an order early in the flight test programme, and by the time the F28 was certified, in February 1969, a total of 22 orders had been received. The initial production version was the 65-seat, 89-ft 11-in (27.16-m) **F28 Mk 1000** and 100 of these were built before production of this version ceased in 1977. Throughout its life the Mk 1000's maximum weight was steadily increased, improving its range to 1,150 miles (1852 km). In 1972 Fokker launched the next model, the **F28 Mk 2000**, which was

Canadian Regional Airlines operates feeder and regional services for Canadian Airlines and operates a large fleet of F28 Mk 1000s.

Beginning in 1993 SAS absorbed the routes and aircraft of Swedish domestic carrier Linjeflyg, including its fleet of F28 Mk 4000s.

stretched to accommodate 79 passengers but had its maximum range reduced to 805 miles (1296 km). Chronologically, the **F28 Mk 6000** came next, in 1975. This combined a slatted wing (to improve take-off performance) with the Mk 2000's fuselage, but airline interest was weak, with only two aircraft ever delivered to individual customers.

Fokker instead turned its attention to the **F28 Mk 4000**, the most popular version. Instigated by a requirement from Swedish domestic carrier Linjeflyg, the Mk 4000 first flew on 20 October 1976. This was the same length as the Mk 2000, but featured an increased wingspan, 85 seats and optional extra fuel. One hundred and eleven Mk 4000s were built, with the last example (also the last F28) delivered on 7 August 1987. The final version to be developed was the **F28 Mk 3000**. This incorporated all the new design features of the Mks 4000 and 6000, but used the short fuselage of the F28 Mk 1000. The first example flew on 23 December 1976, and initial deliveries were made to Garuda. A water/methanol injection version, the **F28 Mk 3000R**, was developed for hot-and-high operations; so too was a cargo door-equipped version, the **F28 Mk 3000C**, in 1978. Twenty-one Mk 3000s were completed. In total 241 F28s were delivered and by September 1999 158 remained in service.

SPECIFICATION:
Fokker F28 Mk 4000
Powerplant: two 9,900-lb (44-kN) Rolls-Royce Spey Mk 555-1P turbofans
Accommodation: two (flight deck), maximum of 85 passengers
Dimensions: span 82 ft 3 in (25.07 m); height 27 ft 9½ in (8.47 m); length 97 ft 1¾ in (29.61 m)
Weights: operating, empty 38,900 lb (17465 kg); maximum take-off 73,000 lb (33113 kg)
Performance: maximum operating speed 380 mph (612 km/h); service ceiling 35,000 ft (10675 m); maximum range, with maximum load 1,295 miles (2085 km)

Fokker 50 and 60

With the success of the F27 Friendship, which has almost become a household name, there was never any doubt that Fokker would launch a successor, taking advantage of all the technological advances that had occurred in the intervening years. On the F27's 25th anniversary in service, in 1983, Fokker announced the **Fokker 50** (**F50**). Similar in size and configuration to the F27, the F50 (so-called because of its seating configuration) features new Pratt & Whitney PW120 series engines with six-bladed propellers, hydraulic gear and flap systems, substantial use of composite materials, and a completely redesigned Honeywell EFIS cockpit. The wing also has been much improved and features small 'Fokklets' (or winglets). From a passenger's point of view, one less satisfactory change was the removal of the F27's large windows in favour of an increased number of smaller ones.

The first two prototypes were modified from F27s, and Fokker's official documentation and some registration certificates still refer to the F50 as the **F27-050**. Ansett Transport Industries, of Australia, placed the launch order for 15 aircraft. The first flight took place from the Fokker plant at Schipol on 28 December 1985, followed by the first production F50 on 13 February 1987. Deliveries commenced to Germany's DLT on 7 August 1987, which later became Lufthansa Cityline. The baseline model is the **Fokker 50 Series 100**, powered by PW125B engines. Depending on the seating configuration, which can range from 46 to 68, the Series 100 is fur-

In 1989 Sudan Airways took delivery of a pair of Fokker 50s, which it operated alongside DHC-6s, 737-200s, an A320, 707-300Cs and A310-300s.

ther divided into **Fokker 50-100** (with four doors) and **Fokker 50-120** (three doors).

By early 1993, Fokker was delivering the **F50 Series 300**. This PW127B-powered, hot-and-high version was first ordered by Avianca, and was again available in **F50-300** and **F50-320** models. Fokker also considered a stretched version, the **Fokker 50 Series 400**, with a 68-seat cabin.

In February 1994 the Dutch air force launched a new development, the **Fokker 60 Utility** (**F60U**), ordering 12 to replace its existing F27 Troopships. The F60U is stretched by 5 ft 4 in (1.6 m) and is fitted with a large cargo door to starboard.

By the mid 1990s Fokker was in serious financial trouble due largely to the cut-throat regional airliner market and its own high manufacturing costs. When various attempts at restructuring failed, it slid in bankruptcy and collapsed, in 1996. Several attempts to revive it, most noticeably the Rekkof Restart bid (Rekkof is Fokker spelt backwards) have come to nothing. As a result an F50 delivered to Ethiopian Airlines on 23 May 1997 became the last Fokker airliner. A total of 232 Fokker 50s were built.

Rio Sul is a subsidiary of VARIG, which flies domestic and regional services from Rio de Janeiro with EMB-120s, ERJ-145s, 737s and four Fokker 50s.

SPECIFICATION:
Fokker 50-100
Powerplant: two 2,500-hp (1864-kW) Pratt & Whitney Canada PW125B turboprops
Accommodation: two (flight deck), maximum of 30 passengers
Dimensions: span 64 ft 10½ in (19.78 m); height 20 ft 10 in (6.35 m); length 65 ft 7½ in (20 m)
Weights: operating, empty 16,457 lb (7465 kg); maximum take-off 25,353 lb (11500 kg)
Performance: maximum operating speed 313 mph (504 km/h); service ceiling 30,000 ft (9150 m); maximum range, with maximum fuel 633 miles (1019 km)

Fokker 70 and 100

Fokker began the search for an F28 replacement with the 110/130-seat '**Super F28**', for service entry in 1984. This became the **Fokker F29**, and the manufacturer even considered using Boeing 737 fuselages to produce a 180-seat airliner. This did not proceed and, along with McDonnell Douglas, Fokker next drew up the 150-seat, 737-lookalike **MDF 100**, before finally returning to the proven F28 design. Stretching the original aircraft, and adding a pair of new Rolls-Royce Tay engines, Fokker launched the **Fokker 100**, simultaneously with the F50, in November 1983.

To build the 107-seat aircraft, Fokker entered into a partnership with MBB (now DASA) to build the mid-section and tail, and Short Bros to build the wing. The F100 won its launch order – 10 for Swissair – in 1984, but it was to be almost three years until another airline signed for the type. A major boost came in 1986 with the signing of an agreement between Ireland-based lessors GPA and Fokker, establishing GPA Fokker 100 Ltd to purchase and place aircraft for airlines. The first Fokker 100 took to the air on 30 November 1986. Swissair took delivery of its first F100 on 29 February 1988, which entered service on the Zürich-Vienna route on 3 April.

On 8 June 1988, Fokker flew an uprated Tay 650-powered version and American Airlines ordered

The worldwide population of Fokker 70s is small and concentrated in a few countries. This Air Littoral aircraft wears Air France Express colours.

Air Gabon was one of several airlines that contracted to lease F100s from GPA Fokker 100, receiving this single example in 1989.

75, with 75 options. Deliveries of this version began, to USAir, in 1989. The 75th aircraft for American was also the 250th F100 to be delivered, in early June 1994. The F100 was also available in an 88-seat **Fokker 100QC** (Quick Change) cargo version and the VIP **Fokker 100 Corporate**.

In 1992 Fokker gave the go-ahead for a short-fuselage variant of the F100, the 79-seat, Tay 620-powered **Fokker 70**. Modification of the second prototype F100 to this configuration began in October 1992, and it flew on 4 April 1993. Measuring 101 ft 4¾ in (30.91 m), the Fokker 70 was built on the same line as the F100 and customers could switch between either version with only 12 months' notice. Launch orders for the F70 came from Pelita and Sempati Air in Indonesia, followed by British Midland and Mesa Airlines, in the USA. On 12 July 1994 the first production aircraft flew at the Schipol plant. The first customer aircraft was handed over to the Ford Motor Company as a 48-seat corporate shuttle and the first airline delivery took place on 9 March 1995, to Sempati Air.

The collapse of Fokker in March 1996 brought an end to the Fokker '**JetLiners**'. The last F100 was delivered to TAM Brasil on 21 March 1996 and the last F70 went to KLM Cityhopper on 18 April 1997. A total of 280 F100s and 45 F70s were built.

SPECIFICATION:
Fokker F100
Powerplant: two 9,900-lb (44-kN) Rolls-Royce Tay Mk 620-15 turbofans
Accommodation: two (flight deck), maximum of 107 passengers (standard 97)
Dimensions: span 92 ft 1½ in (28.08 m); height 27 ft 10½ in (8.5 m); length 115 ft 10¼ in (35.31 m)
Weights: operating, empty 51,260 lb (23250 kg); maximum take-off 91,500 lb (41500 kg)
Performance: maximum operating speed 367 mph (592 km/h); maximum cruising altitude 35,000 ft (10670 m); maximum range, with maximum load 2,222 miles (1380 km)

GAF N.22 and N.24 Nomad

Australia's Government Aircraft factory (GAF) was founded in 1939 to build military aircraft, all largely under licence, for the services. After World War II the company continued in this role producing Avro Lincoln bombers, English Electric Canberra jet bombers, Dassault Mirage III fighters and the indigenously-designed Jindivik target drone. In 1967 GAF moved to diversify into the civil aviation market and drew up a design for a twin-turboprop transport aircraft that was also firmly aimed at the Australian Army.

The **N2 Nomad** was a strut-braced, high-wing aircraft with a mid-set tailplane and a squared-off fuselage that could accommodate 12/13 passengers. It had a retractable tricycle undercarriage with the main gear housed in sponsons that supported the wing braces. The Nomad was optimised for STOL performance, using full-span double-slotted flaps and drooping ailerons. It was powered by a pair of 400-hp (298-kW) Allison 250-B17 turboprops. The prototype first flew on 23 July 1971. A second development aircraft was also built and later handed over to the Army in 1975.

The initial basic models were the **N.22 Nomad** (or **Missionmaster**) for the Australian Army and the 13-seat **N.22B Nomad** for the airlines (and export military customers). Only 14 N.22s were built. The N.22B faired somewhat better with GAF building a total of 96 aircraft. Several domestic airlines and the Royal Flying Doctor Service acquired N.22Bs and it was also exported to operators in New Guinea

New Zealand's Air Safaris operates a fleet of five N.24 Nomads from its home at the popular tourist destination of Lake Tekapo.

and Malaysia. However, most N.22Bs entered service with the military in Australia, Indonesia, the Philippines and Thailand. GAF proposed a number of specialist military versions but the only major developments were the **N.22SB Search Master B**, fitted with a Bendix RDR1400 sea search radar and the more sophisticated **N.22SL Search Master L** (Long) fitted with a Litton APS 504 radar.

On 17 December 1975 GAF flew the prototype of the stretched **N.24 Nomad**, with its fuselage extended by 5 ft 9 in (1.79 m). This version carried four extra seats, had two extra cabin windows and operated at higher weights. A total of 44 were built.

The Nomad proved unpopular in service and gained a bad reputation for technical troubles and failures. GAF closed the line in 1984 after 160 production-standard aircraft had been built.

In July 1987 GAF was privatised, becoming Aerospace Technologies of Australia (ASTA) which today provides technical support for the surviving Nomads. Approximately 20 Nomads are still in commercial service, with the active aircraft now concentrated largely in New Zealand.

Most Nomads in commercial service are the stretched N.24 model – however larger numbers of N.22s and N.24s are still in military service.

SPECIFICATION:
GAF N24A Nomad
Powerplant: two 400-shp (298-kN) Allison 250-B17B turboprops
Accommodation: single-pilot standard (flight deck), maximum of 17 passengers
Dimensions: span 54 ft (16.46 m); height 18 ft 1½ in (5.52 m); length 47 ft 1¼ in (14.36 m)
Weights: operating, empty 5,241 lb (2377 kg); maximum take-off 9,400 lb (4263 kg)
Performance: cruising speed 193 mph (311 km/h); service ceiling 20,000 ft (6100 m); maximum range, with reserves 840 miles (1352 km)

Gulfstream I

In the early 1950s Leroy Grumman, chief of the Grumman Aircraft Corporation, saw the market for a purpose-built executive aircraft, rather than the existing conversions of World War II-vintage types. Using a pair of the newly developed Rolls-Royce Dart turboprops, Grumman started planning a high-wing, S-2 Tracker anti-submarine aircraft derivative – but this proved to be an unsatisfactory starting point Customer response underlined the need for a 350-mph (560-km/h) aircraft with a stand-up cabin, capable of covering up to 2,200 miles (3500 km). By 1957, when the go-ahead was given, the eventual low-wing configuration was evolving and 250 engineers were assigned to the newly christened **Design 159**. The **G.159** would become far better known as the **Gulfstream** (later **Gulfstream I**), yet the origins of the name are somewhat hazy. It was chosen by Leroy Grumman himself, with an eye on the aircraft's transatlantic range, and proved to be a durable one.

On 14 August 1958 the first aircraft emerged from its Bethpage home for its maiden flight. This proved to be one of history's less routine first flights, as an electrical failure shut down the fuel system, forcing a rapid emergency landing before the engines stopped turning. The second aircraft followed on 11 November, delayed by a strike at

French airline Air Provence provides passenger and cargo charter services throughout France with a fleet of six Gulfstream Is, plus HS 748s and FH-227s.

Despite its relative age the Gulfstream I has proved to be a reliable and dependable performer and over the half the aircraft built are still in service.

suppliers, the Pittsburgh Plate Glass Co. The flight test programme was undertaken largely at Stewart Field, Florida, and led to FAA certification to CAR 4B, Part 40 and SR422A 'Special Requirement, Turbine-Powered Airplane' standards, permitting full airline-style operations up to 12192 m (40,000 ft). The first customer delivery (aircraft number four) was made to the Sinclair Oil Company, entering service in October 1959. With firm orders standing at over 30 (early critics of the programme had forecast sales of 15 at best), the production rate was set at three per month; however, the break-even figure was a more daunting 125 to 150 aircraft. By 1965 Gulfstream had delivered its 150th aircraft.

In the early 1960s the type was certified for 24-passenger operations, with an optional 62 x 82-in (1.57 x 2.08-m) aft cargo door plus optional wing slipper fuel tanks. There was also a general rise in fuel capacity and operating weights.

A stretched version, the **Gulfstream I-C** was developed, with the fuselage extended by 10 ft 8 in (3.25 m) to seat up to 37 passengers. This did not prove a success and only five were built. A total of 200 Gulfstream Is (including the I-Cs) were built before production finally ceased in 1969 in favour of the Gulfstream II jet. By June 1999 112 of these were still in corporate and airline service.

Specification
Gulfstream I
Powerplant: two 2,190-shp (1631-kW) Rolls-Royce Dart 529 turboprops
Accommodation: two (flight deck), maximum of 24 passengers (10/12 standard)
Dimensions: span 78 ft 4 in (23.87 m); height 22 ft 9 in (6.94 m); length 64 ft 6 in (19.66 m)
Weights: empty, equipped 21,900 lb (9933 kg); max take-off 35,100 lb (15920 kg)
Performance: max cruising speed at 25,000 ft (7625 m) 348 mph (560 km/h); service ceiling 36,000 ft (11000 m); range, with max fuel and reserves 2,540 miles (4088 km)

Gulfstream II and III

The Gulfstream I competed with the first generation of biz-jets. These aircraft had their advantages, but none could match the G.159 for comfort or range. A jet-powered Gulfstream was a logical progression, and so studies began into a swept-wing aircraft, using the same cabin as the G.159. Power was again provided by Rolls-Royce, in the shape of the Spey turbofan. Cruising at Mach 0.75, at 13100 m (43,000 ft), the T-tailed **G.1159** would have a range of 3,190 nm (5907 km/3670 miles). In 1964 Grumman announced that it would proceed upon the receipt of 50 $420,000 deposits. In the event it went ahead, in May 1965, with substantially fewer but the 50 total was reached before the maiden flight.

The first **G.1159 Gulfstream II** flew on 2 October 1966. The first four production 'GIIs' were dedicated to the flight testing and FAA type certification was awarded on 19 October 1967.

As Gulfstream I production came to an end at 200 aircraft in 1969, over 50 GIIs had been delivered. The G.1159 soon established itself as the fastest biz-jet available. To comply with FAR Part 25 and 36 noise abatement regulations, a hush kit for the GII was developed and fitted as standard from aircraft number 166 onwards. A more radical change came in the tip-tank-equipped **Gulfstream II(TT)**. The modification was certified in September 1976 and led to a slight improvement in performance and handling due to the increased wing area. Available as an option from aircraft number 199 onwards, the GII(TT) offered a 400-nm (740-km, 460-mile)

The Gulfstream III was the yardstick against which all other long-range business jets were measured and remained so until the advent of the GIV.

increase in range at Mach 0.72. Grumman considered the tanks to be standard from aircraft No. 206 onwards, and customers had to specify their exclusion.

The GII benefited from GIII technology and a refit programme added winglets to existing GIIs. Between 1981 and 1987 43 examples were thus transformed into **G.1159B Gulfstream IIBs**. GIIs fitted with new blended winglets developed by Seattle-based Aviation Partners are designated **Gulfstream IISPs** (previously **Gulfstream IIWs**). By 1999 51 GIISP conversions had been undertaken and 246 GIIs (of 258 built) remained in service.

In 1973 the company was reorganised as the Gulfstream American Aviation Co., and the new **G.1159A Gulfstream III** was launched. The original, very ambitious plans for a supercritical-winged aircraft were scaled back to produce a stretched GII, with winglets. The definitive 4,686-mile (6732-km) capable Gulfstream III first flew on 2 December 1979, replacing the GII. Gulfstream III production ended in September 1988, with the arrival of the Gulfstream IV. In September 1999 196 of the 200 GIIIs built remained in service.

Many GIIs have been fitted with winglets, either as GIIBs (seen here) or GIISPs. The extra cockpit side window sets them apart from similar GIIIs.

Specification
Gulfstream III
Powerplant: two 11,400-lb (50.7-kN) Rolls-Royce Spey Mk.511-8 turbofans
Accommodation: two (flight deck), maximum 24 passengers (standard layout for 8/10)
Dimensions: span, over winglets 77 ft 10 in (23.72 m); length 83 ft 1 in (25.32 m); height 24 ft 4 in (7.43 m)
Weights: operating, empty 38,000 lb (17236 kg); max take-off 69,700 lb (31615 kg
Performance: max cruising speed Mach 0.85; max operating altitude 45,000 ft (13715 m); max range, with eight passengers, baggage and VFR reserves 4,686 miles (7542 km)

Gulfstream IV and V

In 1983 the Gulfstream company went public, offering shares to raise working capital for a new project – the **Gulfstream IV** (**G.1159C**). Although the GIII was selling well, new regulations would catch up with its reliable, but loud (and smoky) Spey engines. The answer again lay with Rolls-Royce and the new-technology Tay Mk.611-8 turbofan – which was quieter yet more powerful.

The GIV represented another leap forward in capability. As the GIII had bettered the GII in range by some 37 per cent, so the GIV introduced a 22 per cent improvement over the GIII, carrying eight passengers over 4,600 nm (8519 km, 5294 miles). The GIV would also be longer (by 1.37 m/4.5 ft), faster and fitted with the most modern of cockpits, using the Sperry SPZ-8000 EFIS system. The first GIV was rolled out on 11 September 1985, followed by a first flight eight days later and FAA certification on 22 April 1987. That year the second prototype captured the record for a westbound (against the prevailing winds) circumnavigation of the globe from the Paris air show at Le Bourget. In 1988 the eastbound record (held by a Boeing 747SP) fell too.

The **Gulfstream IV-SP** (Special Performance) was unveiled at the 1992 Farnborough air show. It offered an increase in payload/range capability over the standard GIV of 53 per cent, and a new SPZ-8400

The Gulfstream V was the first business jet with true global range. Perhaps the only way it can be improved is by developing a supersonic version.

The GIV-SP boosts the payload of the baseline GIV with no increase in empty weight. From September 1992, all Gulfstream IVs were built to this standard.

EFIS. The first (converted) GIV-SP flew on 24 June 1992 and the GIV-SP became the sole production GIV variant, from aircraft No. 1215 onwards.

Also at the the 1992 Farnborough show (rather than the traditional venue of the NBAA show) Gulfstream returned to announce its biggest aircraft yet. Stretched by a further 2.13 m (6 ft 10 in) over the GIV, the **Gulfstream V** boasted a new larger wing, along with a larger horizontal tail. The GV is the world's first ultra-long-range business jet, with a non-stop range of 6,300 nm (11667 km, 7,250 miles) placing a New York-Tokyo or London-Singapore sector well within reach.

Cruising at 51,000 ft (15545 m) and Mach 0.90, the GV is powered by two 14,750-lb (65.6-kN) Rolls-Royce/BMW BR 710-48 turbofans. The cockpit is built around a six-screen (colour LCD) Honeywell SPZ-8500 EFIS system and a Honeywell/GEC-Marconi Model 2020 HUD is also available. The first GV flew on flew on 28 November 1995 and full FAA certification was awarded in April 1997. With the GIV-SP and GIV in production side-by-side, Gulfstream (which was acquired by General Dynamics in 1999) is now firmly a 'two aircraft' company for the first time. By June 1999 376 GIVs and 46 GVs had been delivered, with an announced order backlog of 60 GIV-SPs and 60 GVs.

SPECIFICATION:
Gulfstream IV-SP
Powerplant: two 13,850-lb (61.6-kN) Rolls-Royce Tay Mk 611-8 turbofans
Accommodation: two (flight deck), standard seating for 14 to 19
Dimensions: span, over winglets 77 ft 10 in (23.72 m); height 24 ft 5¼ in (7.45 m); length 88 ft 4 in (26.92 m)
Weights: operating, empty 42,500 lb (19278 kg); maximum take-off 74,600 lb (33838 kg)
Performance: maximum cruising speed speed at FL310 Mach 0.85; maximum operating altitude 45,000 ft (13715 m); maximum range, with maximum load 4,856 miles (7815 km)

HAMC Y-12

The 17-passenger **Y-12** (**Yunshuji-12** – transport aircraft 12) traces its origins to the 9/10-seat HAMC **Y-11**, designed and developed by Harbin Aircraft Manufacturing Corporation in China's Heilongjiang Province. Studies to improve the payload/range capabilities of the Y-11 resulted in an initial development version, the **Y-12 I** (originally **Y-11T1**). This had two 500-hp (373-kW) Pratt & Whitney PT6A-11 turboprops replacing the earlier 285-hp (213-kW) Huosai-6A piston engines.

These more powerful engines enabled the basic Y-11 airframe to be scaled up in diameter and from 39 ft 5 in (12.02 m) to 48 ft 9 in (14.86 m) in length, to provide increased seating for 17 passengers. Other changes from the Y-11 included a 9-in (0.23-m) increase in wingspan, a new supercritical aerofoil section, integral fuel tanks and bonded construction.

Two prototypes and a static test airframe were built, and the Y-12 I made its first flight on 14 July 1982. The two flying models were later modified for geological survey work in the Harbin area. About 30 production models of the Y-12 I were also built, for domestic use.

Three further development aircraft followed in 1983 leading to the **Y-12 II** (originally **Y-11T2**). This version introduced yet more powerful PT6A-27s, each flat rated at 620 shp (462 kW). Another major external difference was the deletion of the leading-edge flaps. A larger dorsal fin and tail unit were added in production aircraft. The first Y-12 II flew on 16 August 1984 and it received its domestic

The Y-12 IV is the latest version of HAMC's STOL transport and looks set to continue the trend of modest sales set by the preceeding Y-12 II.

type certification in December 1985. First deliveries of four aircraft to the Sri Lankan government for patrol duties were made in early 1987. Its export potential was considerably improved when it obtained limited certification from the UK Civil Aviation Authority on 20 June 1990. FAA approval is still being sought. By early 1999 approximately 100 Y-12 IIs had been delivered to military and civil customers in Bangladesh, Cambodia, China, Eritrea, Fiji, Iran, Kenya, Kiribati, Laos, Malaysia, Mauritania, Mongolia, Namibia, Nepal, Pakistan, Peru, Sri Lanka, Tanzania and Zambia.

An improved version, the **Y-12 IV**, made its first flight on 30 August 1993. This aircraft incorporates sweptback wingtips, modified control surface actuation, new main gear and brakes, a rear baggage door, and a redesigned interior for 18/19 passengers. Western avionics can also be fitted. Maximum take-off weight has been increased to 12,500 lb (5671 kg). HAMC is attempting to start production of a fully-westernised version of the Y-12 IV, the **Twin Panda**, in association with the Canadian Aerospace Group, based at North Bay, Ontario.

The 1984-vintage Harbin Y-12 I was built in small numbers and owed much to the earlier Y-11 DHC-6 Twin Otter lookalike.

SPECIFICATION:
HAMC (Harbin) Y-12 II
Powerplant: two 680-hp (507-kW) Pratt & Whitney Canada PT6A-27 turboprops
Accommodation: two (flight deck), maximum of 17 passengers
Dimensions: span 56 ft 7 in (17.24 m); height 17 ft 4 in (5.28 m); length 48 ft 9 in (4.86 m)
Weights: operating empty 6,614 lb (3000 kg); maximum ramp 11,747 lb (5330 kg)
Performance: maximum cruising speed 201 mph (325 km/h); service ceiling 22,965 ft (7000 m); range with maximum passenger load 254 miles (410 km)

Hawker Siddeley HS 748

Twin-turboprop airliner and utility transport

The 748 turboprop airliner was the result of a decision by the Avro company to re-enter the commercial market in the late 1950s. Early designs envisaged a 20-seat, high-wing aircraft, but this evolved into a larger 36-seat, low-wing model. Known as the **Avro 748**, it became the **HS 748** when Avro was absorbed into the Hawker Siddeley Group in 1963, then as the **BAe 748** after Hawker Siddeley became part of the new British Aerospace in April 1977.

The first of two prototypes flew on 24 June 1960, and the type received its certification on 7 December 1961. When production finally closed in 1988, a total of 379 748s had been built both in the UK and under licence by Hindustan Aeronautics Limited (HAL) in India, including 31 military **Andover C.Mk 1**s for the Royal Air Force.

The first production batch was the **Series 1**, which flew on 30 August 1961 and was powered by two Rolls-Royce Dart RDa6 Mk 514 turboprop engines rated at 1,880 hp (1402 kW). The Series 1 also differed from the prototype in having an increased wingspan of 98 ft 6 in (30.04 m). Next came the **Series 2** with higher-rated 1,910-hp (1425-kW) RDa7 Mk 531 engines; later 2,105-hp (1570-kW) Mk 533-2s provided improved performance in hot-and-high conditions, but was otherwise similar

For many years the UK Civil Aviation Authority used two HS 748 Srs 2s for airfield and navaid calibration. Both aircraft are now flown by a civilian contractor.

Many of the surviving HS 748s have found favour with charter airlines and cargo carriers who appreciate its roomy cabin and reliable Dart engines.

to the Series 1. The Series 2 was first flown on 6 November 1961 and was certificated in October 1962. Various other versions were considered but not proceeded with, including a longer-fuselage **748E**, a **748 Super E** combining the longer fuselage with new 2,400-hp (1790-kW) Dart RDa10 engines, and the executive **748X** variant.

The Series 2 was superseded by the **Series 2A** with uprated Darts for improved performance. First flown on 5 September 1967, the 2A introduced two versions of the Dart: the 2,280-hp (1700-kW) RDa.7 Mk 535-2 (originally designated 532-2S), and the 2,230-hp (1663-kW) Mk 534-2 (originally 532-2L). Most of the Series 2 models were modified to the 2A standard. As part of a continual updating process, the company developed the **Series 2B**, which made its first flight on 22 June 1979. New features included the latest Mk 536-2 engines with the same rating as the Mk 535-2 but also improved single-engined performance, a 4-ft (1.22-m) increase in wingspan, modified tail surfaces, an optional hush-kit and interior enhancements. The final variant was the **Super 748**, based on the 2B but with a completely new flight deck, Mk 552 engines with hush-kit and water-methanol injection. By September 1999 approximately 250 British- and Indian-built 748s remained in service.

SPECIFICATION:

BAe (Hawker Siddeley) Super 748
Powerplant: two 2,280-hp (1700-kW) Rolls-Royce Dart RDa7 Mk 552 turboprops
Accommodation: two (flight deck), with a maximum of 58 passengers
Dimensions: span 102 ft 6 in (31.24 m); height 24 ft 10 in (7.57 m); length 67 ft (20.42 m)
Weights: operating empty 27,060 lb (12278 kg); maximum ramp 46,500 lb (21098 kg)
Performance: maximum cruising speed 280 mph (452 km/h); service ceiling 25,000 ft (7620 m); range with maximum payload and typical reserves 1,155 miles (1865 km)

Hawker 800

The jet known today as the Hawker 800 is the last (production) aircraft in a long line that began life as the **de Havilland D.H.125 Jet Dragon**. The D.H.125 was designed to succeed the popular Dove in the executive transport market and featured a pressurised cabin for six to eight passengers. The moderately-swept wing gave good range performance, and power came from a pair of Rolls-Royce Viper 20 turbojets. The prototype flew on 13 August 1962. When de Havilland became part of Hawker Siddeley the aircraft became the **HS 125**.

Initial **Series 1** production accounted for eight aircraft, followed by 77 **Series 1A**s (the A suffix being for North American aircraft) and **1B**s (the B for customers in the rest of the world), all with uprated engines. Twenty **Series 2**s were built for the RAF as the **Dominie T.Mk 1** navigation trainer. Production continued with 39 **Series 3**, **3A** and **3B**s, powered by Viper 522s and with many refinements. The 36 **3A-RA**s and **3B-RA**s had longer range. Next came the **HS 125-400**, with uprated engines, a cabin for seven passengers and flight deck improvements. A total of 116 was sold.

On 21 January 1971 the first **HS 125 Series 600** flew. This introduced a 3-ft 1-in (0.95-m) fuselage stretch to seat eight in executive layout or 14 in high-density seating, and Viper 601-22 engines. Production of this model amounted to 72, before the **Series 700** was introduced. This featured new Garrett AiResearch (now AlliedSignal) TFE731 turbofans, offering dramatically improved perfor-

The 15-seat long-range Hawker 1000 (formerly the BAe 125-1000) was the ultimate development of a design that first flew in 1962.

mance. A total of 215 was built, followed by the **Series 800** with many improvements including a 'glass' cockpit and curved windscreen. This variant made its first flight on 26 May 1983 by when it was known as the **British Aerospace BAe 125-800**.

In response to the challenge of the Falcon 50 and 2000, BAe developed the **BAe 1000**, based on the 125-800 but with a 2-ft 9-in (0.84-m) fuselage stretch, greater cabin height, Pratt & Whitney Canada PW305 turbofans and extra fuel for true intercontinental range. First flown on 16 June 1990, initial deliveries began in December 1991.

In 1993 BAe sold its Corporate Jets division to Raytheon and the two production 125s were renamed **Hawker 800** and **Hawker 1000**. In 1994 the US firm announced that it was suspending production of the 1000 and would soon move the 800 line to the United States. Hawker 1000 production ceased at 52 aircraft. The 800 remains in production at Wichita, now as the **Hawker 800XP** – which offers improved payload/range performance. By July 1999 production of all BAe 125-800 and Hawker 800 aircraft had reached 420.

This BAe 125-700B, operated by the Government of Algeria, is typical of the hundreds of early-model HS and BAe 125s still in service around the world.

SPECIFICATION:
Hawker 800XP
Powerplant: two 4,660-lb (20.73-kN) AlliedSignal (Garrett) TFE731-5BR-1H turbofans
Accommodation: two (flight deck), maximum of 14 passengers
Dimensions: span 51 ft 4½ in (15.66 m); length 51 ft 2 in (15.60 m); height 17 ft 7 in (5.36 m)
Weights: empty, operating 16,100 lb (7303 kg); maximum take-off 28,000 lb (12701 kg)
Performance: maximum cruising speed 525 mph (845 km/h); service ceiling 43,000 ft (13100 m); maximum range with maximum fuel 3,251 miles (5232 km)

IAI Galaxy, Astra and Westwind

The Westwind/Astra family was originally a design of the Aero Commander company and known as the **Model 1121 Jet Commander**. First flying on 27 January 1963, it had a mid-mounted wing, podded General Electric CJ610 turbojets, a high-set tail and seating for up to eight passengers. In 1967 Rockwell, which was Aero Commander's parent company, acquired North American, which produced the Sabreliner. US anti-trust laws forbade Rockwell having two business jet production lines, so the Jet Commander programme was sold to Israel Aircraft Industries.

IAI initially built an unchanged Jet Commander, but later came the **1121A** with more fuel and the **1121B** with uprated engines. The **1123 Commodore Jet** followed, with a stretched fuselage for 10 passengers. The first 1123 flew on 28 September 1970, and was later renamed the **Westwind 1123**.

Fuel-efficient Garrett AiResearch TFE731 turbofans were added to produce the **Westwind 1124**. Minor improvements led to the **1124 Westwind 1**, with an optional extra fuel tank. On 24 April 1979 the prototype **1124 Westwind 2** made its maiden flight, using an all-new 'Sigma' wing with winglets and seating options for seven to 10 passengers. A total of 442 IAI 1121, 1123 and 1124s were built by 1987, when production switched to the new Astra.

The Galaxy (originally the Astra IV) is the latest evolution of the Astra design. A mid-size business jet, it offers intercontinental range for a low price.

The original IAI Astra (seen here) has been developed into the wingletted Astra SPX (or simply SPX) now marketed by the Galaxy Aerospace Corp..

The IAI 1125 Astra retained little of the 1124, although it emerged with some similar features, such as the tail and engine pods. The 'Sigma 2' wing was low-set and swept back, and the new cabin was much deeper to allow for standing room. The first flight came on 19 March 1984. Power comes from TFE731-3A-200G turbofans. A total of 40 Astras were built until replaced in 1989 by the **Astra SP** – an improved version with Collins digital autopilot and EFIS cockpit, a new interior and further refined aerodynamics. The first SP flew in 1990 and 37 were built before it was superseded by the **Astra SPX**. First flown on 18 August 1994, the Astra SPX comes with a Collins Pro Line 4 EFIS cockpit and FADEC-equipped TFE731-40R-200G engines. Its 'Sigma 2' wing has been fitted with winglets. By 1999 33 had been built.

In February 1997 IAI teamed with US backers to form Galaxy Aerospace and set up a new production facility at Alliance Airport, Ft Worth, Texas. It introduced the new (**IAI 1126**) **Galaxy** wide-bodied jet which is now in production alongside the (renamed) **SPX**. The Galaxy first flew on 25 December 1997 and FAA certification was awarded in December 1998. The PW306A-powered Galaxy offers full transatlantic range up to 4,169 miles (6708 km) at 541 mph (871 km/h), with seven passengers.

SPECIFICATION:
IAI 1125 Astra
Powerplant: two 3,700-lb (16.46-kN) AlliedSignal (Garrett) TFE731-3A-200G turbofans
Accommodation: two (flight deck), standard layout for six passengers
Dimensions: span 52 ft 8 in (16.05 m); length 55 ft 7 in (16.94 m); height 18 ft 2 in (5.54 m)
Weights: empty 13,225 lb (6999 kg); maximum take-off 23,500 lb (10659 kg)
Performance: maximum cruising speed 533 mph (858 km/h); maximum operating altitude 45,000 ft (13715 m); maximum range with four passengers and reserves 3,241 miles (5215 km)

Ilyushin Il-18

The **Ilyushin Il-18 'Coot'** was designed to meet an Aeroflot requirement for a medium-range transport aircraft for at least 75 passengers, and for operations from primitive unpaved airfields. It featured a conventional low-wing monoplane configuration with a pressurised circular fuselage and retractable tricycle landing gear. The prototype, named 'Moskva', first flew on 4 July 1957, powered by four wing-mounted Kuznetsov NK-4 turboprop engines that each developed 4,000 hp (2983 kW). The five development aircraft and most early production aircraft in a trials batch of 20 were also fitted with the NK-4, while others had the refined Ivchenko AI-20K with the same rating. Aeroflot put the type into service on routes from Moscow to Adler and Alma Ata on 20 April 1959.

The Ivchenko powerplant was adopted as standard on subsequent aircraft, beginning with the **Il-18B**. Maximum take-off weight was also increased from 57200 kg (126,100 lb) to 59200 kg (130,514 lb) and the cabin re-arranged to seat up to 84 passengers. The Il-18B gave way in 1961 to the **Il-18V**, which differed primarily in a revised interior layout for 90 to 100 passengers. This required repositioning of some cabin windows. Further development work resulted in the **Il-18I**, put into production in 1964 as the **Il-18D**. This new version introduced the more powerful AI-20M turboprops, rated at 4,250 hp (3170 kW) and increased fuel capacity through the installation of extra fuel cells in the centre-section to add an additional 6300 litres (1,386 Imp gal). In

Balkan Bulgarian Airlines still has two Il-18s in regular service that can be configured as full-cargo aircraft or for up to 105 passengers.

addition, an extensive internal redesign involved the moving aft of the pressure bulkhead, deletion of the rear cargo hold and increase of the passenger capacity to 110. In the summer months, this could be increased to 122 by removing the coat stowage space required in the winter. The extra fuel provided the aircraft with a long-range capability, serving Aeroflot in the interim period before the arrival of the turbofan-powered Il-62, and found success in the export market. The **Il-18E**, produced in parallel, was identical except for the absence of the extra fuel cells. Both versions entered service with Aeroflot during 1965.

Retired from mainline service, the Il-18 proved useful in a cargo role and remains in limited service. The cargo modifications are distinguished by a large rear cargo door and strengthening of the floor. Production finished in 1970 and is believed to have totalled around 800 units. The demand for second-hand aircraft is strong and over 70 Il-18s are in regular service, chiefly as freighters, working across Africa Eastern Europe, the former Soviet Union, the Middle East and the Far East.

Cuba's Aerocaribbean was one of the last major users of the Il-18 – and, in recent times, the only one in the Americas. Its Il-18s are now gradually being retired.

SPECIFICATION:
Ilyushin Il-18D
Powerplant: four 4,250-hp (3170-kW) Ivchenko AI-20M turboprops
Accommodation: five (flight deck), with a maximum of 122 passengers
Dimensions: span 122 ft 8 in (37.40 m); height 33 ft 4 in (10.17 m); length 117 ft 9 in (35.90 m)
Weights: operating empty 77,140 lb (35000 kg); maximum take-off 141,056 lb (64000 kg)
Performance: maximum cruising speed 418 mph (675 km/h); range with maximum payload and reserves 4,025 miles (6500 km)

Ilyushin Il-62

The **Il-62** 'Classic' was developed as a long-haul jetliner for Aeroflot's International Directorate, primarily as a replacement for the turboprop-powered Tu-114. With its T-tail and pairs of side-by-side turbofans mounted on each side of the rear fuselage, the Il-62 was of a configuration broadly similar to Britain's VC-10. AL-7 turbojet-engined prototypes flew from January 1963, while production aircraft, powered by 22,273-lb (99-kN) NK-8-4 turbofans, were built at Kazan and entered service in March 1967. In high-density configuration, the Il-62 seated 72 in the forward cabin and 114 in the rear, separated by the galley. Seats were six abreast, split into threes by the central aisle.

The availability of the new Soloviev D-30KU engine allowed a redesign as the **Il-62M**, with a new fuel tank in the fin, clamshell-type thrust reversers, and completely new avionics. The cabin was redesigned to seat up to 174, and the aircraft incorporated containerised underfloor baggage and cargo holds. First flying in 1970, the Il-62M entered Aeroflot service during 1974.

Further improvement of the Il-62 design resulted in the **Il-62MK** of 1978. This was externally indistinguishable from the Il-62 but with a completely restressed structure and a redesigned low-pressure undercarriage allowing take-off at higher weights.

This former-Interflug Il-62M is one of those now in service with Uzbekistan Airways. The Il-62 offers long-range performance and is cheap to acquire.

Aeroflot still relies on the Il-62M and Il-62MK for its long-haul services, as the Il-86 is too short-legged and other types are not yet available in quantity.

Payload was increased from 25.4 tons (23 tonnes) to 27.6 tons (25 tonnes) and the cabin was completely redesigned, with provision for up to 195 seats, despite a wider aisle and overhead luggage lockers.

A total of 288 Il-62s had been delivered when production formally ended in 1990 (95 Il-62s, 173 Il-62Ms and 18 Il-62MKs, plus two prototypes), though the last production Il-62 was not handed over until 1996. Many have been updated with a triplex INS and new engine nacelles that reduce noise and emissions. The break-up of the USSR led to the replacement of many Il-62s by more efficient, newer Western wide-bodies like the A310 and Boeing 767. However, retired Il-62s often found new customers in Russia and elsewhere, attracted by their low acquisition costs and familiar with their operation.

The type remains in use with Aeroflot Russian International Airlines, especially on longer-range routes and for VIP flights, for which some are modified with extra communications equipment in an extended dorsal spine. The basic design life has been studied and extended from 30,000 hours to 40,000 hours and further extensions are under review. Approximately 150 Il-62s remain in service today but Stage 3 noise regulations pose a threat to their continued operation on mainstream routes.

SPECIFICATION:
Ilyushin Il-162M
Powerplant: four 24,250-lb (107.9-kN) Soloviev D-30KU turbofans
Accommodation: five (flight deck), with 186 passengers standard
Dimensions: span 141 ft 9 in (43.20 m); height 40 ft 6¼ in (12.35 m); length 174 ft 3½ in (53.12 m)
Weights: operating empty 157,520 lb (71600 kg); maximum take-off 363,760 lb (165000 kg)
Performance: maximum cruising speed 571 mph (920 km/h); range with maximum payload and typical reserves 4,846 miles (7800 km)

Ilyushin Il-76

The Il-76 'Candid' was developed to meet a joint Aeroflot/air forces' requirement for a long-range heavy freighter/transport to replace the piston-engined Antonov An-12. Using a T-tailed, high-wing configuration, with four turbofan engines in under-slung pods, the Il-76 has a similar layout to the Lockheed C-141. The aircraft's military role dictated the use of a low-pressure landing gear and a modestly swept wing to ensure good short-field/semi-prepared runway capability. The aircraft has a weather radar in the nose and a mapping radar below it, but is also provided with a glazed navigator's compartment (especially useful in military paradropping missions and for tactical off-airways navigation). The aircraft has a cargo floor made up of titanium panels, with overhead hoists of 2.5- and 3-tonne (2.8- and 3.3-ton) capacity and with provision for optional rollers in the floor. In an improvement over the An-12, the entire fuselage is pressurised.

The prototype Il-76 made its maiden flight on 25 March 1971, and has been followed by a number of variants. The higher-payload **Il-76T** 'Candid-A' introduced extra fuel tankage in the centre-section, as did the military **Il-76M** 'Candid-B', which also has ECM equipment, provision for chaff/flare dispensers and a gun turret in the tail, with two GSh-23L twin-barrelled 23-mm cannons. Large numbers of 'military' Il-76s were delivered to Aeroflot.

Introduction of the D-30KP-2 turbofan with better hot-and-high performance resulted in the civil **Il-76TD** and the military **Il-76MD**, each of which had

The Il-76 is a popular and profitable type among CIS airlines as its affordable, heavy-lift capabilities are much in demand by western companies.

greater fuel capacity, higher payload and MTOW. Specialised fire-fighting (**Il-76P** or **MDP**), inflight-refuelling (**Il-78T** and **Il-78M** 'Midas') and airborne early-warning (**A-50** and **A-50M** 'Mainstay') versions have also been produced. By June 1999 production of all Il-76 variants had exceeded 900 aircraft. Production continues, at the very decreased rate of 10 per year at the TAPOich plant, in Tashkent, Uzbekistan. In years gone by this factory was building 10 aircraft a month.

Large numbers of Il-76s were delivered to Aeroflot and the military VTA, and with the break-up of Aeroflot the type has gained a large number of new commercial operators. These include military aircraft leased out to civil operators, a practice particularly common in Ukraine.

Ilyushin has now developed a stretched version, the **Il-76MF**, which has been refitted with PS-90AN turbofans. The new aircraft is 6.6-m (21-ft 8-in) longer than the basic Il-76 and has a range of 5200 km (3,230 miles) with a 40,000-kg (88,185-lb) payload. The prototype flew on 1 August 1995 and the first customer is expected to be the Russian air force.

This Il-76TD is flown by Belair, of Belarus. Belair is typical of the plethora of small Il-76 operators that have sprung up around the CIS.

SPECIFICATION:
Ilyushin Il-76T
Powerplant: four 26,455-lb (117.7-kN) Soloviev D-30KP turbofans
Accommodation: five (flight deck)
Dimensions: span 165 ft 8 in (50.5 m); height 57 ft 7 in (17.5 m); length 181 ft 7 in (55.3 m)
Weights: maximum payload 88,185 lb (40000 kg); maximum take-off 374,784 lb (170000 kg)
Performance: maximum level speed 528 mph (850 km/h); range with maximum payload and typical reserves 2,265 miles (3650 km)

Ilyushin Il-86 and Il-96

Intended as a successor to the Il-62 on Aeroflot's international routes, the **Il-86** '**Camber**' was developed in response to the Boeing 747, and intended to be broadly equivalent. Originally designed as a wide-bodied Il-62, retaining the same T-tail and engines but redesigned with a conventional low-set tailplane and with new Kuznetsov NK-86 engines in underwing pods, the prototype Il-86 made its maiden flight on 22 December 1976. The extra power of the NK-86 allowed fuel capacity and MTOW to be increased. The Il-86 has two decks, with passengers carrying on their own luggage and coats, stowing them on the lower deck, before climbing upstairs to be seated. The type entered service in December 1980, but proved seriously deficient in range, resulting in the Il-62 remaining in service in large numbers for use on the longest-distance routes. Maximum accommodation is for 350 passengers (nine abreast) with twin aisles. A total of 104 were built when production ceased in 1994.

Although it is outwardly similar to the Il-86, the **Il-96** is a new aircraft in every respect. The Il-96 introduced Aviadvigatel (formerly Perm) PS-90A turbofans, a new supercritical wing of greater span and slightly reduced sweep, and improved structure and materials to give lower weight and longer life. New avionics and systems are provided, including a

The 'prestige' Il-86 was rushed in to service to coincide with Moscow's 1980 Olympics, but its performance since has been far from medal winning.

triplex fly-by-wire control system. Internal fuel capacity is doubled by comparison with the Il-86, while reduced drag also contributes to the new aircraft's dramatically increased range. The lower deck of the Il-96 is purely for cargo and luggage, and passengers enter only at cabin level.

The basic production version seats up to 300 passengers and was designated **Il-96-300**, but the mixed-class layout that is normally used seats 235. The prototype made its maiden flight on 28 September 1988 and the second aircraft flew on 28 November 1989. Deliveries began to Aeroflot in 1995 and proceeded at a very slow rate. By June 1999 Aeroflot had six aircraft. Another three were in service with Domodedovo airlines along with two operated by the Russian government.

Ilyushin is also developing the stretched **Il-96M** (originally the Il-96-350). This version will have Pratt & Whitney PW2337 turbofans, a smaller tailfin and a cabin that can accommodate up to 375 passengers. The prototype **Il-96MO** was converted from the first Il-96-300 and flew on 6 April 1993. An all-freight **Il-96T** has also been developed with a 15-ft 11-in x 9-ft 5-in (4.85- 2.87-m) cargo door fitted on the port side. It flew on 16 May 1997. The first Il-96M customer will be Aeroflot but a severe shortage of funds is holding back the programme.

The first production-standard version of the Il-96M family was this Il-96T freighter, which was rolled out of the Voronezh plant on 26 April 1997.

SPECIFICATION:
Ilyushin Il-86
Powerplant: four 28,660-lb (127.5-kN) Kuznetsov NK-86 turbofans
Accommodation: five (flight deck), with a maximum of 350 seats
Dimensions: span 157 ft 8 in (48 m); height 51 ft 10 in (15.8 m); length 195 ft 4 in (59.4 m)
Weights: maximum take-off 458,560 lb (208000 kg)
Performance: maximum cruising speed at 36,000 ft (11000 m) 590 mph (950 km/h); range with maximum payload and typical reserves 2,235 miles (3600 km)

Ilyushin Il-114

During the early 1980s several Russian design bureaus drew up plans for an Antonov An-24 replacement. The requirement was for a tough passenger and freight aircraft that could operate in austere conditions from unprepared airfields. The Ilyushin **Il-114** design emerged as the front-runner in this competition. However, even though the Ilyushin design was finalised as early as 1986, the prototype did not make its maiden flight until 24 December 1991. This delay was a reflection of the great political and financial upheavals in the former-Soviet Union at that time.

The 64-seat Il-114 closely resembles the British Aerospace ATP (Jetstream 61) in configuration and is powered by a pair of Klimov TV7 turboprops driving six-bladed SV-34 low-noise propellers. It is being produced in co-operation with the TAPO manufacturing plant in Tashkent, Uzbekistan. After the prototype took to the air in 1990, a second example followed on 24 December 1991. The first production aircraft flew on 7 August 1992 and a flight test schedule involving the first five series production Il-114s was drawn up. Unfortunately, the second prototype was lost in an accident on 5 July 1993 which brought about the withdrawal of all Russian government funding for the programme. As a result of this loss, a major delay was suffered and the Il-114 did not receive its Russian type certification until 26 April 1997.

Ilyushin hopes to build several versions of the Il-114. The basic passenger version will be joined

After many years Ilyushin is still struggling to progress with the Il-114 programme. Two aircraft are in service in Uzbekistan for route proving and trials.

by the **Il-114T** freighter. This all-cargo version has already been ordered by Uzbekistan Airlines and is fitted with a 3.31- x 1.78-m (10-ft 10¼-in x 5-ft 10-in) cargo door in the rear fuselage. The cabin has a removable roller floor, maximum take-off weight is set at 23500 kg (51,805 lb) and the first aircraft flew on 14 September 1996. Customer deliveries were due to begin in 1998 but none are understood to have yet taken place. The collapse of a leasing deal with Moscow's Exim bank in 1998 seriously stalled progress in the home market.

Ilyushin is also attempting to develop the **Il-114-100** (previously the **Il-114PC**), a westernised version powered by two Pratt & Whitney Canada PW127F turboprops driving Hamilton Standard propellers, and equipped with Sextant avionics. This export-dedicated version was initiated by a joint venture between Ilyushin and Pratt & Whitney in June 1997 but a formal launch decision has been hampered by a lack of funding. The ninth production Il-114 has been converted to act as the -100 demonstrator. Ilyushin has also drawn up plans for the **Il-114M**, powered by uprated TV7M-117 turboprops.

The Il-114T should prove to be a popular aircraft in the domestic market and deliveries should now have begun, but Russia's cash crisis has halted matters.

SPECIFICATION:
Ilyushin Il-114
Powerplant: two 2,466-hp (1839-kW) Klimov TV7-117S turboprops
Accommodation: two (flight deck), with a maximum of 64 passengers
Dimensions: span 98 ft 5¼ in (30 m); height 30 ft 7 in (9.32 m); length 88 ft 2 in (26.88 m)
Weights: empty, operating 33,070 lb (15000 kg); maximum take-off 51,808 lb (23500 kg)
Performance: maximum level speed 310 mph (500 km/h); optimum cruising height 23,620 ft (7200 m); range with 64 passengers and typical reserves 621 miles (1000 km)

Jetstream 31 and 41

The **Jetstream** began as a Handley Page design for a 12/20-seat commuter aircraft, the **HP.137** – it was destined to become the last aircraft that the company built before its demise in 1969. The first of five prototypes, powered with Turboméca Astazou XIV turboprops, made its maiden flight on 18 August 1967. Other engines were tried, but 35 production aircraft with Astazous had been completed by 27 February 1970, when Handley Page collapsed. Rights to the Jetstream were acquired by Scottish Aviation, which built 26 navigation-training versions for the RAF. The final version was the **Jetstream 200** with 969-hp (723-kW) Astazou XVID engines.

Following the incorporation of Scottish Aviation into the newly-established British Aerospace Group on 1 January 1978, BAe announced that it would relaunch the aircraft as the **Jetstream 31**. In its reincarnated form, with two 940-hp (701-kW) Garrett TPE331-10UF turboprops, new advanced-technology propellers and systems, revised cockpit layout and redesigned interior, the Jetstream 31 first flew on 18 March 1982. First deliveries were made to German airline Contactair on 15 December 1982, following UK certification the previous June. In addition to the 18-seat commuter versions, corporate and executive shuttle variants with nine- and 12-seat layouts, respectively, were available.

Most Jetstream 41 deliveries were made to existing Jetstream customers – like United Express – which were well-satisfied with their earlier aircraft.

The Jetstream 31/32 was a popular 19-seat feederliner, but it was outgrown by an airline market that was looking for larger and faster aircraft.

The first **Jetstream Super 31**, also referred to as the **Jetstream 32**, was certificated on 7 October 1988. This new variant provided significant improvements in performance and passenger comfort, derived from more powerful 1,020-hp (760-kW) TPE331-12UAR engines giving better hot-and-high performance, recontoured interior providing greater cabin width at head height, and reduced noise and vibration. An improved version, the **Jetstream 32EP**, followed and when Jetstream 31 production halted in 1994 a total of 384 had been built.

Plans for a stretched Jetstream came to fruition in May 1989, when BAe announced the go-ahead of the **Jetstream 41**. Although it retained the same fuselage cross-section, it had a 16-ft (4.88-m) longer fuselage to accommodate up to 29 seats. Other major differences included more powerful TPE331-14GR/HR engines, a lowered wing to provide more baggage space and integral airstairs in the forward door. The first aircraft flew on 25 September 1991. In 1992 Jetstream Aircraft, based at Prestwick, became a subsidiary of BAe, and was responsible for all manufacture and marketing. A corporate Jetstream 41, fitted out in a 14-seat business shuttle configuration, took to the air on 18 May 1994. The last of 104 Jetstream 41s flew on 28 July 1997 and the line closed in 1998.

SPECIFICATION:
Jetstream 41
Powerplant: two 1,500-hp (1119-kW) AlliedSignal (Garrett) TPE331-14GR/HR turboprops
Accommodation: two (flight deck), with a maximum of 29 passengers
Dimensions: span 60 ft 5 in (18.42 m); height 18 ft 10 in (5.74 m); length 63 ft 2 in (19.25 m);
Weights: operating empty 14,040 lb (6370 kg); maximum ramp 23,110 lb (10485 kg)
Performance: maximum cruising speed 340 mph (547 km/h); service ceiling 26,000 ft (7925 m); range with maximum payload and typical reserves 680 miles (1098 km)

Jetstream 61 (BAe ATP)

On 1 March 1984, British Aerospace announced its intention to develop a larger advanced turboprop (**ATP**) regional transport, to succeed the Super 748 (HS 748). This was not a new idea, as Avro had considered similar options, in its **748E** and **748 Super E** projects, some 20 years earlier. The British Aerospace ATP design that emerged had the same cabin cross-section of the Super 748, but a longer fuselage to accommodate 64 passengers in a standard configuration, with up to 72 seats possible. New fuel-efficient 2,150-hp (1604-kW) Pratt & Whitney Canada PW124 turboprops, driving slow-turning propellers with six composite blades, were later replaced by the more powerful PW126A engine.

Other important improvements included the installation of the most modern equipment, including new electrical, hydraulic and environmental control systems, carbon brakes and an advanced flight deck with a four-screen EFIS cockpit. The ATP also introduced separate forward and rear passenger doors, with integral airstairs in the forward door, and separate forward and rear baggage doors.

The prototype ATP flew for the first time on 6 August 1986 and obtained its certification in March 1988. British Midland Airways became the first to put the type into revenue service on 9 May that same year. In spite of good operating economics and figures that showed the ATP to be the quietest aircraft in its class, its slow speed and early technical reliability problems kept sales sluggish.

From its bases in Palma and Barcelona Spain's Air Europa Express is now one of largest ATP operators with a fleet of 10 aircraft.

In a last-ditch attempt to restimulate interest in the ATP, BAe developed the **Jetstream 61** which was to be a major overhaul of the design. It was powered by more powerful 2,750 hp (2051 kW) Pratt & Whitney PW127D engines, providing improved airfield performance, especially in 'hot-and-high' conditions. A completely new interior with new-style seats, better underseat stowage and larger overhead bins were also added to enhance passenger appeal.

The relaunch failed to attract any meaningful new orders and production was finally halted at total of 65 aircraft. The aircraft dubbed the first Jetstream 61 was, in fact, the 64th ATP to fly (on 11 May 1994). Both it and the 65th aircraft, which flew on 26 July 1995, were later broken up (along with several unfinished aircraft on the production line). The last ATP customer delivery came in 1995, with an aircraft built in 1993. However, the fortunes of the 63 remaining aircraft (now referred to only as ATPs) have undergone a small renaissance in the hands of British Aerospace Asset Management – demand for them is solid with all in regular service.

Several of British Airways partner airlines operate ATPs. These include British Regional Airlines (formerly Manx Airlines) and Sun-Air (seen here).

SPECIFICATION:
Jetstream 61 (ATP)
Powerplant: two 2,388-hp (1,781-kW) Pratt & Whitney PW126A turboprops
Accommodation: two (flight deck), with a maximum of 72 passengers
Dimensions: span 100 ft 6 in (30.63 m); height 24 ft 11 in (7.59 m); length 85 ft 4 in (26.00 m)
Weights: operating empty 31,385 lb (14240 kg); maximum ramp 50,692 lb (23000 kg)
Performance: maximum cruising speed 305 mph (493 km/h); range with maximum payload and typical reserves 660 miles (1065 km)

LET 410 and 610

The **LET 410** (LET Akciová Spolecnost – LET aeronautical works) made its first flight on 16 April 1969, as the **XL-410**. While awaiting new Motorlet turboprop engines, the prototype and early models were fitted with 715-hp (533-kW) Pratt & Whitney PT6A-27s driving Hamilton Standard three-bladed props. Known as the **L-410A**, the first revenue service with Slov-Air in late 1971. One of the four prototypes became the **L-410AB** when tested with Hartzell four-bladed propellers. One **L-410AF** was built for Hungary in 1974 with a revised glazed nose for aerial survey work. A photo version was known as the **L-410FG**. A Soviet avionics fit produced the **L-410AS**.

When the Motorlet (Walter) engines became available, the **L-410M** entered production and was put into service in 1976. This model differed only in the installation of the 550-hp (410-kW) M 601A turboprop, but the L-410M soon gave way to the **L-410MA**, introducing M 601Bs rated at 730 shp (554 kW). The **L-410MU** was an MA specifically for Aeroflot, seating up to 17 passengers. The **L-410UVP**, first flown on 1 November 1977, introduced a number of major changes to comply with new Soviet airworthiness regulations and stringent Aeroflot requirements that required operations in temperatures of -50 to +45°C. Major external differences were an

Initial production LET 610s were the L-610M version, powered by Walter M602 engines. The six aircraft built are in Czech military service or on trials duties.

LET 410UVP-E production exceeds 450 and despite difficult financial times the Czech manufacturer has maintained a small steady stream of sales.

increased wingspan and tail area, dihedral tailplane, spoilers and new flaps. Soviet certification was obtained in 1980, and most of the 514 L-410UVPs produced went to Aeroflot.

The improved **L-410UVP-E**, earlier designated **L-410E** and **L-420**, with five-bladed Avia propellers, wingtip tanks and more powerful 750-hp (559-kW) M 601E engines, made its first flight on 30 December 1984 and entered service in 1985. A further improved version, the new **L-420** flew in 1993, powered by M601F engines. A breakthrough order for five L-420s, with 15 options, was signed with US airline Pan Pacific Airways in June 1999 with first delivery due before the end of the year. A re-engined L430 with PT6s is still under study.

LET is also developing the larger 40-seat **L-610**, a new design with a pressurised cabin, APU and 1,822-hp (1358-kW) M-602 turboprops. It first flew on 28 December 1988 and was designed to an Aeroflot requirement. With the disappearance of its Russian market LET moved on to the improved **L-610G** in a joint venture with General Electric. This version, powered by two 1,745-hp (1300-kW) General Electric CT7-9D turboprops, first flew on 18 December 1992 and was certified in 1998. Also in 1998 LET was acquired by the US Ayres Corp. which should greatly boost export prospects.

SPECIFICATION:
LET L-410UVP-E
Powerplant: two 750-hp (559-kW) Motorlet (Walter) M 601E turboprops
Accommodation: one or two flight crew and up to 19 passengers
Dimensions: span, over tip-tanks 65 ft 6½ in (19.98 m); height 19 ft 1½ in (5.83 m), length 47 ft 3¾ in (14.425 m)
Weights: operating empty 9,215 lb (4180 kg); maximum take-off 14,550 lb (6600 kg)
Performance: maximum cruising speed 241 mph (388 km/h); service ceiling 24,300 ft (7410 m); range with maximum fuel and typical payload 843 miles (1358 km)

Learjet 23, 24 and 25

William P. 'Bill' Lear's **Learjet** family has its origins in Switzerland in 1955, when the Swiss air force rejected the indigenous **FFA P-1604** single-seat fighter. Already fabulously wealthy, having founded Motorola and the Lear Siegler Corporation, Bill Lear had retired to Switzerland in the late 1950s with a track record of executive aircraft conversions (such as the Lockheed Lodestar to Learstar modifica-tion) behind him. In 1959 he picked up the P-1604 design and began preliminary development of a new executive jet derivative at St Gallen.

Christened the **Swiss-American Aircraft Corporation (SAAC) Learjet 23**, the company moved work to Wichita, Kansas, where the first aircraft flew on 7 October 1963. The type's high speed and striking good looks, plus the fact that it could be flown by a single pilot (not to mention its low price), ensured success in the face of competition from aircraft such as the Falcon 20. The 43-ft 3-in (13.18-m) Learjet 23 was a five/seven-seat aircraft, powered by a pair of 2,850-lb (12.68-kN) General Electric CJ610-4 turbojets (though the first 30 relied on lower-powered CJ610-1s). Initially, several Learjet 23s were lost, leading to a series of modifications to improve its demanding handling characteristics.

Now named the Lear Jet Corporation, in 1965 the manufacturer began work on a similar but heavier second model that would seat up to eight passengers and fly at a higher cruising altitude. The **Learjet 24** first flew on 24 February 1966. It was followed by the up-engined **Learjet 24B** and longer-range

Original short-bodied Learjet 23s (Gates' 'pocket rocket') are becoming increasingly rare but, as over 350 were built, many remain in the USA and Mexico.

Learjet 24D, which was the first aircraft to do away with Learjet's trademark bullet fin fairing and to introduce square windows. A lightweight **Learjet 24D/A** was succeeded by the **Learjet 24E** and **Learjet 24F**, both of which boasted refined interiors and aerodynamics, while the latter had additional fuel for further increased range.

In 1966 the company was renamed Lear Jet Industries but, in April of the following year, was taken over by the Gates Rubber Company, becoming the Gates Learjet Corp. 1966 also saw the first major development of the basic design, the stretched, 10-seat **Learjet 25**. First flown on 12 August 1966, the improved **Learjet 25B** and longer-range **Learjet 25C** came next. In 1976 a new cambered wing led to the **Learjet 25D** and **Learjet 25F**. Every version still relied on the CJ610 engine. The Learjet 25 led to the **Learjet 28** and **Learjet 29 Longhorn**, the first wingletted Learjets (although they shared the same cabin size as the Learjet 25, they are more fully described under the Learjet 55 entry). Between 1964 and 1982, 105 Learjet 23s, 255 Learjet 24s and 368 Learjet 25s were delivered.

The Learjet 25D was fitted with quieter CJ610-8A engines and a new wing to improve its take-off and low-speed performance.

SPECIFICATION:
Learjet 24F
Powerplant: two 2,850-lb (12.68-kN) General Electric CJ610-8A turbojets
Accommodation: two (flight deck), with a maximum of eight passengers
Dimensions: span 35 ft 7 in (10.85 m); height 12 ft 3 in (3.73 m); length 43 ft 3 in (14.18 m)
Weights: operating empty 7,064 lb (3204 kg); maximum take-off 15,000 lb (6804 kg)
Performance: maximum speed 549 mph (884 km/h); service ceiling 51,000 ft (15545 m); range with four passengers and typical reserves 1,584 miles (2549 km)

Learjet 35 and 36

Increased competition and the availability of newer, more economical and quieter turbofan engines led Gates Lear Jet to introduce the most popular development of the Learjet family so far. The original CJ610 turbojets were finally replaced by Garrett AiResearch TFE731 (now AlliedSignal) turbofans – hence the original designations for the new aircraft, **Learjet 25B-GF** and **Learjet 25C-GF** (Garrett Fan). A single Learjet 26 testbed was re-engined with one TFE731-2 in the starboard nacelle and first flew on 4 January 1973. A second completely re-engined Learjet 25 followed later that year, paving the way for the two new business jets, the **Learjet 35** and **Learjet 36**.

The eight-seat Learjet 35 was essentially a stretched Learjet 25 with a slightly larger wing. The fuselage was extended by 13 in (33 cm) and the wingtip extended by 2 ft (61 cm). The complimentary Learjet 36 was a six-seat, longer-range version with more fuel and a smaller payload to enable a non-stop transatlantic crossing.

The first production-standard Learjet 36 took to the air on 22 August 1973 and FAA type certification was awarded in July 1974. In 1976 golfer Arnold Palmer flew a Learjet 36 around the world to establish a new distance record of 22,984 miles (36990 km) in 57 hours 24 minutes 42 seconds.

Demand for the Learjet 35A and 36A continued into the mid-1990s when the two were finally replaced by the more modern Learjet 31.

The Learjet 35/36 models – this is a Lear 35A – remain the best-selling members of the Learjet business jet family, by far.

As with previous Learjet models, development of an improved cambered wing and other aerodynamic changes brought new versions, the **Learjet 35A** and **Learjet 36A** – the latter with a further increased MTOW of 18,000 lb (8162 kg). Several product refinements were introduced such as the Softflite package which made changes to the ailerons, leading edges and wing fences to improve handling. New T/R-4000 thrust reversers were added in 1983 and an entirely new interior with stereo, improved seats and in-flight telephones was added in 1985.

Many special-mission variants were developed for military duties such as target-towing, electronic warfare and photo/maritime reconnaissance. The USAF is a substantial Learjet 35A operator, flying 85 aircraft as the **C-21A**. The Learjet 36 was hugely outsold by the Learjet 35, as most operators did not require its five-hour endurance.

By the mid-1980s, Gates Lear Jet was looking for a buyer. Several failed deals and changes of factory location (from Tucson back to Wichita) led to the acquisition in June 1990 of the firm by Canada's Bombardier, and a new name of Learjet Inc. Learjet 35/36 production finally came to an end in 1996. A total of 676 Learjet 35/35As was built along with 63 Learjet 36/36As.

SPECIFICATION:
Learjet 35A
Powerplant: two 3,500-lb (15.65-kN) AlliedSignal (Garrett) TFE731-2-2B turbofans
Accommodation: two (flight deck), with a maximum of eight passengers
Dimensions: span, over tip tanks 39 ft 6 in (12.04 m); height 12 ft 3 in (3.73 m); length 48 ft 8 in (14.83 m)
Weights: empty, equipped 10,119 lb (4590 kg); maximum take-off 18,300 lb (8300 kg)
Performance: maximum speed Mach 0.81; service ceiling 41,000 ft (12500 m); range with four passengers and typical reserves 2,528 miles (4069 km)

Learjet 31 and 45

Twin-engined medium- to long-range business-jets

Learjet's acquisition by Bombardier ensured the future of the **Learjet 31**, the successor to the Learjet 35/36 family. The new aircraft wedded the wing of the Learjet 55 to the Learjet 35 fuselage. A longer-range aircraft, it was still powered by a pair of AlliedSignal TFE731-2 turbofans but featured distinctive 'delta fins' beneath the tail to eliminate 'Dutch roll' and to stabilise the aircraft at high speeds. The wingtip tanks of previous Learjets were replaced by a pair of winglets. The Learjet 31 could carry two crew and seven passengers over 1,911 miles (3076 km) and an aerodynamic prototype first flew on 11 May 1987. FAA type certification was awarded on 12 August 1988.

Learjet 31 production continued until July 1991, by which time 38 had been built. It was superseded by the current-production **Learjet 31A** that cruises faster, at Mach 0.81. The Learjet 31A also introduced a five-screen AlliedSignal EFIS 50 system in the cockpit. It was joined on the production line by the extended-range **Learjet 31A/ER**. This version is certified to operate with extra fuel at a higher take-off weight, pushing maximum range out to 1710 miles (2752 km). By June 1999 a total of 140 Learjet 31A/ERs had been delivered.

The latest short- to medium-range Learjet is the **Learjet 45**, which was unveiled at the 1992 NBAA convention. Learjet had begun design work on the new 10- to 11-seat aircraft earlier that year and the prototype first flew from Wichita on 7 October 1995 – the 32nd anniversary of the first flight of the

The 10-seat Learjet 31, seen here in its current Learjet 31A form, is an advanced Lear 35/36 replacement readily identified by its winglets and rear fins.

original Learjet 23. A second prototype followed on 6 April 1996 and a third development aircraft on 24 April. Components for the aircraft are provided by several members of the Bombardier group. Shorts supplies the fuselage and de Havilland Canada builds the wings.

The Learjet 45 is intended to combine the much-praised handling characteristics of the Learjet 31 and 60 with further-improved fuel efficiency and ease of operation. The aircraft has a redesigned stand-up cabin and a larger fuselage, wing and tail unit. Power is provided by two AlliedSignal TFE731-20 turbofans and the cockpit is built around a Honeywell Primus 1000 EFIS system. Initial engine tests were undertaken on a Learjet 31 testbed which first flew on January 1995.

FAA type certification was awarded on 22 September 1997 and the first customer delivery – to the Pistol Creek Financial Company, Seattle – took place in January 1998. Singapore Airlines acquired four Learjet 45s for crew training, replacing Learjet 31s previously serving in that role. By June 1999 a total of 56 Learjet 45s had been delivered.

The Learjet 45 is the latest member of the 'small' Learjet family. It incorporates new technology in a redesigned airframe with the most modern cockpit.

SPECIFICATION:
Learjet 45
Powerplant: two 3,500-lb (15.65-kN) AlliedSignal TFE731-2-2B turbofans
Accommodation: two (flight deck), with a maximum of eight passengers
Dimensions: span, over tip tanks 39 ft 6 in (12.04 m); height 12 ft 3 in (3.73 m); length 48 ft 8 in (14.83 m)
Weights: empty, equipped 10,119 lb (4590 kg); maximum take-off 18,300 lb (8300 kg)
Performance: maximum speed Mach 0.81; service ceiling 41,000 ft (12500 m); range with four passengers and typical reserves 2,528 miles (4069 km)

Learjet 55, 55C and 60

The origins of the wingletted Learjets lie in the development by Gates Lear Jet of the NASA-designed, supercritical 'Longhorn' wing in the late 1970s. This new wing (so called because its Whitcomb winglets resembled the horns of Longhorn cattle) was applied to the Learjet 25D-derived, 10-seat **Learjet 28**, which first flew on 21 August 1978, and to the eight-seat **Learjet 29 Longhorn**, which traded passengers for extra fuel. Both proved unpopular; they were too small and too expensive for their performance benefits to be of any use. Only five and two, respectively, were built by 1982. However, mating the wing with a new stretched fuselage (and Lear Jet's first 'stand-up' cabin) resulted in the **Learjet 55 Longhorn**.

The 10-seat Learjet 55 first flew on 19 April 1979, powered by 3,700-lb (16.65-kN) TFE731-3-100B turbofans. Two other models – the **Learjet 54** (smaller) and **56** (larger) – were later abandoned. Certification and first deliveries were achieved by April 1981. The seven-seat, long-range **Learjet 55LR** featured a fuel capacity of some 1,141 US gal (4319 litres), while the **Learjet 55XLR** was an even longer-range version with a total of 1,231 US gal (4569 litres) of fuel. An improved-performance, glass-cockpit-equipped **Learjet 55B** was introduced in September 1986. One year later the **Learjet 55C** appeared,

The Learjet 55C combined all the features of the Lear 55 Longhorn with a pair of distinctive rear delta fins. Production ended in December 1990.

The medium-range Learjet 60 is the largest Learjet ever built, with a wide cabin, gold-film-covered windscreen and a Collins ProLine 4 EFIS cockpit.

with its distinctive rear delta fins, the first time these had appeared on any Learjet design. The fins improved directional stability and did away with the need for a 'stick pusher' by reducing the type's landing speed. The **Learjet 55C/LR** was fitted with additional tankage in the tailcone and could cover 2,361 miles (3800 km), while the **Learjet 55C/ER** boasted even longer range by adding yet more fuel. Production of all Learjet 55s ended in 1992, with a 147 delivered.

A replacement for the Longhorns has come in the form of the **Learjet 60**, which first flew (as a proof-of-concept airframe) on 18 October 1990. This aircraft was powered by a Garrett TFE331-3A and a Pratt & Whitney Canada PW305 engine, with the latter chosen as the production powerplant. The first production standard aircraft flew on 13 June 1991. The Learjet 60 is the largest Learjet ever built and features the now standard winglets and delta fins, with a Collins ProLine 4 EFIS cockpit and a wide (5-ft 11-in/1.80-m), well-equipped, stand-up (5-ft 7½-in/1.71-m) cabin. Thrust reversers and a 'steer-by-wire' nosewheel are standard. Certification was obtained on 15 January 1993 and deliveries began almost immediately. Several operators including the US FAA, Malaysia and China are acquiring specialist aircraft modified for navaid calibration. By June 1999 a total of 155 Learjet 60s had been delivered.

SPECIFICATION:
Learjet 60
Powerplant: two 4,600-lb (20.46-kN) Pratt & Whitney Canada 305 turbofans
Accommodation: two (flight deck), with a maximum of nine passengers
Dimensions: span 43 ft 9 in (13.38 m); height 14 ft 8 in (4.47 m); length 58 ft 8 in (17.88 m)
Weights: empty, equipped 13,922 lb (6315 kg); maximum take-off 22,750 lb (10319 kg)
Performance: maximum speed 533 mph (858 km/h); maximum operating altitude 51,000 ft (15545 m); range with typical reserves 3,155 miles (5078 km)

Lockheed L-100 Hercules

When Lockheed flew the first **YC-130A Hercules** (actually the second aircraft to be completed) at Burbank on 23 August 1954, few could have guessed quite what an important aircraft was making its first steps. So unorthodox was its boxy and uncompromising shape (which had been designed and built in secret) that one company onlooker could only remark, "well, it's got a great paint scheme." The Hercules has gone on to become the definitive tactical military airlifter and by 1999 had passed 2,150 sales. From the outset, Lockheed was not blind to the type's commercial potential and worked hard to sell it to US airlines.

In 1959 Lockheed announced the sale of 12 **GL-207 Super Hercules** to Pan American, followed by six for Slick Airways, all for delivery in 1962. Powered by four Allison T61 engines, the Super Hercules was to be 23 ft 4 in (7.11 m) longer than the then production standard military **C-130B**. Versions with alternative powerplants, even jet engines, were proposed, but the GL-207 was cancelled, leaving the standard military Hercules as the only version available. Commercially designated **L-100**, the first civil Hercules prototype (**Lockheed Model 382**) made a record 25-hour maiden flight on 20/21 April 1964. Twenty aircraft (**Model 382B**) were sold in the USA – in March 1965 Alaska Airlines became the first commercial operator.

Next came the stretched **L-100-200 (Model 382E)**, which was 8 ft 4 in (2.54 m) longer than its predecessor. This model entered service with Interior

Since 1981 Air Algerie has flown a pair of L-100-30s on freight operations from its base at Algiers. The Algerian air force is also a Hercules operator.

Airways on 11 October 1968. Eighteen were built, including L-100 conversions.

The main commercial Hercules variant entered service in 1970 with Saturn Airways and is still in production. The **L-100-30 (Model 382G) Hercules** is stretched by an additional 6 ft 8 in (2.03 m), which accords it a fuselage volume of 6,057 cu ft (171.5 m³). The stretched Hercules have all attracted military orders, and the line between the legitimate civil, clandestine and even outright military operations of some users has at times been more than blurred. A total of 87 L-100s has been delivered by late-1999 (including 47 L-100-30s), of which over 30 have been lost – some of these shot down or destroyed by groundfire.

For the Saudi Air Force/Saudia Special Services division, Lockheed built five **L-100-30HS** hospital aircraft that boast X-ray and intensive care facilities, operating theatres and fully independent electrical generators. The future of the L-100 lies with the **Advanced L-100** that will incorporate the advances of the next-generation **C-130J**, including its Allison GMA 2100 turboprops.

UK-based specialist cargo charter operator Heavylift has frequently leased in Hercules – such as this Indonesian L-100-30 – to augment its existing fleet.

SPECIFICATION:
Lockheed L-100-30 Hercules
Powerplant: four 3,362-ehp (4508-kW) Allison 501-D22A (T56-A-15) turboprops
Accommodation: three (flight deck)
Dimensions: span 132 ft 7 in (40.41 m); height 38 ft 3 in (11.66 m); length 112 ft 9 in (34.37 m)
Weights: empty 77,736 lb (35,260 kg); maximum payload 51,054 lb (23,158 kg); maximum take-off 155,000 lb (70,308 kg)
Performance: maximum level speed 355 mph (571 km/h): service ceiling 33,500 ft (10,200 m): maximum range, with maximum payload 1,536 miles (2472 km)

Lockheed L188 Electra

In 1954 American Airlines issued a specification for a turboprop-powered airliner, with a greater passenger capacity than the Vickers Viscount, for its short- to medium-haul domestic routes. The Viscount was winning substantial orders in the US at that time and Vickers, along with Lockheed, bid for the new design. Lockheed's attempts proved unsuccessful at first, but in 1955 American revised its requirement and Lockheed got the go-ahead for the 75/100-seat **L188A Electra**. That same year saw the launch of the Boeing 707 and DC-8. In addition to American's interest, Lockheed secured a second launch order from Eastern Airlines for a combined total of 75 Electras.

The Electra was the first turboprop airliner to be built in the United States, and the prototype aircraft took to the air on 19 May 1958. Deliveries commenced to Eastern Airlines in October, with services beginning the following year. Two versions were available: the L188A and **L188C**, with additional fuel. This was a period just prior to the arrival of first short- to medium-range jets, and many operators believed that aircraft like the Electra would be more economical to run, in any case, so orders mounted. However, the 'prestige' to be had in operating jets, and the emerging fact that they could operate profitably, whittled away the Electra's market.

The last scheduled passenger operator of the Electra was Reeve Aleutian Airways, which flew three aircraft from Anchorage-International.

Until recently Hunting Cargo Airlines (now Air Contractors – Ireland) was a major Electra operator flying its aircraft on overnight freight services.

More damaging was a series of accidents that occurred in the L188's first 15 months of operations when an American aircraft, then a Braniff example and finally a Northwest Airlines' Electra all crashed. Modifications undertaken to the propellers and engine nacelles cured the dangerous resonance problems that tore these Electras apart in mid-air, but the L188's fate was sealed. Production abruptly ceased in January 1961 as orders disappeared. Just 170 aircraft, including 55 L188Cs, were built.

From 1968 the Lockheed Aircraft Service Co. began to modify Electras as freighters (**L188AF** and **L188CF**) with reinforced floors and cargo doors on one or either side of the fuselage. Too late, several airlines (such as Eastern) realised what a great design the Electra was, as its early problems never resurfaced and the survivors continued to provide sterling service into the 1980s and even the 1990s. VARIG's famous airbridge between Rio de Janeiro and São Paulo ended in favour of Boeing 737s in 1992, leaving the bulk of approximately 60 remaining Electras in cargo operation. Sizeable populations of L188s are now active in Africa, Europe and the United States, chiefly in the hands of overnight freight carriers who appreciate the type's ability to carry a load superior to that of many jets, without any of the latter's noise restrictions.

SPECIFICATION:
Lockheed L188AF Electra
Powerplant: four 3,750-hp (2800-kW) Allison 501D-13A turboprops
Accommodation: three (flight deck)
Dimensions: span 99 ft (30.18 m); height 32 ft 10 in (10 m); length 104 ft 6 in (31.81 m)
Weights: empty 27,895 lb (61500 kg); maximum payload 26,500 lb (12020 kg); maximum take-off 116,000 lb (526648 kg)
Performance: maximum cruising speed 405 mph (652 km/h); service ceiling 27,000 ft (8230 m); maximum range, with max payload 2,200 miles (3540 km)

Lockheed L1011 TriStar

USA
Three-engined medium- to long-range airliner

Joining battle in what would become dubbed the 'wide-body war' of the late 1960s and early 1970s, the Lockheed-California Company answered a requirement from American Airlines for a twin-engined aircraft to serve on its Los Angeles-Chicago route. Lockheed launched the three-engined, medium-haul **L1011 TriStar** on 1 April 1968 with orders for 144 aircraft, although none came from American. As the first TriStar began assembly at Palmdale, the project was badly affected by Lockheed's severe financial difficulties caused by the C-5 Galaxy military airlifter programme. Then, in 1971, the sole engine supplier, Rolls-Royce, collapsed. New engines could not be accommodated by the design and the TriStar was saved only when Rolls-Royce was effectively nationalised, and the RB 211 turbofan was saved from oblivion.

Despite this, the first **L1011-1 TriStar** flew on 16 November 1970 and Eastern flew the first service on 26 April 1972. One hundred and sixty of this version were built until 1983, though 119 of these were sold between 1973 and 1975. Essentially a US domestic version, the L1011-1 (**TriStar 1**), was followed by the higher gross weight **L1011-100 TriStar**, with additional fuel improving its range by 20 per cent. The first of these was delivered to Cathay Pacific in 1975. In 1974 Saudi placed orders for the **L1011-200**, a 'hot-and-high' TriStar powered by RB211-524 engines. Twenty-four L1011-200s were built, followed by 14 conversions. British Airways inspired the final production version, the

Even early-model TriStars, like this TriStar 1, are still in service. Many aircraft have been converted to the standard of subsequent production aircraft.

L1011-500 TriStar. A long-range development to compete with the DC-10-30 that had won substantial orders, the L1011-500 was powered by RB211-524B engines. The **TriStar 500** is shorter than previous aircraft – 164 ft 2 in (50.09 m) compared to 177 ft 8½ in (54.17 m) – and has a greater wingspan. TriStar production ceased in 1983 at a total of 249 (with some unsold aircraft) and by September 1999 a total of 185 was still in regular service.

Lockheed began to offer a series of conversions for existing aircraft. Beginning in 1981, 28 L1011-1s became **L1011-50**s through an increase in maximum weight from 430,000 lb (195048 kg) to 450,000 lb (204120 kg). A small number of **L1011-150** conversions were undertaken, increasing the range of a Tristar 1 by 10 per cent, slightly better than the marginally transatlantic TriStar 50. In 1986 Delta Airlines pioneered the **L1011-250** conversion. This substantially increased the TriStar 1's MTOW and refitted more powerful RB211-524 engines. Marshall Aerospace in the UK completed 10 freighter conversions for the RAF and Lockheed Martin is now moving to set up a civilian freighter conversion line.

US-based Tradewinds Airlines (formerly Tradewinds International – TIA) operates a fleet of eight TriStars, including this TriStar 200, on passenger charters.

SPECIFICATION:
Lockheed L1011-500 TriStar
Powerplant: three 50,000-lb (222.5-kN) Rolls-Royce RB211-524B4 turbofans
Accommodation: three (flight deck), maximum of 315 passengers (standard 280)
Dimensions: span 164 ft 6 in (50.09 m); height 55 ft 4 in (16.87 m); length 164 ft 2½ in (50.05 m)
Weights: operating, empty 245,400 lb (111312 kg); maximum take-off 510,000 lb (231330 kg)
Performance: cruising speed 595 mph (959 km/h); service ceiling 43,000 ft (13100 m); maximum range, with maximum fuel 7012 miles (11286 km)

Lockheed L1329 JetStar

Together with the smaller Rockwell Sabreliner, Lockheed's four-engined **L1329 JetStar** was the first purpose-built business jet to be developed. Like the Sabreliner, its roots were in a design aimed at the military – one developed for the US Air Force's UC-X competition to supply a high-speed transport and training aircraft. The JetStar programme was launched in March 1957 and the new jet was intended to carry between eight and 10 passengers. Lockheed developed the JetStar as a private venture, in anticipation of major orders from the US military, at some point in the future. In the event, Lockheed did build a small number of military JetStars for the USAF under the designation **C-140** (**VC-140**) but it was not as successful in the military role as the competing Sabreliner. Instead, the JetStar went on to pioneer the early long-range executive jet market.

The **L329** prototype first flew on 4 September 1957, but it was very different to the production aircraft that followed. It was powered by only two engines – a pair of Bristol Siddeley Orpheus turbojets. Despite a successful flight test programme these engines were swapped for four less-powerful 2,400-lb (10.7-kN) Pratt & Whitney JT12A-6 turbojets, in 1959. With these new powerplants the JetStar flew again in 1960 and was certified in August 1961.

This JetStar II was donated by Algeria to the newly-established Government of Palestine, to act as its head-of-state aircraft.

Sixty of the 162 JetStar 6s and 8s built were later re-engined to JetStar 731 standard, making them equivalent to new-build JetStar IIs.

Initial production aircraft, powered by the JT12A-6 engine were known as **L1329-6 JetStar 6**s. These engines were later uprated to 2,570-lb (11.43-kN) JT12A-6A standard. In January 1967 a new version was introduced, the **L-1329-8 JetStar 8**, powered by four 3,300-lb (14.7-kN) JT12A-8 turbojets. This version was fitted with improved anti-skid brakes and an emergency pneumatic extension system for the undercarriage. The JetStar 8 was also re-certified to operate at higher weights.

In October 1972 Lockheed introduced the **L1329-25 JetStar II**. This new-build aircraft was completely re-engined with four Garrett AiResearch (now AlliedSignal) TFE731-3 turbofans. These engines were quieter and more efficient then the older turbojets and improved overall performance. The first JetStar II flew on 18 August 1976 and was certified on 14 December. Lockheed suspended JetStar II production in 1979. However, in a parallel programme, existing JetStar 6s and 8s were re-engined by the AiResearch Aviation Company to become **JetStar 731**s. The first of these made its maiden flight on 10 July 1974 and the first production JetStar 731 flew on 18 March 1976. A total of 202 JetStars were built (plus two prototypes) and by late-1999 about 113 remain in service – almost exclusively JetStar IIs and JetStar 731s.

SPECIFICATION:
Lockheed L1329-25 JetStar II
Powerplant: four 3,700-lb (16.5-kN) Garrett AiResearch TFE731-3 turbofans
Accommodation: two (flight deck), standard 10 passengers
Dimensions: span 15 ft 5 in (16.60 m); height 20 ft 5 in (60.23 m); length 60 ft 5 in (18.42 m)
Weights: operating, empty 24,750 lb (11226 kg); maximum take-off 44,500 lb (20185 kg)
Performance: maximum cruising speed 547 mph (880 km/h); service ceiling 43,000 ft (13105 m); maximum range, with maximum fuel and reserves 3,189 miles (5132 km)

McDonnell Douglas DC-8

One of the great civil aircraft manufacturers, the Douglas Aircraft Corporation (which was taken over by McDonnell in 1967), launched its first jet age competitor, the **DC-8**, in 1955. Boeing was already well advanced with its Model 707 (Dash 80) and, as a result, the DC-8's launch order (from Pan Am) in October 1955 had to be split with the rival Boeing aircraft. The first Pratt & Whitney JT3C-6 turbojet-powered **DC-8-10** made its maiden flight, at Edwards AFB, on 30 May 1958. The first aircraft entered service with United Airlines and Delta Air Lines on 18 September 1959. The 150-ft 6-in (45.9-m) DC-8-10 was offered as the **DC-8-11** and **DC-8-12** with increased weights and wing modifications.

On 20 November 1958 Douglas flew the first **DC-8-21**, powered by JT4A-9 engines. A far more important version was the **DC-8-30** family, an intercontinental development of the Series 20. The first aircraft flew on 21 February 1959. Both the **DC-8-31** and **DC-8-32** featured increased MTOWs, while the **DC-8-33** had modified flaps and JT4A-11/-12 turbojets. Rolls-Royce Conway RCO.12 engines replaced Pratt & Whitney units on the **DC-8-40**, which was delivered to Air Canada, Alitalia and Canadian Pacific from 1960.

Turbojets were replaced by JT3D turbofans in the **DC-8-50**s. Combined with the DC-8-21 airframe, this resulted in the **DC-8-51**, which first flew on 20 December 1960. Five versions were eventually produced, including the **DC-8-52**, **-53**, **-54** and **-55** with a range of JT3D engines and MTOWs. In 1961

Miami-based Fine Air is an important DC-8 freighter operator which flies a fleet of early-model DC-8-50Fs and -60Fs, including this DC-8-54F.

Douglas announced the **DC-8F Combi** (**DC-8-54CF**) freighter, followed by an all-freight **DC-8-54AF**.

With the **DC-8-60**, Douglas stretched the original airframe by 36 ft 8 in (11.2 m). The first **DC-8-61** flew on 14 March 1966 and was followed by the **DC-8-62** (a DC-8-50 stretched by only 3 ft 3 in/1 m with a more efficient wing) and long-range **DC-8-63** (a DC-8-61 with a much improved wing). Combi (**CF**) and all-freight (**AF**) versions were made available, in addition to a passenger freighter (**PF**) stressed for future cargo operations but not initially fitted with a cargo door. DC-8 production ended in May 1972 after 556 aircraft had been completed.

In the early 1980s 110 DC-8-60s were re-engined with CFM56-2 turbofans to produce the **DC-8-70** family. Converted aircraft retain their original sub-type, so a re-engined DC-8-63AF becomes a **DC-8-73AF**, etc.. Cargo conversions are available from Aeronavali, in Italy. Between 1990 and 1995 UPS upgraded 48 of its DC-8s with EFIS cockpits. A number of hush-kits are available for the type, ensuring the current fleet of approximately 260 DC-8-50/-60/-70s will remain active for many years.

Cargo carrying DC-8s are by far the most common aircraft still in service. This DC-8-54F is one of two flown by Swaziland-based African International.

SPECIFICATION:
McDonnell Douglas DC-8-73CF
Powerplant: four 22,000-b (97.9-kN) CFM International CFM56-2-C5 turbofans
Accommodation: three (flight deck)
Dimensions: span 148 ft 5 in (45.20 m); height 43 ft (13.11 m); length 187 ft 5 in (57.12 m)
Weights: operating, empty 141,100 lb (64000 kg); maximum payload 94,000 lb (58410 kg); maximum take-off 355,000 lb (161025 kg)
Performance: maximum cruising speed 551 mph (887 km/h); service ceiling 36,000 ft (10972 m); maximum range, with maximum payload and reserves 5,561 miles (8950 km)

McDonnell Douglas DC-9
USA
Twin-engined short- to medium-range airliner

The search for a smaller companion for the DC-8 led the Douglas Aircraft Company to first propose a four-engined aircraft, two-thirds the size of a DC-8, before scaling back their plans even further to arrive at the **Model 2086** of 1962. Delta Air Lines placed the first orders for this twin-engined type, now known as the **DC-9**, in April 1963. The initial model of the DC-9, the **DC-9-10**, was 104 ft 5 in (31.85 m) long, powered by a pair of Pratt & Whitney JT8D-7 turbofans and able to seat up to 109 passengers; it first flew on 25 February 1965. Two main sub-variants were built, the **DC-9-14** and **DC-9-15** (both with progressively increased MTOWs). Cargo versions included the **DC-9-15MC** (multiple change) and **DC-9-15RC** (rapid change), the latter with a roller floor allowing quick changes in configuration.

Eastern Airlines launched the advanced **DC-9-30** in February 1965, the same month the DC-9-10 flew. The fuselage was increased by 9 ft 6 in (2.92 m), with a 4-ft (1.2-m) increase in wingspan. The first example flew on 1 August 1966 and deliveries began to Eastern in February 1967. This proved to be the most popular DC-9 variant (661 built) and appeared in several versions. The **DC-9-31** and **DC-9-32** were increased max weight aircraft, (usually) powered by JT8D-7 and -9 engines, respectively. Freighter versions included the **DC-9-32LWF** (lightweight

The bulk of surviving DC-9s are in service in the United States. TWA operates a sizeable fleet of 46 DC-9s, including this DC-9-15.

Northwest Airlines is the world's largest DC-9 operator with approximately 182 aircraft still in its active fleet.

freight), which retained full passenger capability, the **DC-9-32CF** (convertible freighter) with no cargo door for small package use, and the windowless **DC-9-32AF** (all freight).

In 1966 SAS asked McDonnell Douglas to produce a version that could operate from short runways. The result was the **DC-9-21**, which combined the fuselage of the DC-9-10 with the wing of the DC-9-30 and two uprated JT8D-11 turbofan engines. The first aircraft flew on 18 September 1968, and 10 were built for SAS alone. At the same time (1966), SAS also ordered the **DC-9-40**, which first flew on 28 November 1967. A high-density, short-range version, the DC-9-40, was further stretched by 6 ft 2 in (1.88 m), and could seat up to 128. Seventy-one were built.

Swissair launched the final 'original' DC-9, the **DC-9-50**. This was stretched by 8 ft (2.43 m) to seat up to 139 passengers, and featured new brakes and redesigned thrust reversers. Ninety-six were completed (from a total of 976 DC-9s) by April 1981, when McDonnell Douglas moved on to the 'Super Stretch' **DC-9-80** (**MD-80**), described later. Attempts to raise airline interest in a multiphased **DC-9X** upgrade ended with the acquisition of McDD by Boeing in 1997. Approximately 770 DC-9s remained in service by September 1999.

SPECIFICATION:
McDonnell Douglas DC-9-30
Powerplant: two 14,500-lb (64.4-kN) Pratt & Whitney JT8D-15 turbofans
Accommodation: two (flight deck), maximum of 115 passengers (standard 105)
Dimensions: span 93 ft 5 in (28.47 m); height 27 ft 6 in (8.38 m); length 119 ft 3½ in (36.37 m)
Weights: operating, empty 57,190 lb (25940 kg); maximum take-off 121,000 lb (54885 kg)
Performance: max cruising speed, at 25,000 ft (7620 m) 563 mph (907 km/h); max cruising altitude 35,000 ft (10670 m); max range, with 80 passengers 1,923 miles (3095 km)

McDonnell Douglas DC-10

The USAF's 1965 CX-HLS programme brought the DC-10 into being. McDonnell Douglas refined a proposal for a 650-seat aircraft to suit the same 250-seat market (and proposed American Airlines requirement) at which the TriStar was aimed. The DC-10 was launched in February 1968 with 50 orders, soon increasing to over 100.

The first **DC-10-10** flew on 29 August 1970, with deliveries following to United and American Airlines. Aimed at the US domestic market, 122 DC-10-10s, including Combi **DC-10-10CF** freighters with side cargo doors, were built – 87 of these in the first four years of production. The DC-10-10 is powered by three General Electric CF6-6D engines, and is 182 ft 3 in (55.5 m) long. Pratt & Whitney JT9D-20s featured on the next version, the **DC-10-40**, at the insistence of launch customer Northwest Orient. The longer-legged DC-10-40 first flew on 28 February 1972, and 42 were ordered by Northwest and JAL (the latter with JT9D-59A engines).

In 1969 KLM, Swissair, SAS and UTA launched the penultimate production DC-10, the long-range **DC-10-30**. Developed alongside the DC-10-40, the DC-10-30 first flew on 21 June 1972 and entered service with Swissair on 15 December. Operating at higher weights the DC-10-30 has an additional undercarriage leg on the centreline, an increased wingspan and more powerful engines.

A small number of extended-range **DC-10-30ER**s were delivered from 1982 to 1988, with extra fuel and CF6-50C2Bs. Seven aircraft were later converted

This particular DC-10-30 of Canadian International has been specially decorated with the signatures of airline employees.

to this standard. Twenty-eight **DC-10-30CF** freighters were built, in addition to nine all-cargo **DC-10-30AF**s, primarily for Federal Express.

The final version was the 'hot-and-high' **DC-10-15**, powered by General Electric CF6-50C2Fs and ordered by Mexicana and Aeromexico. Only seven were built. Plans for a stretched and wingletted **DC-10-60** series lead to the even more advanced MD-11. The USAF ordered 60 **KC-10A Extender** tanker/transports ensuring that DC-10 production continued into the late 1980s. The last aircraft off the line was a DC-10-30 delivered to Nigerian Airlines in 1989, the 266th Series 30 and the 446th KC-/DC-10. By mid-1999 approximately 330 DC-10s were still in service.

Boeing took over McDonnell Douglas in August 1997 and so Boeing is now leading the **MD-10** upgrade, which was launched in September 1996. This programme converts (passenger) DC-10s to freighters – adding a two-crew EFIS cockpit, similar to that of the MD-11. Lead customer is FedEx which has 79 MD-10 conversions on order with 40 options. The first MD-10 flew on 14 April 1999.

Minneapolis-based Sun Country Airlines caters to the US domestic vacation market. This is one of its earlier DC-10-10s, now replaced by DC-10-15s.

SPECIFICATION:
McDonnell Douglas DC-10-30
Powerplant: three General Electric CF6-50A/ -50C/-50C1/-50C2/-50C2B turbofans, rated between 49,000 lb (218 kN) and 54,000 lb (240 kN)
Accommodation: three (flight deck), maximum of 380 passengers (standard 300)
Dimensions: span 165 ft 4 in (50.40 m); height 58 ft 1 in (17.70 m); length 182 ft 1 in (55.50 m)
Weights: operating, empty 267,197 lb (121198 kg); maximum take-off 572,000 lb (259450 kg)
Performance: cruising speed 564 mph (908 km/h); service ceiling 33,400 ft (10810 m); maximum range, with maximum fuel 7490 miles (12055 km)

McDonnell Douglas (Boeing) MD-80

USA
Twin-engined medium-range airliner

McDonnell Douglas realised that the 'stretch' potential of the DC-9 had only begun to be tapped. Further improved JT8D turbofans, coupled with intense customer interest, prompted the study of new larger versions. Designations such as the **DC-9-60**, **DC-9-55RSS** (Refanned Super Stretch) or **DC-9-55** lead to the **DC-9-80**, launched in August 1977. The new aircraft was so named to reflect its proposed in-service date (1980), and early customers included Swissair and Austrian Airways.

The DC-9-80 was offered as a family. The **DC-9-81** was the basic 135-seat, JT8D-209-powered aircraft, which first flew on 18 October 1979. First deliveries commenced to Swissair on 13 September 1980. Announced in April 1979, the **DC-9-82** was powered by higher-thrust JT8D-217s, for hot-and-high operations or improved payload/range in normal conditions. The DC-9-82 made its maiden flight on 8 January 1981, and the first deliveries were made to Aeromexico in August 1981.

In June 1983 McDonnell Douglas dropped its illustrious DC (Douglas Commercial) prefix in favour of the MD designation. Thus, the DC-9-80 family became the **MD-80** family: the **MD-81** and **MD-82**. This meant that the third development of the standard MD-80, launched in January 1983, rapidly became the **MD-83**.

Apart from the short-bodied MD-87, the other versions of the MD-80 family are outwardly indistinguishable. This is an MD-83 of Aeromexico.

Successful US independent Reno Air, operates a fleet of 15 140-seat MD-82s and MD-83s (alongside MD-87s and MD-90s) from its Nevada home.

Featuring increased range, and more powerful JT8D-219 engines, the MD-83 came with two additional fuel tanks fore and aft of its centre-section. Its floor and wings, along with the landing gear, have all been modified to cope with the extra weight. The first MD-83 flew on 17 December 1984 and deliveries commenced to Alaska Airlines in February 1985.

The short-fuselage (DC-9-50 equivalent) **MD-87**, was launched in January 1987. Seating between 109 and 130, this aircraft takes advantage of all the structural and avionics improvements of the MD-80 series. The first aircraft flew on 4 December 1986 and the type entered service with Finnair and Austrian Airlines in November 1987.

In answer to an order for 80 aircraft from Delta Air Lines in 1986, McDonnell Douglas produced the **MD-88**. Similar to the MD-82 or -83, this version boasts a full EFIS cockpit and was certified by the FAA on 8 December 1987, entering service on 5 January 1988.

Following the August 1997 acquisition of McDonnell Douglas by Boeing, Boeing announced that MD-80 production would cease in 2000. By July 1999 MD-80 deliveries totalled 132 MD-81s, 562 MD-82s, 243 MD-83s, 75 MD-87s and 158 MD-88s, with 22 MD-83s still on order.

SPECIFICATION:
McDonnell Douglas MD-83
Powerplant: two 21,000-lb (93.4-kN) Pratt & Whitney JT8D-219 turbofans
Accommodation: two (flight deck), maximum of 172 passengers (standard 150)
Dimensions: span 107 ft 10¼ in (32.87 m); height 29 ft 7¼ in (9.02 m); length 147 ft 10 in (45.06 m)
Weights: operating, empty 79,686 lb (36145 kg); maximum take-off 160,000 lb (72575 kg)
Performance: maximum level speed 575 mph (925 km/h); maximum cruising altitude 35,000 ft (10670 m); maximum range, with 155 passengers 2,880 miles (4635 km)

McDonnell Douglas (Boeing) MD-11

USA
Three-engined long-range airliner

While appearing to be just a DC-10 derivative, the **MD-11** is an advanced design featuring a new wing, tail and a choice of powerplants. By the late 1970s, McDonnell Douglas was examining ways to improve the DC-10. Proposals for a stretched, rewinged **DC-10-61**, **-62** and **-63** series of varying payload range capabilities were shelved by the recession of the early 1980. The design re-emerged as the **MD-100** in 1982, becoming the **MD-XXX** and finally the **MD-11X**. In July 1985 the MD-11 as its exists today was announced, for delivery in 1989. Some 18 ft 7 in (5.69 m) longer than the DC-10-30, and powered by either General Electric CF6-80C2 or Pratt & Whitney PW4000 series engines, the MD-11 was formally launched on 30 December 1986 with 92 commitments. Other versions included the **MD-11Combi** freighter (launch customer Alitalia), the all-cargo **MD-11F** (launch customer Federal Express) and the **MD-11CF** convertible freighter (launched by Martinair Holland).

By the time assembly commenced in March 1988, only 47 firm orders had been received. The programme began to slip, so that the first flight took place eight months behind schedule, on 10 January 1990. This maiden voyage was undertaken by an MD-11F, destined for FedEx. Five aircraft took part in the test programme (four GE-powered, one P&W), which saw certification obtained on 8 November 1990. The first delivery was made to Finnair on 29 November 1990, with the MD-11 entering service on the Helsinki-Tenerife route.

Delta was an early MD-11 customer and placed an order for 15 aircraft in 1988. Its PW4460-powered MD-11s were delivered between 1992 and 1998.

From the outset, the MD-11 was unable to meet its design range guarantees. McDonnell Douglas quickly introduced the **MD-11A-1 PIP** (performance improvement programme) on all new-build aircraft from 1993, and available as a refit. This made changes to the overall weight, aerodynamics, fuel capacity and wing slatting, in addition to improved engine performance. Two optional belly fuel tanks are available, with the result that MD-11 range was extended by up to 690 nm (1278 km, 794 miles)

The final development was the **MD-11ER**, announced at the 1994 Asian Aerospace show. Intended to compete over 747-400 ranges, the MD-11ER can carry 298 passengers 8,331 miles (13408 km). The first customer was World Airways which took delivery of its first aircraft on 11 March 1996, followed by Garuda in December.

Following the August 1997 acquisition of McDonnell Douglas by Boeing, Boeing announced in June 1998 that MD-11 production would cease in 2000. By June 1999 MD-11 deliveries totalled 136 MD-11s, 50 MD-11Fs and five MD-11Cs. Twelve freighters remain on order.

The MD-11 enjoyed some success as a freighter and many surviving aircraft will be converted to cargo configuration. This is a Saudi Arabian MD-11F.

SPECIFICATION:
McDonnell Douglas MD-11
Powerplant: three Pratt & Whitney 60,000-lb (267-kN) PW4460 or 62,000-lb (276-kN) PW4462 or 61,500-lb (274-kN) General Electric CF6-80C2D1F turbofans
Accommodation: two (flight deck), maximum of 410 passengers (standard 298)
Dimensions: span 169 ft 6 in (51.66 m); height 57 ft 9 in (17.60 m); length 202 ft 2 in (61.62 m)
Weights: operating, empty 286,965 lb (130165 kg); maximum take-off 602,555 lb (273314 kg)
Performance: maximum level speed at 31,000 ft (9449 m), 588 mph (945 km/h); max range, with 298 passengers 7,850 miles (12633 km)

McDonnell Douglas (Boeing) MD-90

Intended as an advanced-technology follow-on to the MD-80 series, the **MD-90** is most notable for its use of IAE V2500 turbofans, in place of the Pratt & Whitney JT8Ds that have powered every DC-9 and MD-80. The programme was launched in November 1989, with an order for 50 from Delta Air Lines and a further 115 options (numbers since revised downwards). McDonnell Douglas decreed that the aircraft should be referred to as the MD-90, but when dealing with specific sub-types the hyphen is omitted.

The baseline **MD90-30** has an MD-80-type fuselage stretched by 4 ft 9 in (1.45 m), combined with the enlarged tail of the MD-87. It can carry a maximum of 172 passengers and is powered by V2525-D5 turbofans. A developed version of this aircraft, the **MD90-30ER** was subsequently introduced with an order for two aircraft from Egypt's AMC Aviation. The first of these was delivered on 24 September 1997.

McDonnell Douglas planned two other MD-90 versions, but these were never actually built. They included the **MD90-50**, an extended-range version of the -30 carrying fewer passengers but powered by more powerful V2528-D5 engines and the **MD90-55**, identical to the previous model, but with additional exits fitted for up to 187 passengers.

The MD-90 is a stretched MD-80, powered by a pair of new IAE V2525 turbofans in place of the DC-9/MD-80's faithful Pratt & Whitney JT8Ds.

Japan Air System (formerly Toa Domestic) was a long-term DC-9 and MD-80 customer and acquired a fleet of 16 MD90-30s from 1995 to 1998.

The first MD-90 flew on 22 February 1993 and two aircraft were engaged in the flight test programme that led to certification on 16 November 1994. Assembly of the first production example began at Long Beach in February 1994, and the first aircraft was handed over to Delta on 24 February 1995. It entered service on 1 April. The first European MD-90 operator was SAS which placed its first aircraft into service on 11 November 1996.

Since April 1986 the Shanghai Aircraft Manufacturing Factory (SAMF) has assembled MD-82s and MD-83s for the Chinese airline market. In 1992 SAMF and McDonnell Douglas announced the Trunkliner agreement, to develop the **MD90-30T Trunkliner** with dual main landing gear for operations from rough Chinese airfields. The terms of this long-running deal have been renegotiated several times and now call for the delivery of 20 MD-90s from the US (beginning in 1996) along with 20 built in China. Construction of Chinese-built MD-90s began in 1995, but, by mid-1999, deliveries are not yet understood to have commenced.

Following the August 1997 acquisition of McDonnell Douglas by Boeing, Boeing announced in June 1998 that MD-90 production would cease in 2000. By June 1999 MD-90 orders totalled 114 (excluding MD-90Ts) with 10 still to be delivered.

SPECIFICATION:
McDonnell Douglas MD90-30
Powerplant: two 25,000-lb (111.21-kN) IAE V2525-D5 turbofans
Accommodation: two (flight deck), maximum of 172 passengers (standard 153)
Dimensions: span 107 ft 10 in (32.87 m); height 30 ft 7¼ in (9.33 m); length 152 ft 7 in (46.51 m)
Weights: operating, empty 88,200 lb (40007 kg); maximum take-off 156,000 lb (70760 kg)
Performance: maximum cruising speed at 35,000 ft (10670 m), 503 mph (809 km/h); maximum range, with 153 passengers and reserves 2,400 miles (3862 km)

Mil Mi-8 and Mi-17

Development of the turbine-powered **Mi-8 'Hip'**, derived from the **Mi-4 'Hound'**, began in 1960. Known as the **V-8**, the prototype was a much larger helicopter with a single, more powerful 2,700-hp (2013-kW) Soloviev turboshaft, but retaining the four-bladed main rotor, transmission and tail boom of the Mi-4. The Mi-8 was first seen by the public at the 1961 Soviet Aviation Day display. A second twin-engined prototype flew for the first time on 17 September 1962, and this introduced the standard 1,500-hp (1119k-W) Isotov TV2-117 turboshafts and a five-bladed rotor system adopted in 1966 for the first production aircraft. The 1,700-shp (1268-kW) TV2-117A was fitted later. Production was initiated and is continuing at two locations, the Kazan Helicopter Plant and the Ulan-Ude Aviation Industrial Association. Kazan also independently markets its own versions of the Mi-17.

The Mi-8 is of typical pod-and-boom construction, which provides accommodation for 28 passengers and two or three crew. Large clamshell doors at the rear facilitate the loading of bulky freight. The basic utility version was the **Mi-8T** (and later improved **Mi-8AT** and **Mi-8TM**) for both civil and military use, distinguished by circular windows, aluminium cargo floor, hook-on ramps, electric winch, and optional rescue electric hoist and 24 tip-up seats along the walls. In an ambulance role, the Mi-8 can accommodate 12 stretchers and attendant. The **Mi-8P** passenger version differs in having rectangular windows, airstairs in the clamshell doors and comfortably furnished

The Mi-8 and Mi-17 are versatile types in regular commercial service worldwide. These Aeroflot examples wear a non-standard 'high-viz' scheme.

accommodation for up to 32 passengers. A nine/ 11-seat deluxe version had the designation **Mi-8 Salon**, but is now referred to as the **Mi-8 VIP**.

In the mid-1970s production switched to the improved **Mi-17** (still referred to as the Mi-8 in Russian military service). First displayed at the Paris air show of 1981, the Mi-17 combines the airframe of the Mi-8 with uprated Isotov TV3-117MTs, as fitted to the Mi-14. The tail rotor was also moved to the port side. Current production versions include the **Mi-17/P** (basic 28-seat version, military designation **Mi-8MT**; **Mi-17-1V** or **Mi-8MTV** (uprated TV3-117VM engines and optional nose radar, flotation and fire-fighting gear); **Mi-17-1VA** (Russian flying hospital); **Mi-171** (export version of basic **Mi-8AMT** military transport); **Mi-172** or **Mi-8MTV-3** (Kazan-built 26-seat model with new avionics, systems and TV3-117VM Srs 2 engines for improved performance)

Together with Mil and Kelowna Flightcraft of Canada, Kazan has developed the **Mi-17KF** fitted with a Honeywell EDZ-756 six-screen EFIS cockpit. Kazan also offers the **Mi-17MD**, equivalent to the military **Mi-8MTV-5** with a one-piece rear ramp.

Large square cabin windows mark this Polish-registered Mi-8 as the passenger transport Salon version, known by its NATO codename of 'Hip-C'.

SPECIFICATION:
Mil Mi-17P
Powerplant: two 1,874-hp (1397-kW) Isotov TV3-117MT turboshafts
Accommodation: three (flight deck), with a maximum of 32 passengers
Dimensions: main rotor diameter 69 ft 10¼ in (21.29 m); height 15 ft 7½ in (4.76 m); fuselage length 60 ft 5¼ in (18.42 m)
Weights: empty 15,653 lb (7100 kg); maximum take-off 28,652 lb (13000 kg)
Performance: maximum cruising speed 155 mph (250 km/h); service ceiling 18,380 ft (5600 m); range with maximum payload and reserves 307 miles (495 km)

Mil Mi-26

Design of the **Mi-26** 'Halo' began in the early 1970s to a requirement for a large helicopter for all-weather operations. The specification stipulated an empty weight half of the take-off weight, maximising payload capacity, with total reliability for operations into unprepared sites. Two powerful 11,240-hp (8380-kW) Lotarev D-136 turboshafts and the first-ever eight-bladed rotor system, with an aluminium rotor hub, were fitted. The prototype first flew on 14 December 1977, several pre-production models entered operational trials with the Soviet air force in 1983 and the type was fully operational by 1985. India took the first export deliveries in June 1986.

In 1982, the Mi-26 set a number of impressive payload-to-height records. On 2 February, it lifted a 10000-kg payload to 6400 m, followed the next day by a 25000-kg load to 4100 m and a total 56769 kg to a height of 2000 m. On 4 February, more records were established when lifting a 15000-kg payload to 5600 m and 20000 kg to 4600 m. Everything about the Mi-26 is impressive. It can carry a payload of 20000 kg (44,080 lb), both internally or externally. Its cavernous hold is 15.00 m (49 ft 3 in) long, 3.25 m (10 ft 8 in) wide and up to 3.17 m (10 ft 5 in) high, adding up to a volume of 121 m³ (4,273 cu ft). The hold is loaded via a hydraulically-actuated lower door with folding ramp, and two clamshell upper doors.

The Mi-26TM is the dedicated flying crane version of the Mi-26T, which can be fitted with an observer's 'gondola' under the fuselage or under the rear ramp.

The Mi-26's lifting ability is unrivalled, and underslung loads have ranged from artillery pieces to huge water-filled fire-fighting 'buckets'.

Two electric overhead hoists with a capacity of 2500 kg (5,511 lb) each enable loads to be shifted along the cabin. In typical cargo configuration, the Mi-26 has a crew of five: two pilots, flight engineer, navigator and loadmaster, and a four-seat passenger compartment behind. It can also accommodate 85 combat-ready troops, or up to 100 passengers in a civilian layout.

Current versions include the: Mi-26 basic military transport; **Mi-26A**, with PNK-90 automatic flight control and navigation system; **Mi-26T**, civil transport version also available as **Mi-26 Firefighter** carrying 15,000 litres (3,300 gal) of water/fire retardant in the cabin or 17,260 litres (3,796 gal) in an underslung bucket; **Mi-26TS**, Mi-26T certified for western operations, also known as **Mi-26TC**; **Mi-26MS**, medical evacuation version with accommodation for up 32 stretchers, intensive care and surgery units; **Mi-26P**, 63-seat transport version with 'airline' seating; **Mi-26TH**, flying crane with underfuselage gondola; **Mi-26TZ**, tanker capable of carrying 14040 litres (3,088 gal) of fuel and 1040 litres (228 gal) of oil/lubricants. An **Mi-26M** upgrade, with 14,350-hp (10700-kw) ZMKB Progress D-127 turboshafts, EFIS cockpit and redesigned all-GFRP rotor blades, is under development. By mid-1999 approximately 100 Mi-26s have been built for domestic and export customers.

SPECIFICATION: Mil Mi-26T
Powerplant: two 10,000-hp (7460-kW) ZMKB Progress (Lotarev) D-136 turboshafts
Accommodation: four (flight deck) plus loadmaster and 44,091 lb (20000 kg) of freight or 100 passengers
Dimensions: main rotor diameter 105 ft (32 m); height 38 ft 1 in (11.60 m); length, fuselage 117 ft 9¾ in (35.91 m)
Weights: empty 63,052 lb (28600 kg), maximum take-off 123,450 lb (56000 kg)
Performance: maximum level speed 183 mph (295 km/h); service ceiling 15,100 ft (4600 m); range with maximum payload and reserves 366 miles (590 km)

NAMC YS-11

Yet another aircraft designed in the hope of replacing the world's DC-3/C-47 fleet, the **NAMC YS-11** was a bold attempt by the Japanese aviation industry to satisfy its own airliner requirements. Launched in 1956, the YS-11 programme combined the talents of six established manufacturers, who were rebuilding their capability after World War II. The Nihon Aeroplane Manufacturing Company (NAMC) was in fact a consortium of Fuji, Kawasaki, Mitsubishi, Nippi, Shin Meiwa and Showa. The resulting aircraft was similar in layout to the Avro 748, with high aspect ratio wings with considerable dihedral, circular pressurised fuselage and Rolls-Royce Darts mounted in nacelles above the wing, the nacelle also housing the main undercarriage units. Where it differed was in being appreciably larger, able to accommodate 60 passengers.

The first YS-11 took to the air on 30 August 1962; the second followed it on 28 December. Japanese certification was awarded on 25 August 1964, while the FAA seal of approval came on 7 September 1965.

From the outset, the design of the YS-11 had been driven by the needs of the large Japanese domestic market, where the size of the aircraft was appreciated by the three major carriers. Toa Airways put the first **YS-11-100** into service on 1 April 1965. In May, Japan Domestic Airlines followed (soon to merge with Toa) and then All Nippon in July. Forty-eight YS-11s were built, the hoped-for foreign sales amounting to only seven.

Trinidad-and-Tobago-based Air Caribbean operates a fleet of six YS-11As, acquired in the mid-1990s, on inter-island services from its home at Port of Spain.

To make the aircraft more attractive to foreign operators, it was redesigned with uprated Dart Mk 542 engines and an increase in payload as the **YS-11A**. The **YS-11A-200** was the most successful model, a 60-seat airliner that sold moderately in North and South America, where Piedmont (22) and Cruzeiro (12) were two notable customers. The **YS-11A-300CP** was a mixed passenger/freight carrier, while the **YS-11A-400** was a pure freighter with a rear cargo door that found favour with the Japanese air force. The final variants were the **YS-11A-500, -600** and **-700**, which were similar to the -200, -300 and -400 but had increased take-off weights. Only four -500s and five -600s were built, bringing total production of all variants to 182, the last aircraft being delivered in early 1974.

The YS-11 has proved to be a reliable workhorse and the largest active fleet today belongs to one of the original customers, Japan Air System (formerly Toa Domestic), which currently operates 12 aircraft. By mid-1999 approximately 97 YS-11s were still in civil and military service, chiefly in Japan, the Philippines, the Caribbean and the United States.

Export sales of the robust YS-11 (like this YS-11-100) were hampered because it was tailored too closely to the needs of its original Japanese customers.

SPECIFICATION:
NAMC YS-11A-200
Powerplant: two 3,060-shp (2282-kW) Rolls-Royce Dart Mk 542-10K turboprops
Accommodation: two (flight deck), standard layout for 60 passengers
Dimensions: span 104 ft 11¾ in (32.00 m); length 86 ft 3½ in (26.30 m); height 29 ft 5½ in (8.98 m)
Weights: empty 33,993 lb (15419 kg); maximum take-off 54,010 lb (24500 kg)
Performance: maximum cruising speed 291 mph (469 km/h); service ceiling 22,900 ft (6980 m); range with maximum payload 680 miles (1090 km)

Pilatus PC-12

The Swiss aircraft manufacturer Pilatus has carved a niche for itself by building a succession of specialist STOL transport aircraft and turboprop military trainers. When it launched the **PC-12** (or **PC XII**) it was in an attempt to translate this experience into a whole new market. The PC-12 is unique in being a large, high-speed, pressurised single-engined turboprop that combines a capacious cabin with a sleek design. It is aimed at business or corporate customers, and freight or passenger carriers that operate in rough and spartan conditions.

The PC-12 was unveiled in October 1989 at the NBAA show. The aircraft is built around the proven and reliable Pratt & Whitney Canada PT6A turboprop, driving a four-bladed prop. Its airframe is largely metal, with some composites used to save weight. The PC-12 has a swept T-tail and winglets were incorporated in the early stages of flight testing. Central to the aircraft's design is the ability to undertake single-pilot IFR operations which, coupled with its single engine, offers great operating cost savings to potential customers. The PC-12 has a cabin volume of 330 cu ft (9.34 m³), which is much larger than the similar SOCATA TBM 700, and also beats many twin-engined aircraft such as the Cessna CitationJet and Beech King Air – all aircraft with which the PC-12 is competing.

One of the most important features of the PC-12 is its upward-opening side cargo door which measures 53 x 52 in (1.35 x 1.32 m).

The basic passenger version of the PC-12 carries nine, while the Executive version is configured for six. An all-cargo version is also available.

The prototype PC-12 made its maiden flight on 31 May 1991, followed by a second example on 28 May 1993. Initial Swiss certification was awarded on 30 March 1994 and FAA approval came on 15 July. Expanded FAA clearance, including flight into known icing conditions, came in 1995. The critical certification for full commercial single-engined operations came in 1997, finally allowing the PC-12 to operate to its full potential. The first customer deliveries were made in September 1994, to a US leasing company. The first scheduled airline operator was Canada's Kelner Airways, in 1997. Other significant customers include Australia's Royal Flying Doctor Service, the Royal Canadian Mounted Police and the Red Cross. Sales have been concentrated in the USA, Canada and South America. Pilatus has also developed a range of military special mission variants, as the **Pilatus Eagle**, which can carry a variety or radar and senor systems for maritime patrol and surveillance missions.

PC-12s are built at the Pilatus factory in Stans, Switzerland, where production was stepped up from four to five aircraft per month during 1998. They are then ferried to Pilatus' US completion centre at Broomfield, Colorado, for fitting out. The 100th PC-12 was delivered in April 1998 and by mid-1999 Pilatus had over 250 orders.

SPECIFICATION
Pilatus PC-12
Powerplant: one 1,605-hp (1197-kW) Pratt & Whitney Canada PT6A-67B turboprop
Accommodation: one or two (flight deck) plus 3,364 lb (1526 kg) of freight or nine passengers
Dimensions: wing span 53 ft 3 in (16.23 m); height 14 ft (4.27 m); length 43 ft 3 in (14.40 m)
Weights: empty 5,732 lb (2600 kg), maximum take-off 9,920 lb (4500 kg)
Performance: max cruising speed at 25,000 ft (7620 m) 311 mph (500 km/h); service ceiling 35,000 ft (10670 m); range with maximum payload and reserves 2,602 miles (4187 km)

Reims F406 Caravan II

The French-built Reims **F406 Caravan II** inherits the traditions of a long line of twin-engined aircraft designed and built by Cessna, in the USA. Reims Aviation was established in 1956 and later made its name as the European licence-builder of Cessna's single-engined piston aircraft. Reims built over 6,300 Cessna 'singles' before Cessna halted all production in January 1997 – US production has since been restarted, but not at Reims. In 1989 Cessna sold its 49 per cent stake in Reims Aviation and the company is now wholly French owned.

As an extension of its Cessna experience, Reims announced it was working on its own twin-engined design in 1982. The F406 (all Reims-built aircraft had an F prefix) was named the Caravan II, in an attempt to line up a family of aircraft alongside the highly successful Cessna 208 Caravan I. The new twin was to be a modern version of the Cessna 401, 402 and 404 family and, outwardly, it closely resembled the Model 404 Titan. In fact, the design was based on the Cessna Conquest but with expanded dimensions and a more 'squared-off' shape.

The Caravan II has a conventional light metal structure and a two-spar wing with a failsafe three-spar centre section. It is powered by a pair of Pratt & Whitney Canada PT6A turboprops, each driving a three-blade reversible pitch propeller. The cabin can accommodate up to 14 passengers, in two forward-facing rows. A business version with six reclining seats was also developed, with a partition between the passenger cabin and a special rear toilet. An all

The PT6A-powered Reims F406 Caravan II is today the only in-production twin in its class, and it has secured a solid niche in the market.

freight version could be fitted with an optional double cargo door (4 ft 2 in x 1 ft 10¾ in/1.27 x 0.58 m), on the port side. An underfuselage cargo pod can also be fitted. Baggage compartments are located in the nose, engine nacelles and at the rear of the cabin.

The prototype F406 made its maiden flight on 22 September 1983. French certification was obtained on 22 September 1994 and the first production aircraft flew on 20 April 1985. Reims has developed a family of military variants of the F406, known as the **Vigilant**. Versions of the basic aircraft are aimed at a range of maritime patrol and surveillance missions and the F406 is also in use as an aerial target tug.

By mid-1999 Reims had 89 orders for the F406, with deliveries proceeding. The special missions market is now the most important and new FLIR, camera and radar equipment will be added. At the 1999 Paris air show Reims announced it would develop a new type, described as 'a cargo aircraft with a range of 700-2000 km (435-1242 miles) and a payload of 4000-4500 kg (8,818-9,920 lb)'. It is expected that this will entail a licence-production deal with a Russian manufacturer

Aviation Lease Holland is the largest Caravan II operator with a fleet of 28 dedicated to overnight parcel services and cargo charters.

SPECIFICATION
Reims Aviation F406 Caravan II
Powerplant: two 500-shp (373-kW) Pratt & Whitney Canada PT6A-112 turboprops
Accommodation: two (flight deck) plus 4,892 lb (2219 kg) of freight or 14 passengers
Dimensions: wing span 49 ft 5½ in (15.08 m); height 13 ft 2 in (4.01 m); length 39 ft ¼ in (11.89 m)
Weights: empty 5,033 lb (2283 kg), maximum take-off 9,850 lb (4468 kg)
Performance: maximum cruising speed 283 mph (455 km/h); service ceiling 30,000 ft (9154 m); range with maximum fuel and reserves 1,327 miles (2135 km)

Rockwell Sabreliner

Twin-engined short- to medium-range business jet

The JT12-powered Sabreliner 40 was the initial production variant and is identifiable by its three, distinctively teardrop-shaped, cabin windows.

Inspired by its famed F-86 Sabre fighter, in 1952 North American Aviation (NAA) began work on a twin turbojet-engined transport. Its early studies were rejuvenated when the USAF launched a competition in 1956 for an off-the-shelf transport and training aircraft. North American entered its earlier design as the **N.A.286 Sabreliner** (underlining its links with the F-86) and rolled out the first example on 8 May 1958, at Inglewood. This aircraft made its maiden flight from Palmdale on 16 September, and its successors won substantial orders from the USAF, USN and USMC as the **T-39 Sabre**.

While the first Sabreliners had been built for the military, by 1962 NAA began to turn its attention to commercial versions. The Sabreliner was already certified to CAR 4b jet transport standard, so NAA launched a version essentially similar to the USAF's **T-39A** transport, the **Sabreliner 40**. To the FAA, the military Sabreliner was the **N.A.265**, so the Sabreliner 40 became the **N.A.265-40**. This version had its Pratt & Whitney JT12A-6A engines replaced by 3,300-lb (14.7-kN) JT12A-8 turbojets and featured an additional cabin window (for a total of three).

A single **Sabreliner 50** was built chiefly for test duties with NAA before the stretched **Sabreliner 60** was introduced in 1967. This version could seat 10 passengers and featured five cabin windows on

each side. In September 1967 NAA merged with the Rockwell-Standard Corporation, and Sabreliner production became the responsibility of the Sabreliner Division of Rockwell International.

On 17 June 1970 the **Sabreliner 70** was certified, with a 'stand-up' cabin, and square windows in place of the original triangular ones. This version was soon redesignated **Sabre 75**, and when mated with new General Electric CF 7002D-2 turbofans became the **Sabre 75A** (initially **Sabre 80**) from 1972. This re-engining greatly improved its sales performance. The final production Sabre was the **Sabre 65**, powered by Garret TFE731-3 engines. This transcontinental version first flew on 8 April 1979 and featured a new supercritical wing developed by the Reisbeck Group, of Seattle.

Reisbeck became heavily involved in modifying Sabres, retrofitting its new wing and 'Mark Five' aerodynamic improvement package to Sabre 75As (as the **Sabre 80A**) and TFE731 engines to the Sabre 60. Rockwell planned the stretched and improved **Sabre 85**, but production finally ceased on 1 January 1982 at a grand total of 441. Approximately 333 of these are still in use. Product support for all Sabreliners/T-39s is now undertaken by the St Louis-based Sabreliner Corporation, which acquired the production rights in 1983.

The Sabre 60 was the most numerous version to roll off the NAA production line, with 146 delivered. It was replaced by the much-changed Sabre 75.

SPECIFICATION:
Rockwell (North American) Sabre 65
Powerplant: two 3,700-lb (16.46-kN) Garrett (now AlliedSignal) TFE731-3-D turbofans
Accommodation: two (flight deck), maximum of 12 passengers (nine standard)
Dimensions: span 55 ft 5⅛ in (15.37 m); height 16 ft (4.88 m); length 46 ft 11 in (14.30 m)
Weights: empty 13,350 lb (6055 kg); maximum take-off 24,000 lb (10886 kg)
Performance: maximum speed Mach 0.85; service ceiling 45,000 ft (13715 m); maximum range, with maximum fuel 3351 miles (5393 km)

Saab 340

A unique US/European aviation collaboration was announced in January 1980 when Saab-Scania and Fairchild Industries announced a new jointly-developed, 35-seat, twin-turboprop design, the **Saab-Fairchild 340** (**SF 340**). Fairchild undertook to manufacture the wings, tail unit and engine nacelles, while Saab was responsible for 75 per cent of the development costs, systems integration and certification. The SF 340 made its maiden flight on 25 January 1983. The launch customer was Switzerland's Crossair, to whom deliveries began in July 1984.

Two versions were initially on offer, the basic air transport configuration or an executive model. Five VIP aircraft entered service, including one for the Swedish Royal family. At the 1985 Paris air show the manufacturers announced the next development, an increased MTOW (27,275 lb/12872 kg) version with uprated engines and larger Dowty propellers.

Fairchild's ailing financial position forced it to withdraw from the project in October 1985, and production was gradually transferred to Saab's Linköping home. The Swedish company next launched the **Saab 340QC**, a quick-change freighter aircraft, the first of which was sold to Finnaviation in 1987. That same year, as links were finally severed with Fairchild, the SF 340 became the **Saab 340**.

In 1987 Saab announced the **Saab 340B**, the final production version. Featuring higher-powered CT7-9B engines, a larger-span tailplane and a further increased maximum weight, Crossair was again the

Skyways is a successful domestic Swedish carrier based at Linköping, Gothenburg and Stockholm. Its fleet includes 11 Saab 340Bs.

launch customer. The arrival of the Saab 340B invigorated sales that had slowed to around the 200 mark at that point. A substantial order was won from American Eagle, American Airline's commuter arm, for 100 Saab 340Bs (it already flew the SF 340). On 8 June 1993 American Eagle's 100th aircraft, the 340th Saab 340, was handed over.

Saab improved hot-and-high and short-field performance by fitting (optional) wingtip extensions. These increased the aircraft's take-off weight by 1,200 lb (544 kg), equivalent to six/seven passengers. Advances made in the Saab 2000 cabin design (including the active noise system) were also applied to all late-production Saab 340Bs, the 'Generation 3' aircraft dubbed **Saab 340B Plus**.

However, faced with a dramatic drop in demand for regional turboprop airliners Saab was forced to announce the closure of the production line in 1998. The last two Saab 340Bs were handed over on 21 May and 4 June 1999, to Hokkaido Air System and Japan Air Commuter respectively. In all 459 aircraft were built and almost all are still in regular airline service worldwide.

In August 1988 Taiwan's Formosa Airlines became the first Asian operator of the Saab 340. Today it still has two aircraft in service.

SPECIFICATION:
Saab 340B
Powerplant: two 1,750-hp (1305-kW) General Electric CT7-9B turboprops
Accommodation: two (flight deck), standard load of 35 passengers
Dimensions: span 70 ft 4 in (9.50 m); height 22 ft 10½ in (6.97 m); length 64 ft 8¾ in (19.73 m)
Weights: operating, empty 18,133 lb (8225 kg); maximum take-off 29,000 lb (13155 kg)
Performance: maximum cruising speed 325 mph (522 km/h); service ceiling 25,000 ft (7620 m); maximum range, with 35 passengers, baggage and reserves 1,047 miles (1685 km)

Saab 2000

Experience with the Saab 340 convinced the Swedish manufacturer that there was a market for an advanced, high-speed turboprop regional airliner. The **Saab 2000** would be a 50-seat aircraft, capable of matching jet performance and block times over a range of sectors, and the project was formally launched in December 1988, with an order for 25 (with 25 options) from Crossair.

Saab spread the development burden of its new aircraft, entering into agreements with CASA, of Spain, to build the wing, Finland's Valmet to build the tail unit and elevators, and Westland to build the rear fuselage. A Collins Pro Line 4 avionics system was selected and a radical reduction in cabin noise became a major design goal. To this end, Allison GMA 2100 turboprops (now AE2100) driving six-bladed propellers were selected. Saab also developed an active noise reduction system that detected airflow and vibration noise and rebroadcast an equal, opposite waveform, thus effectively 'switching off' cabin noise.

First metal was cut at Linköping in February 1990, and the prototype flew on 26 March 1992. A four-aircraft test programme was established. Early in the programme, all Saab's performance requirements were met or exceeded. Underlining this, a Saab 2000 set a new time-to-climb record of 29,527 ft

Moritz Suter's Crossair, already a firm Saab 340 operator, was the Saab 200 launch customer. Today Crossair operates half the aircraft built.

SAS Commuter acquired six Saab 2000s in 1997 and 1998, but even its vote of confidence in the type could not save it from cancellation.

(9000 m) in 8 minutes 8 seconds, bettering that set previously by an E-2 Hawkeye. Maximum cruise speed was well above the promised 360 kt (413 mph; 665 km/h) and in a dive the aircraft attained 430 kt (493 mph; 794 km/h) with no ill effect.

However, the certification timetable was set back by problems with the aircraft's high-speed longitudinal stability, and a new Powered Elevator Control System (PECS) had to be initiated in late 1993. First delivery dates were thus delayed into the fourth quarter of 1994 – 18 months behind schedule. European certification of the Saab 2000 was received on 31 March 1994, with a redesigned elevator spring tab. The full PECS modification followed later. FAA certification was achieved on 29 April 1994. Deliveries to Crossair finally began on 30 September 1994, and these were followed by the first aircraft for Deutche BA on 17 March 1995.

The Saab 2000 suffered from several early teething troubles but these were nothing compared to the explosive arrival of competing regional jets, which emerged just as the Saab 2000 was trying to find its feet. Orders, which had always been slow, stopped and the Saab 2000 was discontinued in 1998. Production ceased at 63 aircraft, though a 64th undelivered airframe (for the Japan Maritime Safety Agency) was laid down on the Linköping line.

SPECIFICATION:
Saab 2000
Powerplant: two 4,152-hp (3096-kW) Allison AE2100A turboprops
Accommodation: two (flight deck), maximum of 58 passengers
Dimensions: span 81 ft 2¾ in (24.76 m); height 25 ft 4 in (7.73 m); length 89 ft 6 in (27.28 m)
Weights: operating, empty 30,423 lb (13800 kg); maximum take-off 50,265 lb (22800 kg)
Performance: maximum cruising speed 423 mph (681 km/h); service ceiling 31,000 ft (9450 m); maximum range, with 35 passengers, baggage and reserves 1,782 miles (2868 km)

Shorts Belfast

The **Short SC.5 Belfast** was designed as a strategic military freighter for the RAF, with a cavernous hold that could accommodate bulkier and more awkward loads than the Boeing 747 or Lockheed C-5 Galaxy, and with a removable 'stub deck' that could be installed in the roof of the hold for mixed freight/passenger duties. Drawing on Short's experience in licence-producing the Bristol Britannia, the company designed a high-winged freighter version, initially dubbed **Britannic**. A stretched centre-section was added (but wings and tail surfaces were still built in Britannia jigs) and the aircraft was formally named Belfast in 1959. Ten were built for the RAF, the first of these making its maiden flight on 5 January 1964, and the type entering service with No. 53 Squadron in 1966.

Short-sighted defence cuts led to a dramatic down-sizing of the RAF's transport fleet and No.53 Sqn disbanded in 1977. Its Belfasts were put into storage. A sale of all 10 to Pan African (possibly a CIA front company) fell through, but three aircraft continued to be modified for civil use (for Liberian certification) by Eurolatin. The other seven were sold to Rolls-Royce for recovery of their Tyne engines, for use on Aeritalia G.222s – effectively a death sentence, after unsuccessful bids by Transmeridian Air Cargo, Tradewinds and IAS. One was presented to the RAF Museum by Rolls-Royce, and two were sold to Transmeridian, who had taken over the three Eurolatin aircraft and who became TAC Heavylift and eventually Heavylift Cargo Airlines.

Today the Belfast is an asset unique to Stansted-based Heavylift Cargo Airlines, which has seen other rival types come and go.

Civil certification proved time-consuming and costly, but the aircraft began earning their keep in March 1980. The Belfasts were soon breaking records for bulk cargo moved by civil aircraft, especially for the oil, gas and mining industries. Flying BAC One-Eleven components to Romania, SEPECAT Jaguar sub-assemblies to India, and transporting components for Boeing 767s were all early jobs. MoD charters during the Falklands War alone reportedly cost the taxpayer more than would the cost of keeping every aircraft on in Royal Air Force service until 1990.

The end of the Cold War and the gradual change of Russia and other former USSR states into market economies has led to a flood of high-capacity transport aircraft (such as the An-22, An-124 and Il-76) and freighters entering the market. As a result, the ageing Belfast has lost its unique selling point, although it continues to represent an extremely low-cost solution to bulk transport requirements. The Heavylift fleet is now down to two of these massive and reliable (if ponderous) giants but there are no immediate plans for their retirement.

G-BEPE was the first civilian Belfast, and at its unveiling TAC Heavylift announced it as the "first aircraft that could carry a Hercules."

SPECIFICATION:
Shorts S.C.5 Belfast
Powerplant: four 5,730-hp (4273-kW) Rolls-Royce Tyne Rty.12 turboprops
Accommodation: three or four (flight deck) plus a loadmaster
Dimensions: span 158 ft 9 in (48.40 m); height 47 ft (14.33 m); length 136 ft 5 in (41.48 m)
Weights: operating empty 127,000 lb (57606 kg); maximum take-off 230,000 lb (104326 kg)
Performance: maximum cruising speed 352 mph (566 km/h); service ceiling 30,000 ft (9145 m); range with maximum payload and typical reserves 1,000 miles (1609 km)

Shorts 330 and 360

Having perceived an emerging market for a 30-seat commuter aircraft, Shorts began to study a development of its 19-passenger SC-7 Skyvan. The company decided to base the new aircraft, then known as the **SD3-30**, on the small, boxy Skyvan using the same square fuselage cross-section, twin tail unit and outer wing panels. However, the wingspan was increased, as was the fuselage length, and a retractable landing gear replaced the fixed gear of the Skyvan. The Garrett engines were changed to 1,156-hp (862-kW) Pratt & Whitney PT6A-45A turboprops. The first of two prototypes flew on 22 August 1974 and, after receiving UK and US certification, the type entered service with Time Air of Canada on 24 August 1976.

The **Shorts 330**, as it became known soon after, underwent a number of progressive upgrades. The first of these was the introduction of the PT6A-45B after 26 production aircraft, followed by the PT6A-45R with slightly greater power, which allowed a gross weight increase from 22,690 lb (10295 kg) to 22,900 lb (10390 kg). When the fuel capacity was increased in January 1985, the designation was changed to **330-200**. Earlier models then became known as the **330-100**. A quick-change version was made available, and Shorts produced the military **330-UTT** (utility tactical transport) with a strength-

The Shorts 330 has increasingly been acquired by small cargo airlines who appreciate its square, roomy fuselage and ease of access for loading.

The Shorts 360 still appeals to small airlines which need a reliable aircraft that is cheap to acquire and easy to operate.

ened cabin floor, inward-opening rear door for paradropping, and some structural beefing-up. The **C-23A Sherpa** was a cargo version for US forces.

The relaxation of US regulations, which prior to deregulation in 1978 had prohibited commuter airlines to use aircraft with more than 30 seats, led to the **Shorts 336**, distinguished by a lengthened and more streamlined fuselage that permitted six extra seats, a swept-back conventional tail and more powerful 1,327-hp (990-kW) PT6A-65Rs. By the time the prototype made its first flight on 1 June 1981, the aircraft had become known as the **Shorts 360**. The Shorts 360 entered service with Suburban Airlines, Reading, Pennsylvania, on 1 December 1982.

The **360 Advanced**, of 1986, introduced 1,425-shp (1062-kW) PT6A-65ARs. This was followed in 1987 by the final variant, the **360-300**, which featured PT6A-67ARs, an autopilot and substantially enhanced passenger comfort. Previous models were then redubbed the **Shorts 360-100** and **360-200**. By the time production of the 330/360 family ceased in 1991/92, Shorts had produced a total of 136 Shorts 330s, including military variants. By September 1999 approximately 77 of these aircraft remained in service, alongside 153 of the 164 Shorts 360s built.

SPECIFICATION:
Shorts 360-300
Powerplant: two 1,424-hp (1062-kW) Pratt & Whitney PT6A-65AR turboprops
Accommodation: two (flight deck) with a maximum of 39 passengers
Dimensions: span 74 ft 9 in (22.80 m); height 23 ft 10 in (7.27 m); length 70 ft 9 in (21.58 m)
Weights: operating empty 17,356 lb (7875 kg); maximum ramp 27,198 lb (12340 kg)
Performance: maximum cruising speed 244 mph (343 km/h); range with maximum payload and typical reserves 460 miles (745 km)

Sikorsky S-61 Sea King

On 24 December 1957, the US Navy issued a contract for a new high-performance helicopter to replace the Sikorsky S-58. Sikorsky submitted a design for a large twin-turbine aircraft with a boat-type hull and retractable undercarriage for amphibious operations. Given the Sikorsky model number **S-61**, the prototype made its first flight on 11 March 1959. This was followed by seven pre-production models, which began trials on 8 February 1961. First deliveries of the **S-61B** (Navy designation **HSS-2**), later **SH-3A Sea King**), for anti-submarine duties, were made in September that same year.

The S-61 was powered by two 1,250-shp (932-kW) General Electric T58-GE-18 turboshafts, driving a fully-articulated all-metal rotor system with five main interchangeable blades that could be folded. The specially-shaped fuselage was sealed to permit emergency landing on water, with the landing gear retracting hydraulically into stabilising floats on each side of the fuselage. The success of the naval trials, which proved the safety, survivability and reliability of the S-61, encouraged Sikorsky to develop a civil transport version. The first to be built was the **S-61L**, a non-amphibious model that first flew in prototype form on 6 December 1960.

The S-61L retained the rotor system of the military S-61s, but without the blade-folding feature. Other differences included a fixed landing gear and a longer fuselage to provide accommodation for up to 28 passengers. Powerplant was the 1,350-shp (1007-kW) CT58-140 turboshaft. The S-61L received

The twin-engined, long-range Sea King is almost the universal helicopter of choice for search and rescue operators, like the Canadian Coast Guard.

its FAA type certificate on 2 November 1961 and entered scheduled revenue passenger service with Los Angeles Airways on 1 March 1962.

The **S-61N**, which followed, was generally similar but had a sealed hull for amphibious operations, retractable undercarriage and stabilising floats. It was first flown on 7 August 1962. Later production aircraft introduced more powerful 1,500-shp (1119-kW) CT58-GE-140-1/2 engines, better baggage facilities and damping to reduce rotor-induced vibration. This model was designated **Sikorsky S-61N Mk II** and became highly popular in the offshore market, where it is still used by many operators. Sikorsky also produced a heavy-lift version, known as the **Payloader**. This reverted to a fixed landing gear and had all non-essential fittings and equipment stripped to increase the payload. Production of commercial Sea King versions ceased in June 1980, after the completion of a grand total of 13 S-61Ls and 123 S-61Ns. A potential successor, the **S-92 Helibus**, made its maiden flight in 1998. The Helibus can carry up to 19 passengers or three standard LD3 freight containers.

Dutch-based KLM Helicopters was typical of most S-61 Sea King operators, flying aircraft like this S-61N on offshore support missions.

SPECIFICATION:
Sikorsky S-61N Mk II
Powerplant: two 1,500-shp (1119-kW) General Electric CT58-GE-140-1/2 turboshafts
Accommodation: three (flight deck), with a maximum of 30 passengers
Dimensions: main rotor diameter 62 ft 0 in (18.90 m); height 17 ft 6 in (5.32 m); length 72 ft 10 in (22.20 m)
Weights: empty 12,510 lb (5676 kg); maximum take-off 20,500 lb (9300 kg)
Performance: maximum cruising speed 150 mph (241 km/h); service ceiling 12,500 ft (3810 m); range with maximum fuel and reserves 495 miles (797 km)

Sud-Est S.E.210 Caravelle

France

Twin-engined short- to medium-range airliner

France's **Caravelle** was a pioneering design, the first short- to medium-range jet and the first rear-engined jet to be developed. It began life as a Sud-Est design, the 65/90-seat **X210**, and was launched as the **S.E.210 Caravelle** in January 1953. Rolls-Royce Avon turbojets were chosen and the Caravelle's nose section and cockpit were derived from the de Havilland Comet. The French government-funded prototype first flew, from Toulouse, on 27 May 1955 and soon afterwards the Caravelle attracted its first orders from Air France and SAS. The initial Avon Mk 522-powered **Caravelle I** was delivered the former on 2 April 1959, but entered revenue service with SAS on 26 April. A second version, the **Caravelle IA**, featured Mk 526 engines, but both aircraft shared the same 105-ft (32-m) fuselage and 79-seat layout. Thirty-four Caravelle I/IAs were built

The second true production type was the **Caravelle III**, which first flew on 30 December 1959. This featured Avon Mk 527s and improved range. Seventy-nine were built and 31 Series I/IAs were later converted to this standard. The **Caravelle VI** was another up-engined development built in two variants. The **Caravelle VIN** was powered by Avon Mk 531 engines, while the **Caravelle VIR** was fitted with Mk 532s or Mk 533s with thrust

The last operational Caravelle in Europe was this 1964-vintage Caravelle 10B flown by Swiss airline Aero Jet, from Zurich and Geneva.

reversers. The first Caravelle VI flew on 10 September 1960 and 109 were completed.

The **Caravelle 10B** (or **Super B**) of 1965 was a major development replacing the original noisy and thirsty engines with Pratt & Whitney JT8D turbofans. This version also had a fuselage stretch of 3 ft 3½ in (1.02 m) to accommodate 109 passengers. Many Caravelle VIRs were brought up to so-called **Caravelle 10R** standard through the refitting of JT8D-7 engines. Twenty-two Caravelle 10Bs and an equal number of 10Rs were built. Combi freight services could be undertaken by the **Caravelle 11R**, which first flew in June 1967. A fuselage stretch of 2 ft 4in (0.73 m) allowed the fitting of a forward cargo door to port and six were built.

The final production version was the **Caravelle 12**, which was some 10 ft 6¼ in (3.23 m) longer than the Caravelle 10B. This could carry up to 140 passengers (though 128 was the norm) and the first aircraft flew on 29 October 1970. A total of 12 aircraft was built before production ended in 1973.

No Avon-powered Caravelles remain, although by mid-1999 approximately 13 late-model aircraft were still surviving, largely in South America and Africa. No Caravelle is Stage 3/Chapter 3 compliant and no hush-kit has been developed, so any current operations are confined to remote locations.

Colombia is one of the last outposts of Caravelle operations. This Caravelle 10B3 was one of two converted to serve as freighters by Aerosucre.

SPECIFICATION:
Sud-Est S.E.210 Caravelle 10B
Powerplant: two 14,000-lb (62.3-kN) Pratt & Whitney JT8D-7 turbofans
Accommodation: two (flight deck), standard layout for 89 passengers
Dimensions: span 112 ft 6 in (34.30 m); height 28 ft 7 in (8.72 m); length 108 ft 3½ in (33.01 m)
Weights: operating, empty 66,259 lb (30055 kg); maximum take-off 123,457 lb (56000 kg)
Performance: maximum cruising speed, at 25,000 ft (7620 m) 512 mph (825 km/h); maximum cruising altitude 35,000 ft (10670 m); range, with max payload 1,668 miles (2685 km)

Tupolev Tu-134

The world's second turbofan-powered short-haul jetliner (after the **Tu-124**), the **Tu-134** 'Crusty' was Russia's first entirely new jet airliner, previous aircraft having been derived from the Tu-88 bomber (Tu-16 'Badger' prototype). The glazed navigator's compartment in the nose and Tupolev's trademark undercarriage fairings on the wing trailing edge gave the new aircraft a distinctively Soviet appearance. By comparison with the earlier Tu-124, the engines were moved to the sides of the rear fuselage. The aircraft also introduced a T-tail, while more powerful anti-skid brakes removed the need for a brake parachute. A redesigned wing allowed the aircraft to have a level cabin floor. The 11,905-lb (52.9-kN) Soloviev D-20P-engined prototype was designated **Tu-124A** and first flew in December 1963.

The more powerful 14,990-lb (66.7-kN) Soloviev D-30 turbofan was adopted on pre-production aircraft, which gained the new designation **Tu-134**. This basic version entered service in 1967, and could carry 64 passengers – typically 16 first class and 48 tourist class. An APU and clamshell thrust reversers were added during production.

In 1970 production switched to the **Tu-134A**. This was lengthened by 2.1 m (6 ft 10 in), mainly ahead of the wing, and retained the original 28-seat rear cabin, but new front/middle cabins gave a capacity of up to 80 or, exceptionally, 84 passengers. The Tu-134A also introduced the D-30-II engine, which could maintain the same thrust ratings at higher temperatures and which had a higher take-off

This Tu-134A-3 is one of several flown by Rossia, the Russian state transport company, which undertakes VIP missions for the Russian government.

rating of 15,608 lb (69.4 kN). The wing structure was strengthened and the tailfin/tailplane bullet fairing was extended to house a new VHF antenna.

The Tu-134's glazed nose and chin radome were replaced with a more modern radar at the 1971 suggestion of Yugoslav charter airline Aviogenex. The new solid nose was subsequently made an option on all Tu-134As. The **Tu-134A-3** was powered by D-30-III engines, and introduced lightweight seats allowing up to 96 passengers to be carried. The **Tu-134B** had a revised flight deck with no navigator, and modified spoilers. Later improvements came in the form of the D-30-II-powered **Tu-134B-1** and the D-30-III-powered **Tu-134B-1-3**.

Production slowed to a trickle in the early 1980s and ceased in 1984/85 after a total of 852 aircraft had been built. The Yak-42 took the place of the Tu-134 in Aeroflot's fleet – and Aeroflot was the driving customer. By mid-1999 over 400 Tu-134As were still believed to be in service. The Minsk Aircraft Repair Plant (MARZ) has launched a programme to re-engine aircraft with quieter and more efficient D-436T1-134 turbofans.

Air Moldova is one of the many new national airlines that sprang up in the newly-independent republics of the former-USSR. It operates nine Tu-134A-3s.

SPECIFICATION:
Tupolev Tu-134A
Powerplant: two 14,990-lb (66.7-kN) Soloviev D-30 Series II turbofans
Accommodation: three (flight deck), maximum of 84 passengers (standard 76)
Dimensions: span 95 ft 1¾ in (29 m); height 30 ft (9.14 m); length 121 ft 6½ in (37.05 m)
Weights: operating, empty 64,045 lb (29050 kg); maximum take-off 103,600 lb (47000 kg)
Performance: max cruising speed, at 27,890 ft (8500 m) 558 mph (898 km/h); max cruising altitude 36,000 ft (10973 m); range, with maximum payload 1,174 miles (1890 km)

Tupolev Tu-154

The **Tupolev Tu-154 'Careless'** was designed as a replacement for the Tu-104 and Il-18 on Aeroflot's medium-range, medium-density routes. The new airliner had to seat at least 120 passengers, fly sectors of up to 6000 km (3,728 miles) and operate from short gravel or packed-earth runways. This contradictory requirement demanded a greater thrust-to-weight ratio than was expected of Western jetliners, so that although weight and seating capacity were lower than the similar Boeing 727, the engines were more powerful.

The prototype made its maiden flight on 4 October 1968, powered by 20,950-lb (93.2-kN) Kuznetsov NK-8-2 turbofans. Domestic passenger services were initiated in February 1972 and Balkan Bulgarian became the first export customer in July.

In 1973 the **Tu-154A** introduced the 23,150-lb (103-kN) NK-8-2U which allowed operation at higher weights. The aircraft also featured a new fuel storage tank in the centre-section. This could not be used in flight, and merely allowed an aircraft to take fuel with it for refuelling at its destination. Seating was increased to 168 and there were other minor improvements. Deliveries began in 1974.

The **Tu-154B**, introduced in 1975 (from the 120th aircraft onwards), gained two extra emergency exits to allow the carriage of up to 180 passengers,

Russia's Samara Airlines is based in the eastern town of the same name where all Tu-154M production is undertaken.

In addition to a redesigned wing and tail, the Tu-154M has gained an enlarged centre intake to improve the airflow to its new D-30KU engines.

and had a higher MTOW. It was also fitted with Thomson CSF/SFIM avionics to allow Cat II operations. A refined **Tu-154B-1** followed and, in the further developed **Tu-154B-2** the centre-section fuel tank became part of the normal fuel system.

The **Tu-154S** designation is applied to dedicated freighters, which feature a large side cargo door and a strengthened cargo floor with roller tracks. All were converted from Tu-154As and Tu-154Bs.

The improved **Tu-154M** was originally designated **Tu-164**, and switched to 23,380-lb (104-kN) Soloviev D-30KU-154-II turbofans in redesigned nacelles with larger intakes. Slats and spoilers were redesigned, and the entire horizontal tail was redesigned with greater area. Most noticeably, the centre intake has been enlarged. The performance gains which might have been expected are negated by an increase in empty weight that reduces payload to a figure less than that of the original Tu-154. Deliveries of the Tu-154M began in December 1984 and production at the Samara plant is believed to total some 930 aircraft. Tu-154Ms are still being built at a very slow pace. A version dubbed the **Tu-154M-100** with a new Aviacor-designed interior is the latest production aircraft on offer, while an attempt to re-engine Tu-145s with Perm PS-90A turbofans, as the **Tu-154M2**, has been shelved.

SPECIFICATION: Tupolev Tu-154M
Powerplant: three Aviadvigatel (Soloviev) 23,380-lb (104-kN) D-30KU-154-II turbofans
Accommodation: three (flight deck), maximum of 180 passengers (standard 154)
Dimensions: span 123 ft 2½ in (37.55 m); height 37 ft 4¾ in (11.40 m); length 157 ft 1¾ in (47.90 m)
Weights: operating, empty 121915 lb (55,300 kg); maximum take-off 220,460 lb (100000 kg)
Performance: max cruising speed 590 mph, (950 km/h); max cruising altitude 39,000 ft (11900 m); range, with maximum payload 2,425 miles (3900 km)

Tupolev Tu-204, Tu-214, Tu-224 and Tu-234

Twin-engined short- to medium-range airliners

The **Tu-204** was developed as a replacement for the Tu-154 on Aeroflot's medium-range routes. The Tu-204 is Tupolev's first truly modern airliner, with extensive use of composites (18 per cent by weight), a triplex digital fly-by-wire control system and an EFIS cockpit. A Tu-154 development hack even tested sidestick controllers, but these were rejected in favour of central yokes.

A PS-90AT-engined prototype made its maiden flight on 2 January 1989. Tu-204 production is undertaken at the Aviastar plant, in Ulyanovsk. An all-cargo version of the basic 214-seat aircraft, the **Tu-204C**, was also developed. This was joined, in 1993, by the **Tu-204-100**, an extended-range passenger version with extra fuel and an increased MTOW. A similarly-improved cargo version, the **Tu-204-100C**, became available in 1994.

A major change came in the form of the Rolls-Royce RB211-535-E4-powered **Tu-204-120**. The prototype flew on 14 August 1992 but the first production aircraft did not fly until 7 March 1997. This version was originally funded and marketed by the British Russian Aviation Corporation (BRAVIA) as the **BRAVIA Tu-204**. BRAVIA announced over 20 orders for the type but the joint-venture team has since been dissolved. Tupolev has continued with Tu-204-120 development, leading to the Tu-204-120C freighter, which first flew on 10 November 1997.

The **Tu-204-200** brought a further increase in payload, fuel load and MTOW. The first example to fly was actually a Tu-214 (see below) in March 1996. A full

The Tu-204-100C is an extended-range freighter development of the basic passenger aircraft. Only a very small number have yet entered service.

freighter version, the **Tu-204-200C** is on offer. Tupolev hopes to add RB211 turbofans to the -200 airframe to produce the **Tu-204-220** and associated **Tu-204-220C**. A series of proposed aircraft fitted with Collins avionics is designated **Tu-204-122** and **Tu-204-222**, but none have yet been built.

The **Tu-214** is a combi freighter version of the Tu-204-200 also known as the **Tu-204C[3]** (Cargo, Converted, Containerised). It can carry a mix of 30 passengers and 16 LD3 containers or six LD3s and 130 passengers, for example. Production of this version is undertaken at the KAPA plant, in Kazan, and the prototype first flew on 21 March 1996. The **Tu-224** (formerly **Tu-204-320**) and **Tu-234** (formerly **Tu-204-300**) are proposed trunk route versions with shorter fuselages to seat between 90 and 160.

Deliveries have been very slow. The first aircraft, a Tu-204C, was handed over to ARIA in April 1995. Sirocco Aerospace International which is marketing the RB211-powered aircraft secured 20 orders from Egypt's Kato Group. These will be leased to KrasAir (Siberia) and Air Cairo. A handful of Tu-204s are also in service with other smaller Russian airlines.

This 1994-production Tu-204 is one of three such aircraft in service with Moscow's Vnukovo Airlines, which also operates a single Tu-204-100C.

SPECIFICATION:
Tupolev Tu-204-120
Powerplant: two 43,100-lb (191.7-kN) Rolls-Royce RB211-535F turbofans
Accommodation: three (flight deck), maximum of 214 passengers (standard 190)
Dimensions: span 137 ft 1¼ in (41.80 m); height 45 ft 7¼ in (13.90 m); length 151 ft 3 in (46.10 m)
Weights: operating, empty 130,070 lb (59000 kg); maximum take-off 244,155 lb (110750 kg)
Performance: cruising speed at 40,000 ft (12200 m) 528 mph (850 km/h); maximum range, with maximum payload and reserves 2,858 miles (4600 km)

Yakovlev Yak-40

The **Yak-40** 'Codling' represents the USSR's most successful (and perhaps most radical) attempt to develop a DC-3 replacement. Powered by three turbofan engines, with clamshell thrust reversers, the Yak-40's performance gives it a still-enviable mix of high sector speeds and excellent short/rough-field capability. The aircraft can take off and climb with two engines, and can maintain height in the cruise on one engine. With its rear-mounted engines and slightly swept fin, the Yak-40 resembles a miniature Tu-154, although it has an unswept, tapered wing with hydraulically operated three-section plain flaps and conventional, manually actuated ailerons. The simple but rugged undercarriage has single nose and mainwheels.

The main cabin is usually configured to seat 27 passengers, in nine three-abreast rows, with two seats on the starboard side of the aisle. Alternatives include a layout with eight four-abreast rows, or a mixed-class layout with six or eight seats (including a four-place inward-facing settee) in the forward cabin and 12 seats (in standard three-abreast rows) in the rear cabin. An 11-seat executive configuration is another option.

First flown in prototype form on 21 October 1966, the Yak-40 entered production in 1967, and began passenger-carrying operations with Aeroflot

Yakovlev's small tri-jet is fading from regular airline service, although many VIP-configured versions remain – such as this Orel Air Enterprise aircraft.

Transeast Airlines is actually a Latvian-based airline, though here one of its Yak-40s is seen wearing a Kazakhstan registration.

during September 1968. The Yak-40 rapidly became the most popular short-range aircraft on Soviet domestic routes, and huge numbers were procured for Aeroflot and its regional directorates; most of these remain in service with the various private companies that have been established across the former-Soviet Union. The Yak-40 also enjoyed considerable export success and was exported widely to both civilian and military customers.

A 40-seat high-density variant announced in 1971 was stillborn, as was the stretched **Yak-40M** and the **Yak-40B** and **Yak-40V** – both of which were versions with uprated AI-25T engines. An intended freighter variant reached the prototype stage.

Production continued at the Saratov plant until 1980, by which time approximately 1,000 aircraft had been built. About 700 of these are still in service. Plans were drawn up to restart production in the USA during the early 1980s, as the **Avia LC-3**, powered by Garret (now AlliedSignal) TFE731-5 engines, but these came to nothing. Garret and Yakovlev again discussed re-engining existing aircraft with TFE731s in 1991, but in 1992 Yakovlev and Textron Lycoming signed an agreement to undertake a re-engining programme using two LF507 turbofans. These 'new' aircraft would be known as **Yak-40TL**s, but the project has stalled.

SPECIFICATION:
Yakovlev Yak-40
Powerplant: three 3,300-lb (14.7 kN) Ivchenko AI-25 turbofans
Accommodation: two (flight deck), maximum of 32 passengers (24 standard)
Dimensions: span 82 ft 0¼ in (25.0 m); length 66 ft 9½ in (20.36 m); height 21 ft 4 in (6.5 m)
Weights: empty 20,725 lb (9400 kg); maximum take-off 35,275 lb (16000 kg)
Performance: maximum cruising speed 342 mph (550 km/h); maximum range with 27 passengers at 292 mph (470 km/h) 1,118 miles (1800 km) with reserves

Yakovlev Yak-42

Yakovlev developed the **Yak-42 'Clobber'** as a short-haul medium-capacity airliner to replace the Il-18, An-24 and older Tu-134s in Aeroflot service. Design work commenced in the early 1970s, and the aircraft emerged as a scaled-up Yak-40. It retained its predecessor's austere strip capability, needing the minimum of ground support equipment for operations in the Soviet Union's more remote regions. The Yakovlev Bureau suffered some obvious difficulties in the type's early stages as three prototypes were built, all with differing wings, to determine the optimum angle of sweep (which was settled on 23°). The first of these flew on 7 March 1975 and the aircraft entered initial production at Smolensk. Much refinement remained to be done, as Aeroflot only placed its Yak-42s into service on the Moscow-Krasnodor route in 1980/81.

Production Yak-42s could carry 120, using the uniquely Soviet system of passengers carrying on their own luggage and stowing it in the cabin. They also featured four-wheeled main undercarriage bogies instead of the prototype's two-wheeled units. The type suffered many difficulties once in service and was withdrawn from use after accidents in 1982. By October 1984 aircraft with modified wings had been returned to Aeroflot service.

The first major development was the **Yak-42D**, which first appeared in 1989. This version offered an increased fuel load to extend range with 120 passengers to 2200 km (1,365 miles). It also incorporated a larger passenger door and remains the

Cubana has a fleet of four Yak-42Ds which it took delivery of in 1990/91. Each aircraft is configured with 120 seats.

current production variant. Specialist versions include the **Yak-42E-LL**, a testbed for ZMKB Progress D-236 propfan engines, which first flew in 1991, and the **Yak-42F** with two large underwing sensor pods for survey and earth science duties, several of which were delivered to Aeroflot.

Yakovlev is now working on an improved version of the Yak-42A, formerly known as the **Yak-42B**, but now redesignated as the **Yak-142D-100**. This version was first displayed at the 1993 Paris Air Show, where the designation **Yak-142** was briefly attached to it. The Yak-42D-100 has an AlliedSignal EFIS cockpit, flight-deployable wing spoilers, a wider range of flap settings, an air-operable TA-12 APU and redesigned engine intakes that cut noise levels. Yakovlev is also developing a **Yak-42T** freighter with a side cargo door and payload of 12000 kg (25,455 lb). Work on the Yak-42-derived twin-engined **Yak-242** was halted in 1997.

Yak-42 production continues at a slow rate at Saratov. Approximately 200 have been built and they serve largely with Russian operators, with some exports to China and Cuba.

Based at Moscow's Bykovo Airport, Bykovo Avia operates a large fleet of Yak-42s and Yak-42Ds, including this early production Yak-42.

SPECIFICATION:
Yakovlev Yak-42D
Powerplant: three 14,330-lb (63.74-kN) Ivchenko Progress D-36 turbofans
Accommodation: two (flight deck), maximum of 120 passengers
Dimensions: span 114 ft 5¼ in (34.88 m); height 32 ft 3 in (9.83 m); length 119 ft 4¼ in (36.38 m)
Weights: empty, equipped 76,092 lb (34515 kg); maximum take-off 126,765 lb (57500 kg)
Performance: maximum cruising speed 503 mph (810 km/h); maximum cruising height 31,500 ft (9600 m); maximum range, with 120 passengers and reserves 1,180 miles (1900 km)

INDEX

Text entries appear in plain face
Pictures appear in **bold**

Picture Credits